The Belly Fat Fix

TAMING GHRELIN,
Your Hunger Hormone,
for QUICK, HEALTHY WEIGHT LOSS

MARJORIE NOLAN COHN, MS, RD

RODALE.

© 2013 by Marjorie Nolan Cohn

Illustrations © 2013 by Scott Cohn
Exercise photographs © Rodale Inc.

Printed in the United States of America
Rodale Inc. makes every effort to use acid-free ♾, recycled paper ♲.

Ghrelin Masters photographs courtesy of test panel participants
Exercise photographs by Mitch Mandel/Rodale Images
Book design by Christina Gaugler

Library of Congress Cataloging-in-Publication Data is on file with the publisher.

ISBN 978-1-60961-966-4 hardcover

2 4 6 8 10 9 7 5 3   hardcover

We inspire and enable people to improve their lives and the world around them.
For more of our products visit rodalestore.com or call 800-848-4735

TO MY PARENTS,
CRAIG AND LISA NOLAN.

Thanks, Dad, for believing in me so much as a child
that even after your passing, I carry your love and
support with me along this journey.

Mom, your participation means the world to me.
Thank you for trusting me and my work so much
that you put yourself out there for the world to see.

CONTENTS

ACKNOWLEDGMENTS

I want to acknowledge every one of my clients. If it were not for you sharing your struggles, pain, stories, and successes, I would not have been inspired to create the Belly Fat Fix. Thank you for trusting me enough to show you the way, and for your encouragement and support in writing this book. You will see a piece of your story on every page. Your dedication and effort to improve your health kept me inspired throughout this process. I thank you all eternally for every bit of it.

I am grateful to have met Deborah Grandinetti, my writing coach and teacher. Thank you, Deborah, for leading by example and showing me how to work on my own as we completed this manuscript. You are truly an amazing writer, coach, and leader. I am captivated by your craft and am indebted to you for sharing it with me. Thank you for believing in me and my work.

Thank you to my husband and artist, Scott Cohn, for your creative talent. I am grateful to have you part of my team, helping me balance my science research with practical images—in the same way you balance my life with your patience and love.

Thank you, Claire Gerus, my literary agent, for believing in me. It was only after you took me on as a client that I fully believed in myself. Thank you to my supportive editor, Nancy Fitzgerald, for your advice, guidance, and coordination to complete this project. I was able to have a stress-free honeymoon thanks to your willingness to shift deadlines and coordinate the Rodale team on my behalf.

Many thanks to my graduate intern, Christina Harvey. Your hard work not only made my life easier, it brought even more practical information to *The Belly Fat Fix*. Thank you for helping me analyze seemingly endless recipes, create meal plans, and complete research—and for all the countless tasks you took on to support my work. You will be an excellent dietitian. I am proud to call you my colleague.

Finally, thank you to my family. Your support and infinite encouragement have given me the time and energy to complete this dream you have shared with me for so many years. Special thanks to my mom for participating in my book and proving that the Belly Fat Fix is the way to live. Thank you to my in-laws, Dr. Robert and Nancy Cohn, for your help in researching and teaching me about the science of ghrelin. I am so happy to call you my family.

INTRODUCTION

"Ghrelin" is new to me in comparison with dieting. The first time I ever heard the word *ghrelin,* I was 24 years old and almost 180 pounds. Yup, in the not-so-distant past, I was you. I was *always* on a diet. You name it; chances are I've tried it. I may not look like it now, but the truth is, I was fat kid. I know "fat" is a bad word. It is politically incorrect and considered *way* more of an insult than "obese." But let's be real: Who looks in the mirror and tells themselves, "I'm *so* obese"? I use the word *fat* because that is how I felt every time I'd look in the mirror. At 12, I weighed more than I do now. I am a living, breathing example that you *can* beat the odds.

When I was 12 years old, I weighed 150 pounds. At 5 foot 2 inches I was, without a doubt, obese. I was teased by my classmates: "Large Marge" was my nickname. Luckily, I was quick-witted enough to throw a zinger right back to defuse the situation and distract my classmates, at least for a little bit. As I grew into my teens and adult years, I stopped being obese. Now I was "overweight" or "big." However I still felt fat.

I became a dietitian and personal trainer years before I fully figured out how to control my weight—it goes to prove that even if you have knowledge, putting it into practice is a whole different story. I've drawn from my weight-loss experience while writing this book. I know how hard it is to lose weight and keep it off. But I promise you this: Once you learn the ways of ghrelin, that task will get easier. It did for me.

Only after I was well established in my career did I begin learning more and more about ghrelin. What was this hormone? Where did it come from? And how was it affecting me and countless other people trying to lose weight? I was fascinated—and I still am. Ghrelin, quite literally, will make or break you. This one hormone has helped the human race (along with most other animals) survive. It's also helped keep them healthy. Balancing your ghrelin will not only help you to lose more weight with less effort but it will also improve your overall health in many significant ways.

Once I learned the science of ghrelin and started eating in a way that balanced it, a funny thing happened. I lost weight and kept it off, *and it was not hard*. That's when I started to create the Belly Fat Fix.

In the pages ahead, I'll share with you all the strategies, tricks, and tips I have developed throughout the years. I know they work because I use them—and so do my clients—with great success. I have reached my weight goal. But even though I am 5 foot 8 and 135 pounds, I *still* use them today.

I said earlier that I beat the odds. Well, that's sort of a lie. Weight loss is about the odds, but not in the way it seems. Losing weight—and keeping it off—isn't a game of chance. It's a matter of playing your cards the right way. If you keep at it consistently, you always beat the odds eventually. I've designed this plan so that you can easily continue on a healthy path for the rest of your life. By following the Belly Fat Fix, you, too, will beat the odds!

Learn It

CHAPTER 1

Meet Ghrelin, the Hunger Hormone

Imagine reaching your ideal weight without having to fight yourself each step of the way. Imagine going from where you are now—not *quite* the size and shape you wish you were—to where you want to be, without feeling that gnawing sensation of hunger throughout the day. Imagine slimming down as you eat three delicious, balanced, and filling meals—plus an afternoon snack—each day.

It's not only possible, it's easy when you make ghrelin, the hunger hormone, your ally instead of your enemy. In the pages ahead, I'll teach you how to eat and how to time your meals so you never again have to rely on willpower alone to stop you from eating what you know you shouldn't. (After all, willpower hasn't been much help in the past, has it?)

When you learn the ways of ghrelin, you'll gain *biological control* of your appetite. That's because this weight-loss plan works *with* your body, giving it what it needs, when it needs it. The result? You feel satisfied and full. Since you aren't hungry, you're not tempted to nosh between meals. You don't experience the same strong cravings for high-calorie foods. Once you know how to work with ghrelin, you'll even find it easier to stop at "just a little" of those foods you love—whether it's pizza or ice cream or whatever you tend to gorge on because you just can't find it within yourself to stop till it's all gone.

That sounds like quite a promise. Yet this is exactly what my clients report. "I feel like I have a true hold on my eating problem," says Lisa N., a 55-year-old nurse who's struggled with her weight all her life. "I'm finally learning to eat the way a thin woman eats."

"I really don't feel like I'm on a diet," says Nichole D., a working single mom with a 6-month-old baby. "I eat plenty of food on this plan. Sometimes I may have to stop and think about making the better choice, but I don't ever feel deprived."

Donna, a stay-at-home mom with a 1-year-old son, agrees. "I was constantly hungry on other diets and always fighting with myself not to eat," she says. "The best part about this plan is that I don't feel like I'm on a diet at all. I'm finally eating the way a normal person should. And I'm having fun cooking and eating without guilt!"

Donna, who started this program at her highest weight ever, reports that she and her husband were even able to break their tradition of popcorn and a few mixed drinks after dinner—without feeling deprived. To make the evening feel special and set a mood of relaxation, they've opted for ice water with lemon in highball glasses instead.

"I think it was because our ghrelin levels were finally balanced and stable that we felt full—so we painlessly bypassed our habit-related craving and were completely fine the rest of the night," she reports. "It really does feel empowering to 'reprogram' myself and to see a very clear difference between hunger and habit."

The truth is, when it comes to losing weight, willpower alone does not work when you're confronted with a strong biological drive like hunger. Only when you give your body what it needs, *when* it needs it, can you reach your weight goal without a fight. That's the beauty of the Belly Fat Fix.

I've based this plan on the most recent science, plus widely accepted principles of the professional nutrition community. This is the very first program to incorporate what science knows about ghrelin in a holistic plan that puts together all the pieces of the weight-loss equation:

- Calorie needs
- Meal timing
- Protein/fat/carbohydrate breakdown
- The right kind—and amount—of exercise (it's less than you imagine!)

Best of all, this is a simple, easy-to-follow plan designed for people who lead full, hectic lives. Because I coach a wide variety of clients, I'm familiar with

What *Exactly* Is Ghrelin?

Ghrelin is a potent peptide hormone, or chemical messenger. The message it sends? *I'M HUNGRY. FEED ME!* It's the primary and most powerful hunger stimulator for almost all animals, including human beings. It's also fast acting. That's why your appetite can come on *like that*, seemingly from out of nowhere.

Special cells in the lining of the stomach produce ghrelin in very minute amounts—not continuously, but on a predictable schedule. Even smaller amounts of ghrelin are secreted by other organs, such as the pancreas and the hypothalamus, the part of the brain that controls appetite and weight. Once ghrelin is produced, it's secreted into the bloodstream, which enables it to travel throughout the body and affect every single organ and system.

Your body produces only a little bit of ghrelin, but that's enough to drive your appetite and determine—to a large degree—your overall health. When ghrelin is working optimally, it's easier for you to control your weight and stay healthy. When it's out of balance, it's difficult for you to slim down, and your general health suffers, too, as your body unleashes a cascade of degenerative processes that lead to killer diseases such as fast-growing cancers.

The body makes two forms of ghrelin: *unacylated* and *acylated*. Both forms are always in circulation, though unacylated ghrelin is present in higher concentrations. Scientists originally thought that acylated ghrelin was biologically active and the unacylated form was inactive, but they've since learned that's not true. In humans, for instance, unacylated ghrelin counteracts the influence of acylated ghrelin on insulin secretion and glucose metabolism.[1]

the kinds of challenges that arise for all sorts of people—from new mothers to businesspeople to folks whose jobs or lifestyles require them to eat out a lot. The Belly Fat Fix can accommodate them all. I've included lots of coaching tips throughout the book to make it as easy as possible for you to follow the plan. There's even advice on how to make the meals ghrelin friendly for the entire family.

Bottom line: The Belly Fat Fix will bring your body back to health by balancing your ghrelin. Let's take a brief look now at the components of the plan and how it can work for you.

(Without unacylated ghrelin, acylated ghrelin might bring about too rapid a rise in glucose and insulin levels.[2]) Unacylated ghrelin also enhances insulin sensitivity and inhibits the breakdown of lipids, molecules that contain fats, vitamins, and triglycerides. (Under stress, this breakdown—called lipolysis—occurs in the fat cells. If the stress is chronic, this breakdown in the fat cells increases cholesterol.)

Long story short: Both forms work cooperatively to regulate metabolism.[3] They need to be present in the right proportions for the body to function at its best. Scientists have found that the ratio of unacylated to acylated ghrelin in the body may determine the overall effects of total ghrelin.[4]

Studies have shown that in cases of ghrelin imbalance, the body tends to produce excessive amounts of unacylated ghrelin relative to acylated ghrelin. Diseases occur when there's an imbalance in the ratio of unacylated ghrelin to acylated ghrelin—and also when overall ghrelin isn't present in the right amounts.

After all, both types of ghrelin play an important role in regulating metabolism, and a ghrelin imbalance has a negative effect on other regulatory hormones. That's because the hormones function interdependently. The functioning of one hormone is determined by the functioning of another, and that hormone, in turn, exerts its influence on yet another hormone, and so on.

Think of ghrelin as the first domino in a long line of dominos. When ghrelin falls out of balance, it knocks the others off balance, too, initiating processes that lead to insulin resistance, diabetes, and many other diseases.

THE BELLY FAT FIX

With the Belly Fat Fix, there are three simple steps to a slimmer, healthier you:

In **Step 1**, you start the 3-Day Fast-Track, outlined on page 122. This step will stabilize your ghrelin and help you lose a quick 3 to 5 pounds. It's also a pattern breaker—a way to signal to yourself that you're ending your old, counterproductive eating patterns and beginning a new, healthier way of life.

In **Step 2**, you use the rest of the month to master this new way of eating. On the plan, there are just two hard-and-fast eating rules:

1. Use the G-Scale (see page 40) to discover your personal hunger quotient, then time your meals accordingly.

2. Consult the handy ghrelin-suppressing food list (see page 79) to create your meal plan.

To make the month as delightful as possible, we've included simple recipes for delicious, satisfying foods that will help stabilize your ghrelin levels. There are dozens of recipes exclusively for people on this plan to prove that you don't have to sacrifice taste in order to slim down. When it came to creating recipes for this plan, the words of the day were "simple" and "assembly based." After all, hardly anyone has much time to spend in the kitchen these days. (There are a few recipes that are a bit more involved, but they're special-occasion treats, not everyday meals.)

You'll embark on **Step 3**, the No-Sweat Exercise Program (see Chapter 8), after you've taken a month to strengthen your new eating habits and to learn more about yourself by using the 30-day food tracker. You'll work out with hand weights (or substitute other household items) for a half hour three or four times a week. This exercise program is specifically designed to stabilize ghrelin even as it helps you build lean muscle.

The No-Sweat program is an important part of the plan. Studies show that moderate exercise reduces inflammation in fat tissue by regulating ghrelin's function within the body's white blood cells. This reduction in inflammation won't just improve overall weight loss, it'll improve your ability to keep the weight off, too. It'll

Balancing Act

Sound familiar? If two or more of these statements apply to you, your ghrelin may be off balance—and getting it back on track could lead to a slimmer, healthier you.

1. **You can't lose weight even when you don't eat—or when you eat very few calories.** That's due to ghrelin's conservation effect, which once conferred an evolutionary advantage in times of famine.

2. **Your sleep schedule is erratic.** You find yourself staying up late and choosing to overeat or snack at night.

3. **You experience extremes in hunger levels.** For instance, when clients tell me that they get up at 7:00 a.m. but don't feel hungry all morning—then by midafternoon they're starving and can't stop eating—I know their ghrelin is out of whack.

4. **You feel depressed or suffer from depression-like symptoms such as fatigue, anxiety, irritability, poor concentration, or headaches.** That could be because of ghrelin's influence on the reward and pleasure centers of the brain.

5. **You find that eating certain foods is soothing.** Maybe you reach for a gooey chocolate brownie at the end of a tough workday or a big bag of chips when you're annoyed at your mother. This, too, may be due to ghrelin's role in the brain's pleasure and reward centers.

6. **You tend to be impulsive about your food choices.** Instead of choosing the foods you *know* you should eat to help you lose weight, you select the high-fat, high-calorie options. That's ghrelin at work.

also boost your mood, since you'll be relying less on food and more on movement as a feel-good strategy.

Notice the emphasis on "moderate" exercise. In Chapter 8, I'll explain why you don't need to overdo it—workouts that are too intensive can actually sabotage your ghrelin-balancing efforts.

Each step in this book will give you a new tool you can use to get closer to your ideal weight. And each of these tools is designed to help you get ghrelin working optimally in your body. When it does—when your body produces enough ghrelin to stimulate your appetite when you need to eat, then eases back when you've had your fill—all your other regulatory hormones receive the biological support they need to remain in balance, too. In short, the choices you make either help ghrelin function at its best, keeping you slim and healthy, or throw your ghrelin levels off-kilter, causing weight gain and putting you at greater risk of developing a wide range of degenerative disease, including cancer. (For more on the link between ghrelin and disease, see Chapter 9.)

GHRELIN POWER

If you're struggling to lose weight, following the Belly Fat Fix can make a huge difference in your life. In fact, you'll find that the benefits extend far beyond your weight and your waistline. Stabilizing your ghrelin levels will also:

- Give you more energy
- Make your thinking clearer
- Sharpen your memory
- Improve your digestion
- Help balance your blood sugar
- Increase your metabolism
- Boost your immune system
- Protect against cancer, heart disease, arthritis, and diabetes
- Help reverse the processes that lead to these diseases

How can stabilizing a single little hormone bring such big results? Ghrelin is small but powerful—and it really gets around! At various times during the day and night, on a schedule we can influence but can't control, ghrelin makes its way around our body, sending its signals to the brain primarily via the vagus nerve, one of a pair of cranial nerves that resemble two thick ropes. These ropelike nerves, made of sensory nerve fibers, extend from the brain stem, past the heart and lungs, and deep into the abdomen, where they branch into a network of nerves that gather intelligence from abdominal organs like the stomach, pancreas, kidneys, liver, and gallbladder. This system of nerves facilitates ongoing two-way communication between the brain and the belly. Without this communication, you'd never know you were hungry.

The takeaway: When you consciously eat to support ghrelin balance, you're working *with* your body—and your brain—to bring about a greater state of health. So you not only slim down, you also become measurably healthier.

YOUR BRAIN ON GHRELIN

Let's take a look at the most important ways ghrelin affects your brain—it may help you better understand some of your own eating behaviors, including the ones you *know* sabotage those numbers on the scale. Understanding ghrelin's effects on the brain will also help you see why you should follow the Belly Fat Fix—not just for a month but forever.

When Japanese researchers first identified ghrelin in 1999, they thought its primary role was to stimulate the pituitary gland to release human growth hormone (HGH). They named it ghrelin after the word root *ghre*, which comes from a Proto-Indo-European word meaning "to grow." Ghrelin *does* stimulate the pituitary gland to release HGH, which spurs growth in children and teens. In adults, HGH helps regulate body composition, muscle and bone growth, and sugar and fat metabolism.

But scientists have come to realize that ghrelin was designed to fulfill a more crucial function. Nobel laureates Joseph L. Goldstein and Michael Stuart Brown discovered that ghrelin's essential purpose is to prevent living beings—from fish to people—from starving to death in times of famine. When blood sugar falls as a person starves, a cascade of activity is initiated in the brain and belly, leading to the release of ghrelin. Ghrelin also acts on the hypothalamus, the part of your brain that controls hunger, thirst, metabolism, and body temperature, as well as the pituitary (or "master") gland, which oversees every single hormone secretion throughout your body. By acting on the pituitary gland, ghrelin stimulates the production of even more HGH. That, in turn, restores blood glucose levels so the starving person can survive.[5] Ghrelin levels are highest in people with anorexia nervosa, a condition in which people literally starve themselves, often to the brink of death.

(continued on page 12)

Donna and Dave H.

DONNA

AGE: 38

POUNDS LOST:

FAST-TRACK: 3.5 TOTAL: 21

ALL-OVER INCHES LOST: 19

DAVE

AGE: 39

POUNDS LOST:

FAST-TRACK: 6

TOTAL: 30 in 60 days

OVERALL INCHES LOST: 26

Donna and Dave, married for more than a decade, came to the Belly Fat Fix from different ends of the dieting spectrum. Donna was overweight as a child and teenager, so she pretty much knows her way around a diet. But for Dave, it was a different story. Though he weighed in at 336 pounds when he started on the plan, he'd grown up tall and thin. He could eat whatever he wanted and not gain an ounce—until recently. "I didn't have good eating habits at all," says the 39-year-old lawyer. "I figured it was okay to eat anything I wanted." When he and Donna met, Dave, at 6 foot 7, was a lanky 180 pounds.

Eventually, though, his poor eating habits caught up with him, and the pounds began to pile on. He tried to shake them with the Atkins and Zone diets, but the minute he deviated, the weight came right back on—and he eventually gave up because the meals were so restrictive that he couldn't dine out with

BEFORE

AFTER

friends. "That's no way to live," he says. On those plans, he was always hungry.

Donna's lifelong weight problem got worse after she gave birth to the couple's son, Jonah. Instead of losing weight after the pregnancy, she gained it. "I was waking up around the clock with my newborn," she said. Every 4 hours when she fed the baby, she grabbed something for herself. When she started on the Belly Fat Fix, she was at her highest weight ever.

"It was hard for me at the beginning," Donna admits. "Doing *anything* when you're tired is hard. And doubling the recipes—but in slightly different portions, since we weren't splitting them exactly in half—also took some figuring out."

"Within a couple of meals, I got it down to a system," she says. (If you're using the Belly Fat Fix with your partner, you'll find tips on how to cook your meals and divvy up portions correctly on page 105.)

For Dave, breakfast was the first challenge. In the past, he'd head off to work on an empty stomach, saving his appetite for a big lunch that would keep him full through his long days on the job. Problem was, that big lunch usually made for sleepy afternoons. These days, Donna packs a breakfast for him to bring along to work, plus an afternoon snack. "If you take care of your appetite at breakfast," he explains, "when lunchtime comes around, you're not feeling desperate, so it's easier to make the better choice."

Donna and Dave had a summer packed full of social activities, which made it difficult for them to follow the plan 100 percent every single day. But that wasn't all bad. Being able to deviate so they could enjoy a normal social life—and then go back on the plan without having to start from square one—was liberating. In fact, that's one of the things they like about the Belly Fat Fix over other diets. "With this plan," says Dave, "I can go out and enjoy dinner with family or friends and either compensate by eating a bit less earlier in the day or getting right back on track the next day."

For Donna and Dave, all their dedication has paid off in big ways. In addition to dropping 30 pounds, Dave has experienced major improvements in his snoring, and he feels much more well rested. He's also seen improvements in his triglyceride levels.

And Donna, now 21 pounds lighter, is back in her prepregnancy jeans. Even more important, eating on the plan helps her regulate her blood sugar, keeping it from dropping—and that's helped her curb her habit of snacking throughout the day. Not an easy feat for a stay-at-home mom, but that's just one of the healthy new habits she's developed.

The verdict on the Belly Fat Fix? "It's a brilliant concept," says Dave. "You lose weight by eating foods that suppress your appetite. That way—since you aren't starving—you can follow your instincts about what your body needs."

Donna agrees. "I love this plan," she says. "I know that 5 years from now, I'll still be following the principles, even if I'm not following the diet exactly. Dave and I don't even feel like we're dieting—that's something I associate with being hungry or with being so restricted that we can't enjoy good times with friends. The Belly Fat Fix is different—for us, it's become a way of life."

Low blood sugar levels stimulate not only a spike in ghrelin but also the activity of the neurotransmitter neuropeptide Y (NPY) in the hypothalamus, ramping up your desire for sweet and starchy food. And what activates NPY? You guessed it: ghrelin. The evolutionary logic is clear—it's a process elegantly designed to keep us alive! When people are starving, sweet and starchy foods are ideal because they're easy to digest and they raise blood sugar quickly. And that's exactly what needs to happen when blood sugar drops to a critical low point, as it does during extreme hunger. The faster you can stimulate that blood sugar to rise, the better. That's why ghrelin and NPY work in tandem.

The peculiar problem now, though, is that we're living in times of plenty, not famine. We have a lot more appetite-stimulating input barraging our senses—food advertisements online, on television, in magazines, and on billboards, plus the aroma from the fast-food chain just around the corner—than our ancestors ever had to contend with. We're also living far from nature and experiencing stressors that drive ghrelin levels up even though food is anything *but* scarce. Maybe you're a working mother with more errands than hours in the day. Maybe your spouse or child is ill and you're worried about medical bills. Or maybe your job requires you to go, go, go—rushing from meeting to meeting, without a break, for hours on end. Stressors like these can send ghrelin through the roof. And high ghrelin levels cause you to eat more while slowing down your metabolism—a double whammy. No wonder people get fat.

APPETITE OR HUNGER?

You probably already know that there's a big difference between hunger and appetite. But you may not know that ghrelin plays a role in both. Hunger is physiological. Appetite, on the other hand, is a learned behavior that depends on lots of external cues. Think of Thanksgiving, for instance. You may be hungry when you sit down at the table, but it's not hunger that induces you to have a second helping of pecan pie after a full plate of turkey with all the fixings. *That's* appetite at work.

Ghrelin triggers appetite in purely physiological ways—and in psychological ways, too. Let's look at the physiological way first.

Ghrelin and True Hunger

True hunger—that's when your stomach is empty and your body is low on nutrients—stimulates the release of ghrelin. And eating puts a stop to ghrelin production. In fact, eating's the only way to turn ghrelin off.

Ghrelin levels rise and fall throughout the day. About 45 minutes to an hour after you finish a meal, the cells in the lining of your stomach (as well as other cells in your pancreas) begin to make more ghrelin. (See the True Hunger loop on page 14.) These cells secrete ghrelin into your blood, causing levels of the hormone to rise. If you abstain from food for another half hour, the ghrelin factory in your belly revs up again and starts producing even more. As this newly produced ghrelin makes its way to the receptors in the hypothalamus in your brain, you start becoming *aware* of your hunger.

This process repeats itself every 30 minutes until you've gone 4 hours without eating. That's when ghrelin gets *really* insistent. At the 4-hour mark, special cells lining your stomach begin producing ghrelin *every 10 minutes*. This is your body's way of saying, *"Hey you! Eat something! Now!"*

Why does your body care if—or when—you eat? That's simple. Because every single one of the *hundred trillion* cells in your body requires huge amounts of energy moment to moment to sustain the processes that maintain life. Your cells "liberate" energy by transforming the food you eat into ATP, a form of energy they can use. In the space of just a few minutes, a single cell can use up *one billion* ATP molecules. So your body is constantly replenishing its supplies.

Ghrelin to the rescue. It comes galloping in to remind you to eat and to prevent you *and* your cells from starving.

Let's use an example. Imagine you sit down to breakfast at 7:30 and finish at 8:00 a.m., then head off to work. Since you've eaten a big breakfast, your ghrelin levels drop and continue to decrease over the next hour, returning to baseline levels.

At 9:00 a.m., you start working, and so does your body's ghrelin factory. The internal production line starts up, and tiny amounts of ghrelin begin circulating in your bloodstream. Around 9:30 a.m., your body produces a new batch of ghrelin, raising its level in your blood even higher. Then—if you don't eat—it does the same at 10:00 and again at 10:30 a.m., when you're probably contemplating a bagel and a cup of coffee. If you skip that bagel, your body will pump out more ghrelin at 11:00

and still more at 11:30 a.m. And if you manage to hold off until noon, some 4 hours since you took your last bite of breakfast, ghrelin revs up into overdrive.

But let's say a noontime conference call forces you to put off lunch a bit longer. As your body releases another batch of ghrelin and your stomach growls, you put the phone on mute. It's a wonder you can concentrate at all. To make matters worse, the aroma of chicken soup and leftover lasagna waft in from the cubicles around

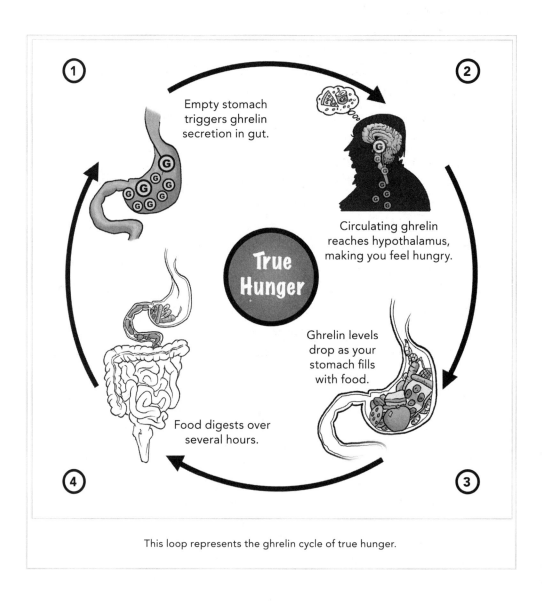

1. Empty stomach triggers ghrelin secretion in gut.

2. Circulating ghrelin reaches hypothalamus, making you feel hungry.

3. Ghrelin levels drop as your stomach fills with food.

4. Food digests over several hours.

True Hunger

This loop represents the ghrelin cycle of true hunger.

Spend More, Weigh Less

Everyone knows that packing on the pounds comes with a steep health cost. But did you ever think about how being overweight hurts you economically? Here's the paradox: When you add up the economic costs of obesity, it's clear that you actually *save* money if you spend *more* on good-quality food.

Think of it this way: If someone told you it would be 10 degrees below zero tomorrow and all you own is a pair of shorts and a tank top, what would you do? Would you go to a discount store and buy a cheap coat without a lining? Or would you spend a few extra bucks for a long down coat to protect you from the cold? What's the better deal in the long run?

It's the same with food. We all know that healthy foods cost more than junk. In the short term, this can be scary. You might be on a set budget. You might think: *But I can't afford it. Where's the extra money going to come from?* My suggestion: Look at good-quality food as an investment—in your health, your well-being, your body image, and your sense of yourself. A long-term investment in your health is worth a lot more than any savings you might get on those buy-one/get-one frozen waffles.

Put a dollar value on the guilt you feel after eating the second (free) bag of chips. Put a dollar value on your loss of self-esteem when you can't fit into your "fat jeans" anymore. Put a dollar value on all the time you spend wishing you weighed less, had more energy, or could keep up with your kids. How much is all of that worth to you?

There are hard costs as well. In fact, the George Washington University School of Public Health and Health Services did a review of all the studies that looked at the economic costs of obesity and excess weight. The review estimates that "the overall, tangible annual costs each year of being obese are $4,879 for an obese woman and $2,646 for an obese man." If you're simply overweight but not quite obese, the annual costs are less—but still significant: $524 for men and $432 for women.[6]

How come? Studies show that obese Hispanic and Caucasian women are less likely to be employed than their normal-weight counterparts—that's a big economic impact. Other studies show that obese women earn less than normal-weight women. Still other studies show that individual medical costs creep up with the number on the scale and that overweight and obese office workers are more likely to suffer from disability and limitations on the job than normal-weight workers. And let's not forget clothing. Many of my clients tell me how difficult it is to find clothes they like, that fit well, and that fall within their budget.

When you add up all the costs, it's easy to see how spending a little more to eat healthful food can save you thousands of dollars a year.

SUGGESTION: Name three things you'd do with the money you'd save if you reached a healthy weight.

you, making you hungrier still. (After all, elevated blood levels of ghrelin make you more sensitive to food smells.)

The conference call finally finishes up at 1:30 p.m., more than 5½ hours since your last morsel of food. Ravenously hungry, you head down to the cafeteria. The "rational" you knows that you're watching your weight, and you're fully aware of the cafeteria's low-calorie selections. But the part of your brain that's been hijacked by high blood levels of ghrelin steers you straight to the special of the day—a gooey bread crumb–encrusted, three-cheese, deep-dish macaroni-and-cheese entrée. You pick up a side salad with a roll and butter, and before you know what's hit you, you're adding a slice of peach pie with a scoop of vanilla ice cream to your tray. (That's neuropeptide Y kicking in.) And then—by now you've thrown caution to the wind—you add a whole-milk latte to top it off.

This is your brain freaked out on too much ghrelin.

First, your body is trying to get you to eat on *its* schedule, not yours. That's why it's been sending out those every-10-minute bursts of ghrelin starting when your stomach has been empty for 4 hours.

What About Weight-Loss Surgery?

Research shows that weight-loss surgery changes the gut-brain connection by altering the anatomy of the digestive tract and affecting gut hormone production and secretions[7]—including ghrelin. That makes sense since ghrelin is secreted from the stomach lining, which is reduced to about 25 percent of its original size after surgery.

Studies have indicated that weight-loss surgery, such as gastric bypass, generally results in reduced production and secretion of ghrelin.[8] After surgery, many people report lower levels of hunger and experience sig-

nificant weight loss in a short amount of time—they often say that "the weight just falls off," mainly because they're simply not hungry. Researchers speculate that the change in ghrelin production is one of the reasons weight loss surgery is successful.

But the role of ghrelin in the success of weight-loss surgery needs much more research.[9] And a recent study reported that those ghrelin levels eventually creep back up.[10] So your best bet: Instead of going under the knife, follow the Belly Fat Fix for similar results without the risks associated with surgery.

THE HUNGER TRAP

Chronically high circulating ghrelin leads to weight gain

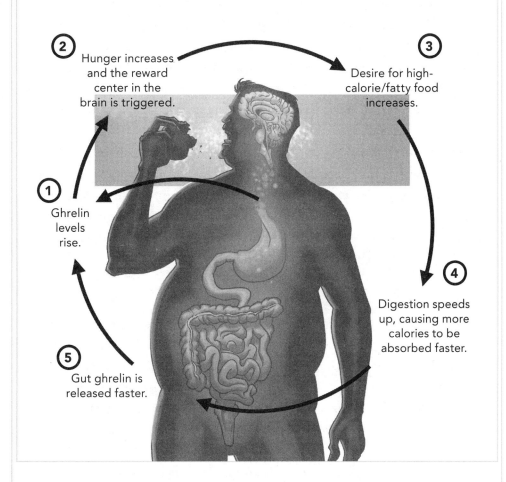

② Hunger increases and the reward center in the brain is triggered.

③ Desire for high-calorie/fatty food increases.

① Ghrelin levels rise.

④ Digestion speeds up, causing more calories to be absorbed faster.

⑤ Gut ghrelin is released faster.

After gobbling down your lunch, you stare at your empty tray in dismay. *What happened to my willpower?* you lament, overcome with remorse. But willpower is *not* the problem. Here's what's going on *inside* your body and mind, beneath the level of rational thinking and a world away from the realm of willpower.

Second, high blood levels of ghrelin make you more likely to choose high-calorie foods and to eat more than you would otherwise. If you were living in a time of famine, it would be smart to load up on those starchy macaroni-and-cheese calories when they're available—after all, who knows when you might get a chance to eat again? But you're not living in famine conditions. In fact, there's probably a vending machine down the hall and a McDonald's down the block.

Research has shown that elevated ghrelin levels lead to overeating. In one study, scientists divided participants into two groups. They injected people in the control group with a saline solution and the other group with a high enough concentration of ghrelin to raise their blood levels to 24-hour fasting levels. Then they set both groups loose at an all-you-can-eat buffet.

Guess which group ended up eating 30 percent more food than normal? Yep, it was the ghrelin people.

The takeaway: If you'd eaten before your ghrelin levels had risen so high, you'd have had an easier time choosing a healthy lunch. And chances are, your lunch also would have cost you less money. One study showed that people under the influence of high levels of ghrelin were willing to pay more for food than those in a control group without elevated ghrelin levels. High levels of ghrelin are hard on your waistline—and your pocketbook![11]

Ghrelin and Psychological Hunger

Of course, we don't eat just because we're hungry. Sometimes we eat because food looks delicious. Maybe we've had that strawberry shortcake before and we remember the pleasure eating it. Or maybe we're stressed and soothing ourselves with ice cream. (See "Are You a Stress Eater"? on pages 22–23.) Sometimes we eat because we're bored, so we may look to food to provide some sensory excitement.

Ghrelin also plays a role in the brain's pleasure circuits. In fact, the brain reward centers linked to ghrelin are the same ones involved in drug and alcohol addiction. Scientists have found a link between high blood levels of ghrelin and some aspects of binge eating and compulsive overeating.[12] (See Psychological Hunger, opposite.)

Ghrelin even heightens our sensitivity to the aroma of food and increases food-sniffing behavior.[13] The higher the ghrelin level, the greater the sensitivity and the more frequent the sniffing. Something similar goes on with the brain's ability to recall food pictures. The higher the level of ghrelin, the more firmly that picture etches into your memory, since ghrelin acts on the areas of your brain involved in memory formation. Ever had a whiff of a dish that sparked a childhood memory? Maybe you smell a muffin as you walk past a bakery, reminding you of your grandmother's house on Sunday mornings. Yep—that's ghrelin at work.

In our hunter–gatherer past, these abilities conferred an evolutionary advantage. The pain of hunger drove our ancestors to seek out food, relying on sight and smell to locate it and on memory to recall where they'd last seen fish or game, fruit or berries. The pleasure of eating rewarded them for their efforts.

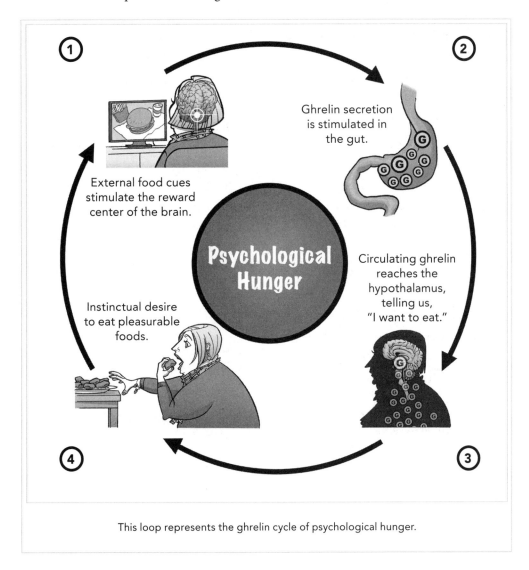

① External food cues stimulate the reward center of the brain.

② Ghrelin secretion is stimulated in the gut.

③ Circulating ghrelin reaches the hypothalamus, telling us, "I want to eat."

④ Instinctual desire to eat pleasurable foods.

Psychological Hunger

This loop represents the ghrelin cycle of psychological hunger.

It was ghrelin that gave them the drive to look for food, *plus* the ability to find it, *plus* the reward for their efforts. "Until food became abundant," my physician father-in-law pointed out to me recently, "ghrelin was the most important factor in preserving the human species." Ghrelin provides the neurochemical link between the areas of the brain that regulate energy balance (the number of calories you take in versus the number you burn) and those involved in memory, learning, and pleasure. Short-term learning and memory are enhanced during food deprivation, since in our evolutionary past we needed enhanced cognitive skills to track down food.

Fast-forward to 21st-century North America, where we have supermarkets in the suburbs, greengrocers on every city corner, and drive-thru lanes at all the fast-food chains. Here's the problem: Sensory cues can stimulate appetite even in the absence of true physiological hunger. In fact, if you've ever wondered what it is that causes you to head for the nearest McDonald's soon after you've driven by a billboard with a giant picture of a Big Mac—that's ghrelin at work. The remembered pleasure of eating your last delicious hamburger gets triggered by the picture as the memory and reward centers in your brain come together under the influence of ghrelin. When food is as plentiful as it is today, though, it's all too easy to continue eating for pleasure long after your true appetite has been satisfied.

Too Little Sleep? Too Much Weight!

Researchers have found that how much—and how soundly—you sleep sets into motion a cascade of hormonal activity that affects your appetite. Lack of sleep causes blood levels of leptin—the hormone that makes you feel full—to fall and ghrelin—which stimulates your appetite—to rise. Studies have shown that people who are sleep deprived crave high-carbohydrate, calorie-dense foods.

Put this all together—the craving for high-calorie foods, the inability to feel full as quickly as usual, and the enhanced hunger signals—and you have a perfect recipe for a high-calorie eating binge.

Here's how to head that off at the pass: If you know you're sleep deprived, sometimes the best way to stave off hunger—or stop that craving for food you *know* you shouldn't eat—is to take a nap.

Incidentally, when ghrelin is working as it should, it promotes deep sleep. (We'll talk more about the relationship between ghrelin and sleep later in the book.)

Ghrelin and Stress

But it's not all about hunger—real or imagined. One of the reasons we seek out food when we don't need it is stress. When we're feeling down or anxious, what we really want is comfort, so we instinctively seek to soothe ourselves by reaching for another piece of fresh-from-the-oven bread or pie or another handful of chocolate chip cookies. At some level, our bodies know that eating carbohydrates like these causes

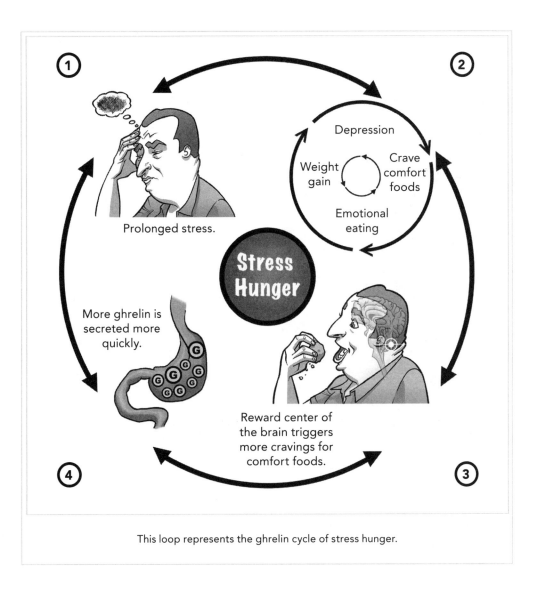

This loop represents the ghrelin cycle of stress hunger.

the brain and central nervous system to release an amino acid called serotonin, which calms our nerves and boosts our mood.

Scientists have discovered that psychosocial stress—the kind that arises in social situations when, say, your boss is condescending and you can't tell him off or when you have to spend an afternoon with that mother-in-law who grates on your nerves—not only boosts the body's level of the stress hormone corticosterone but

Are You a Stress Eater?

This easy quiz can help you learn more about yourself and why you pop those chocolate chip cookies in your mouth every time a deadline looms. Find out if you're a stress eater—just answer the questions below. Check your score at the end.

1. When I feel stressed, I eat without thinking . . .
   a. Most of the time
   b. Sometimes
   c. Rarely

2. When I'm stressed, I crave sweets and desserts, bread, pasta, or chips . . .
   a. Most of the time
   b. Sometimes
   c. Rarely

3. When I'm stressed, it's hard to stop eating . . .
   a. Most of the time
   b. Sometimes
   c. Rarely

4. When I'm stressed, I find myself distracted with thoughts about food . . .
   a. Most of the time
   b. Sometimes
   c. Rarely

5. When I'm stressed, I look for something to eat even when I'm not hungry . . .
   a. Most of the time
   b. Sometimes
   c. Rarely

6. When I'm stressed, I make unhealthy decisions about my food . . .
   a. Most of the time
   b. Sometimes
   c. Rarely

revs up production of ghrelin as well. Those scientists devised an experiment designed to provoke what psychologists call "social defeat stress" (a type of psychosocial stress) by taking male mice and exposing them to bouts of social subordination by an older, aggressive male mouse. As predicted, the subordinate males showed higher levels of corticosterone after these episodes. Curiously, they also exhibited higher levels of circulating ghrelin. Scientists took the study a little

7. When I'm stressed, I prefer to eat alone . . .

   a. Most of the time

   b. Sometimes

   c. Rarely

8. When I'm stressed, I feel powerless against food . . .

   a. Most of the time

   b. Sometimes

   c. Rarely

9. When I eat a dessert that's not part of my plan, I feel more stressed . . .

   a. Most of the time

   b. Sometimes

   c. Rarely

10. After a stressful day, I tend to eat in the evening . . .

   a. Most of the time

   b. Sometimes

   c. Rarely

Tally up your score:
A = 1 point
B = 2 points
C = 3 points

Red Light: You're a Stress Eater (10–14 points) Stop before you munch! You're prone to mindless stress eating. Instead of eating when you're hungry, you turn to food (usually comfort and junk foods) when you're feeling emotions like boredom, anger, anxiety, or stress. Though filling up on these foods helps you feel better now, you end up feeling more stressed out later.

Yellow Light: You Have Stress-Eating Tendencies (15–23 points) Slow down! Most of the time you have a fairly balanced attitude toward food, but on bad days, you're vulnerable to stress eating. You've caved in to stress eating at some point but tend to get back on track pretty easily.

Green Light: You're Not a Stress Eater (24–30 points) Cruise right along. You're dealing with your stress in healthy ways—without food! Your choice of when and what to eat has little to do with your mood.

further and devised a chamber with two sides. On odd days, they confined the stressed, subordinate males to one side of the chamber—the side that contained high-fat food. On even days, they confined them to the other side of the chamber, where regular food was available.[14]

What do you think happened? Yup, the socially stressed mice ate more high-fat food when they had access to it. They also spent more time on the side of the chamber where the high-fat food had originally been placed.[15]

The scientists who carried out that study speculate that "a stress-induced rise in ghrelin levels may facilitate coping mechanisms." They also note that ghrelin has potent anti-inflammatory effects. Inflammation is the body's way of protecting cells, but in stressful situations, cellular components of the immune system attack the body's own tissues as if they were foreign matter. That's when ghrelin comes to the rescue, as levels of the hormone rise, temporarily offsetting this self-attack consequence of stress.[16] This is nature's way of preserving the immune system when chronic stress causes inflammation.

But ghrelin can cause stress, too. Other research has shown that injecting people with high doses of ghrelin increases blood levels of ACTH (adrenocorticotropic hormone), a substance often released under biological stress, and cortisol, a stress hormone that increases blood sugar and aids in the metabolism of fats, protein, and carbohydrates. (See Stress Hunger on page 56).

Coping with Stress Eating

Take the "Are You a Stress Eater"? quiz (pages 22–23). Did that red light flash on? Or did the yellow light slow you down and make you think twice? If you're a stress eater—or have a tendency to be one—here are some strategies to help just say no to noshing when you're stressed out.

1. **Take a time-out.** Imagine that the part of your brain cuing you to stress-eat is your 5-year-old misbehaving kid. What would you do? If you're a healthy disciplinarian, you'd tell your kid to sit in the corner for 10 minutes, right? Well, you don't have to sit in a corner, but take 10 to reflect on your urge to eat. That'll help you resolve whatever's going on in your life right now and move past it—without food.

2. **Write it down.** The process of keeping track of your food will slow you down and increase your awareness of your stress-eating patterns. And increased awareness will go a long way toward decreasing stress eating.

3. **Tune in.** Most of us have smartphones and computers at our fingertips, night and day. Tempted to grab a snack when life throws you a curveball? Pick up your electronic device instead. Send a text to a friend. Zap yourself a reminder to stay positive. Download an app to help you keep track of your food and exercise.

4. **Plan ahead.** Stash a low-calorie snack in your desk drawer, pocket, or purse. You can't always shut off the stress-eating switch at will, so be prepared with a planned snack. A handful of baby carrots is a great choice because the crunch helps release tension.

YOUR BELLY ON GHRELIN

Ghrelin has lots of effects on your brain. Since it's produced in the stomach and the pancreas, you'd expect it to have an impact on your abdominal organs, too—and you'd be right. In the stomach, ghrelin stimulates the release of hydrochloric acid, which assists in the digestion of protein and fat. It increases the secretion of gastric acid, a fluid that activates the enzymes that help digest proteins. Ghrelin also affects the speed at which food is moved along through your gut, aided by rhythmic contractions of the smooth muscle of your gastrointestinal tract. The rhythmic contractions start in your esophagus and travel down through your stomach and intestines all the way into your colon in a process called *gastric motility*.

Elsewhere in the abdomen, ghrelin and insulin—a hormone, secreted by the pancreas that helps keep the level of glucose (or sugar) in the blood from becoming too high—engage in a complex feedback loop. Insulin, produced in response to eating, inhibits ghrelin secretion in healthy, normal-weight people. The glucose that the insulin acts on also plays a role in suppressing ghrelin. For people suffering from a severe deficiency of insulin, however, it's a different story: After they finish a meal, ghrelin isn't turned off. So they never quite feel full—and that leads them to eat more than they need.

But if things are working as they should, after you finish a meal, leptin, the hormone that makes us feel full, kicks in and ghrelin production is suppressed, leaving you with no biological urge to eat for now. Over the next hour, as your food is digested, blood levels of ghrelin drop to their lowest level and your body goes to work transforming the food you've eaten into end products that can be burned for fuel rather than stored as fat. Your body now has all the energy it needs to function optimally. You feel vital and alive. That's how things are supposed to work.

Unfortunately, it's all too easy to—unwittingly—muck up the mechanics and throw that ghrelin cycle out of whack. Any number of things will do it, especially prolonged stress, erratic eating habits, crash dieting, eating the wrong combination of foods, or grazing every couple of hours. You can also derail the ghrelin train by starving yourself until you can't stand it anymore and then overeating, or by not getting enough sleep. Any and all of these can tip the balance, turning ghrelin from a literal lifesaver into a foe in your fight to lose weight.

Let's look at one common way this happens. Say you put yourself on a crash diet. Starving yourself causes your body to produce more ghrelin, which only makes you hungrier. Weight loss from extreme dieting causes elevated ghrelin levels. When ghrelin levels remain chronically elevated, you digest food more quickly, since your body, tricked by high ghrelin into thinking it's starving, can't get those nutrients

---

COACHING TIP

Lose Weight Together!

The Belly Fat Fix was designed with couples in mind—after all, weight loss is easier when you take a team approach. You'll see in Chapter 5 that the 3-Day Fast-Track plan lists the same foods for men and women; only the portion sizes are different. In Chapter 6, you'll notice that your meal plans are all the same foods but, depending on the specific amount of weight you want to lose, the portions are different.

This makes it a snap for both of you to follow the plan and eat the same foods. The only difference: how *much* you put on your plate! This definitely works, as my clients have shown. One couple, Donna and Dave, successfully lost 51 pounds together on the Belly Fat Fix eating all of the same foods.

fast enough. Your stomach empties more quickly, too, and the quicker your stomach empties, the sooner ghrelin starts to rise again and the sooner you feel hungry. You eat again, and the cycle continues.

I call this the ghrelin Hunger Trap. The faster you get hungry, the more often you eat. The more often you eat, the more calories you ingest. The more calories you ingest, the heavier you become, and so on and so on. (Again, see The Hunger Trap on page 17).

But it's not just the extra calories that make you fat. Elevated levels of ghrelin cause your body to convert excess calories from nonfatty foods into fat and then to store that fat for future use. That's not ghrelin being obstinate. It's simply a "miscommunication." The high ghrelin levels trigger a "starvation signal" within your cells. That's because your cells are registering that they don't have enough energy—so your body goes into conservation mode. From your body's perspective, you've starved yourself before, and who knows when—and for how long—you'll attempt that again. Somewhere in your biological memory, the threat of famine is ever present.

Your body, by the way, contains a type of fat cell especially designed to store energy in case of such emergencies. These are the cells that make up *white fat* (as opposed to *brown fat)*. White fat cells can plump up to about four times their size before dividing and increasing the absolute number of fat cells present.[17] The DNA of white fat cells is replicated on a daily cycle. Scientists suspect this cyclic replication makes white fat cells more prone to expand in people who graze, since they have more frequent exposure to ghrelin, than in those who eat three square meals a day. They suspect the same is true in people who eat at times that are at variance with the body's own natural hunger cycles, which also have their own daily rhythm.[18] (See The Survival Effect on page 28.)

White fat, in the presence of chronically high levels of ghrelin, expands, particularly in your belly. Those conditions cause your body to defend against the breakdown of that fat. The end result? Belly fat that won't budge, no matter how many calories you cut or crunches you do.

Can you see now how elevated levels of ghrelin can lead to the development of obesity? Curiously, at a certain point, once someone becomes obese, ghrelin levels drop and stay at a level that is below that of normal-weight individuals. Why do ghrelin levels drop? It's a bit complicated. Ghrelin, of course, triggers hunger, working in opposition to the hormone leptin, which triggers a sense of fullness. People who are obese have high leptin levels because leptin is produced in the fat cells. As leptin levels rise, ghrelin levels drop. Think of a seesaw. As one end rises up, the other dips down. (I'll talk more about leptin in Chapter 2.) This creates a real problem for people watching their weight because as leptin shoots up, the body starts to ignore it. This is called leptin resistance.

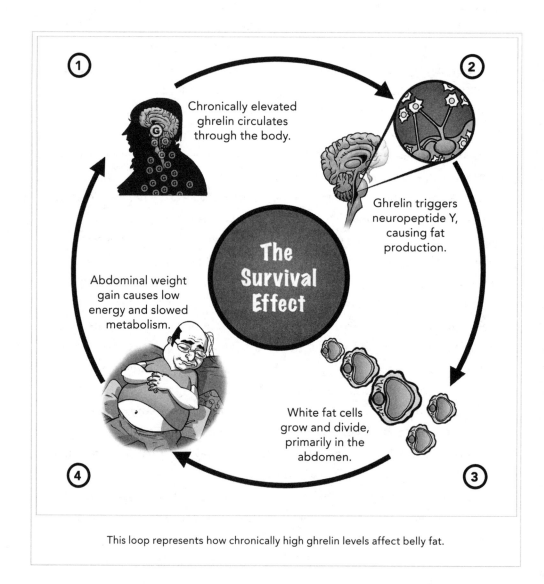

①

Chronically elevated ghrelin circulates through the body.

②

Ghrelin triggers neuropeptide Y, causing fat production.

The Survival Effect

Abdominal weight gain causes low energy and slowed metabolism.

White fat cells grow and divide, primarily in the abdomen.

④

③

This loop represents how chronically high ghrelin levels affect belly fat.

And when you become resistant to leptin, you stop experiencing that satisfying sense of fullness after a meal. In short, you never quite feel full. You've lost that biological signal that tells you to stop eating when you've had enough.

To complicate things, after people become obese and their internal leptin–ghrelin seesaw shifts from the balance position to the high-leptin–low-ghrelin position, insulin resistance becomes a real threat. Once you become insulin resistant (similar to leptin resistance), ghrelin drops even lower, initiating a disease process very likely to erupt into full-blown diabetes. People who are insulin resistant can't make effective use of insulin. When the body can't use insulin effectively, blood sugar and fat levels rise. In short, chronically elevated ghrelin levels lead to obesity; obesity causes a rise in leptin and insulin resistance; and insulin resistance spurs the development of type 2 diabetes. It becomes a vicious cycle.

Another big problem: Eating doesn't suppress the production of ghrelin in people who are obese or insulin resistant, even though baseline levels of the hunger hormone are lower than in normal-weight people. And when the appetite remains continually on, guess what people do?

The Belly Fat Fix Plan

If you're reading this book, chances are you're somewhere on that downward cycle I described. Maybe you're at the beginning; maybe you're significantly along the curve, like some of my clients. It doesn't matter. The Belly Fat Fix can help you reverse the spiral.

Here's how the plan works *with* your body:

1. **It teaches you how to time your meals around true biological hunger.** (See Chapter 2.) Evidence shows that people who eat three meals a day may be less prone to accumulating fat, especially around their middle. The Belly Fat Fix is built around three balanced meals, plus a daily snack.

2. **It teaches you what to eat to experience a biological feeling of fullness.** How full you feel isn't just a function of how much you eat but also of the kinds of food you put on your plate. (See Chapters 3, 5, and 6.) The Belly Fat Fix will teach you what kinds of foods to eat—and in what proportions—to nourish yourself and create that satisfying feeling of fullness. In fact, if you're not full on this plan, I advise you to eat *more* instead of *less*.

3. **It teaches you portion control, so you don't take in calories you don't need.** In my experience as a dietitian, few people understand what a single serving or appropriate portion size is. But don't worry. The portions I recommend won't leave you hungry. In fact, most of my clients are surprised by how much I tell them to eat! I ask them to get a food scale and extra measuring spoons and cups to help with portion control. (See Chapter 4.)

4. **It teaches you how to distinguish biological hunger from nonphysical hunger.** (See "Are You a Stress Eater"? on pages 22–23.) In Chapter 11, you'll keep track of your experiences with food and hunger so you become more self-aware and better and better at determining whether you hunger for food or for something else, like comfort or relief from boredom.

5. **It provides you with a 3-day plan to "reset" your eating switch anytime you need to get back on track with your diet.** (See Chapter 5.) We all know how easy it is to fall off the wagon, especially during vacations or holidays. Consider the 3-Day Fast-Track plan your reset button.

6. **It teaches you how to exercise to keep ghrelin levels in balance.** (See Chapter 8.) There's a specific way to exercise to suppress ghrelin. The exercises I'll teach you will also help you keep the weight off. Bonus: They're easy and quick!

The takeaway: Ghrelin is a hormone you need to support—not undermine—if you want to reach your weight goals easily. Because the Belly Fat Fix works *with* your body, it's safe for just about everyone, except those whose health conditions require them to be on very specific dietary regimens. The Belly Fat Fix—with one important caveat—is safe for people with diabetes. Here's the warning: If you are insulin dependent, then I urge you to consult a registered dietitian or a diabetes educator to make the adjustments that are right for you. That's because this plan isn't set up to count grams of carbohydrates, something you must do if you're taking insulin.

COMING UP NEXT: Chapter 2, where I'll introduce you to the Ghrelin Hunger Scale, created to help you time your meals around your body's natural hunger cycles.

CHAPTER 2

Using the G-Scale to Eat on *Your Body's* Schedule

What makes the Belly Fat Fix different? The emphasis on timing your meals. And that's what also makes it effective and easy to stay with. When you eat the right amount of food at the right times, you lose weight and stay healthy, even while feeling full throughout the day. That's the beauty of the plan.

But meal timing isn't a gimmick. It's a way to return to how nature wants all of us to eat.

Here's what you need to do: Eat three meals a day, plus an afternoon snack. Simple. You'll eat on a regular schedule with your meals timed to keep your ghrelin levels stable rather than elevated. In this chapter, you'll learn how to time your meals around your true appetite to overcome that ravenous hunger that flares up when your ghrelin levels become so elevated you can polish off a quart of ice cream in no time flat.

RETHINKING THREE SQUARE MEALS

Three square meals a day? In the history of the world, that's a pretty recent innovation. Our hunter-gather ancestors didn't have the luxury of sitting down to breakfast, lunch, and dinner at preappointed times. After all, there was no telling when that wild boar might show up—and no supermarket where they could pick up a quart of milk or a loaf of bread. For most of human history, people hunted wild animals and foraged for wild plants, says author Jared Diamond.[1] "The quest for food was driven largely by the hunger pangs ghrelin caused, which helped early man survive," he writes in his essay "The Worst Mistake in the History of the Human Race." "We ate *only* when physically hungry; otherwise, there was no reason to make the effort to find or hunt down food."

Diamond offers the following analogy to show just how long human beings lived that way. Imagine a 24-hour clock in which each hour represents 100,000 years of real past time:

"If the history of the human race began at midnight, then we would now be almost at the end of our first day," he says. "We've lived as hunger-gatherers for nearly the whole of that day, from midnight through dawn, noon, and sunset. Finally, at 11:54, we adopted agriculture."[2]

That was some 10,000 years ago.

But as soon as the first farmer planted those first tidy rows of corn and wheat, it became possible to predict when food would be available—and the art of meal planning was born. Until then—for a span of some 200,000 years—human behavior was largely driven by ghrelin-induced cycles of appetite and leptin-induced cycles of satiety (or fullness), all within the larger natural rhythms of day and night and the human rhythms of activity and rest.

Remember leptin from Chapter 1? That's the hormone produced in the fat cells that sends a "fullness" alert to the brain, telling it, "Stop eating! We've got all the nutrition we need for now!" That back-and-forth banter promotes long-term energy balance, a term that refers to the equilibrium between the amount of food we eat and the amount of energy we use. Too much food in—along with too little energy out—packs on the pounds. When we bring in too many units of food energy—we call them calories—our body converts them into fat, saving it for a rainy day.

In prehistoric times, humans hunted for food during the day and slept at night, so it made sense for ghrelin to be most active when the sun was shining. And that's the same pattern ghrelin follows today. It's secreted into our body on a proven schedule, and its levels in the blood peak three times a day. The last peak coincides with the dinner hour. (See the Healthy 24-Hour Ghrelin Pattern below.)

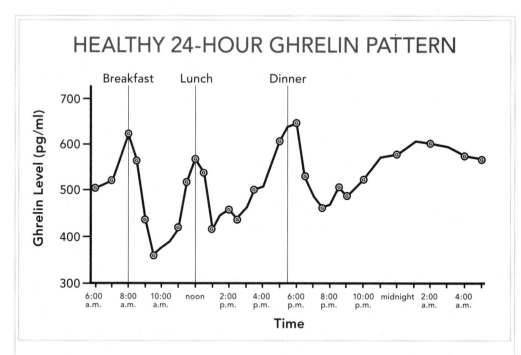

HEALTHY 24-HOUR GHRELIN PATTERN

This graph shows the ebbs and flows of ghrelin throughout the day. Notice the hours when it peaks and the way levels fall sharply once appetite has been satisfied.

If our ancestors were lucky enough to find food during the day, ghrelin secretion would subside after the last meal of the day and drop down to baseline levels within the hour. Then it would begin to climb back up again, until precipitously dropping off in the wee hours of the morning. This allowed the hunter-gatherers to sleep through the night to gather strength for the next day's hunt. It's hard to sleep when you're hungry, so the steep drop-off of ghrelin in the early-morning hours gave our ancestors the luxury of a nice, long siesta. That made for an intelligent interplay between the body's need for food and the body's need for rest.

For most of human history, ghrelin drove human beings to do their primary work—finding food to fill their hungry bellies. A long time between boars and berries? Ghrelin levels shot up, prompting those humans to gorge on anything handy— another intentional part of ghrelin's "design," ensuring that starving humans would not only make up for calories missed but also create reserves of stored fat just in case food remained scarce.

But if those early humans weren't starving—literally—they'd eat only until they'd had their fill, just as animals do. That's different from the way most of us today eat for pleasure—probably more often than we realize.

Our ancestors' way of living, regulated by the hunger fullness cycles in the body and by the rising and setting of the sun, is still deep in our cellular memory, and we can retrieve it with conscious effort and awareness. I'll share tips with you to help you regain this ability to eat in a way that's in harmony with your body's true needs. But you must be willing to abandon your old patterns of reaching mindlessly for food because it's a) available; b) something you use to soothe yourself; c) something from which you are seeking pleasure (pleasure, perhaps, that might better be pursued in nonfood ways); d) a way to be social; or e) any of a number of reasons that have nothing to do with your body's nutritional needs.

If you eat for pleasure, by the way, you have plenty of company. Mahatma Gandhi observed that "99 percent of men and women in this world eat merely to please the palate. They never pause to think of the after-effects at the time of eating."

But if you want to lose weight, keep it off, and end your struggle with the scale once and for all, you'll have to come back to our ancestors' natural patterns of eating. In the most practical sense, that means you have to:

1. Ask yourself: Am I *really* hungry? (We'll use the G-Scale for that.)

2. Change your habits: Eat four times a day—three balanced meals plus an afternoon snack—at the right time for *your* body. (I'll explain why this is critical.)

3. Focus: Pay attention to what you're eating so you'll enjoy each bite. My clients who take the time to do this consistently report that they eat much less while still feeling satisfied.

The more consistently you do all three, the easier it'll be for you to distinguish between true physiological hunger and the kind whipped up by outside cues or by internal stress—which have nothing to do with your body's need for nourishment. Then the weight will come off and, even more significantly—as you'll see in the stories of our "Ghrelin Masters" who've lost pounds permanently—stay off.

Is That My Stomach Growling?

The digestive system is a long tube that starts at your mouth and ends you know where. Even before it begins the task of digesting your food, it initiates strong muscular contractions called peristalsis. That's hard, noisy work, and it's this movement that causes your stomach to make such a ruckus when you're hungry.

But how come your stomach growls before you eat and not after? That's because when there's food in your stomach or small intestine, the growling becomes quieter. It's like putting a pair of sneakers in the dryer by themselves rather than throwing them in with a load of towels. The towels muffle the noise of the shoes as they bounce around. In the same way, food in your stomach muffles the sound of the growls.

But if your stomach is completely empty, here's what happens: The ghrelin-producing cells secrete the hormone into your bloodstream, where it travels to your brain and into your hypothalamus. Once it gets there, it signals your digestive muscles to contract, preparing you for the next round of digestion. This preparation is important for two reasons: First, the contractions remove any remaining food missed from your last meal. Second, an empty stomach stimulates ghrelin secretion, and that's what sends the hunger signals to your brain. Muscle contractions come and go—about every hour—until you eat again. The contraction period—those insistent growls—generally lasts 10 to 20 minutes.

THE G-SCALE AND THE RHYTHMS OF TRUE HUNGER

How do you learn to distinguish your natural hunger from other kinds of hunger? The best way is to gradually become more attuned to the signals your body is sending out—signals that say, *Feed me* or *I'm thirsty* or even *I'm anxious* or *I'm stressing out—attend to me.*

That's what the G-Scale is designed to do. It may seem artificial at first, or just another task to add to your already busy day. But give it a try. Make a copy of this template and take it with you wherever you go, then use it throughout the day. Practice noticing when you're hungry and when you're not. And then feed yourself accordingly.

I can't stress how important—and helpful—it is to make a habit of using the G-Scale. It'll bring you back to your body's natural, healthy way of timing your meals.

And we need all the help we can get. After all, many of us have trouble distinguishing pure hunger from wanting to eat for any number of other reasons. By using the G-Scale regularly, you'll become more tuned in to your real hunger, leading you to eat at appropriate times and avoiding that ghrelin Hunger Trap we learned about back in Chapter 1. I've seen it work time and time again in my practice. When you're in the throes of the Hunger Trap, you've pretty much lost control over how much you eat.

That needs to change. You need to learn to eat when you have true body hunger and then, just as your ancestors did way back when, to stop when you've had your fill. You need to learn to heed the subtle signs of satiety, brought about by the release of leptin and the drop-off of ghrelin after you've eaten. (See Leptin: The "I Feel Full" Hormone on page 49.)

Here's more good news: On the Belly Fat Fix, you'll never feel a sense of deprivation. You'll eat enough to feel full, appeasing your appetite in a biochemically intelligent and efficient way—and gaining control of it at last. This *is* possible. In fact, my clients often tell me how surprised they are that they can feel full and lose weight at the same time.

(continued on page 40)

The Long Journey from Hunting and Gathering to Three Meals a Day

Ten thousand years ago—give or take—human beings took up gardening, and that changed life on the planet forever. That's when our ancestors learned to cultivate grains like wheat, whose wild relatives were first grown in the Middle East.[3]

For the first time, people no longer had to wander to kill animals or pick berries. Now they could stay put and produce food for themselves by planting crops and breeding animals for meat or eggs—or both. Over time, advances in food cultivation led to permanent settlements and, for some, a stable food supply. Agriculture gave rise to trade, and then commerce, and finally to the global economy of the 21st century. Here in the First World, food is more than plentiful, and our hunter-gatherer days are gone for good.

Even after the appearance of agriculture, though, as food continued to remain scarce, two "meals" a day was the norm. By the medieval era, however,

"slightly better-off peasants" were eating three meals daily. Breakfast was served up early, probably soon after dawn, "dinner" by 10:00 in the morning, and supper before the sun set— in the winter, that could be as early as 3:00 in the afternoon.[4] Check out the 24-hour ghrelin level chart on page 34 and it all makes perfect sense. After all, ghrelin levels between 1 and 3 o'clock in the afternoon are— to this day—23 percent higher than they are between 9:00 in the morning and noon. Even now, the 1:00 to 3:00 p.m. period is a high-risk time for dieters—that's why the Belly Fat Fix features an afternoon snack.

In the colonial period, American meal patterns followed European practices, although customs varied across different regions of the country and were determined by occupation, social class, gender, ethnicity, and personal preferences. The extended family sat down to eat three times a day. The afternoon snack, in the form of English tea and sandwiches or pastries, emerged sometime in the 19th century.[5]

Turns out, it's a good thing our eating patterns evolved the way they did. Modern science tells us that three meals a day, plus a snack, is the best way to maintain ideal weight and body composition, even in our age of plenty, when so many of us live sedentary lives. The science is irrefutable: Skipping breakfast or eating just one big meal a day works against weight-loss efforts. In fact, a US Department of Agriculture study found that eating one large meal a day raises blood pressure, while three meals per day lower it.[6] And a National Institute on Aging study reports that eating a single meal a day, rather than three meals, raises insulin resistance and glucose intolerance, key features of type 2 diabetes.[7] The truth is, you need to eat enough to satisfy your physiological hunger. Eating too little doesn't serve you any more than overeating does. In fact, I encourage some clients to eat more, helping them prevent the ghrelin Hunger Trap, in which cycles of self-starvation are followed by guilt-inducing eating binges that pack on the pounds. (Sometimes, these binges also cause digestive upset, which, when added to the guilt and disappointment, feels *bad* all around.)

But here's the good news: If you're one of those people trying to slim down by cutting way back on calories during the day or eliminating breakfast entirely—only to be blindsided by uncontrollable hunger at night—guess what? You'll actually be able to eat *more* food on the Belly Fat Fix—without the daily hunger pangs and the nightly attack of guilt. *And* you'll lose the weight.

Sounds crazy; sounds counterintuitive. But it's absolutely true. In your quest to lose weight, three balanced meals and a snack trumps a starvation diet or a two-meal plan.

USING THE G-SCALE

Let's get started. Pretty soon, with the help of the G-Scale, you'll know your hunger signals well enough to assess your true appetite all on your own. Make a copy of the G-Scale and keep it in your pocket or purse.

GHRELIN HUNGER SCALE

STEP 1 Hunger/Fullness

1	**Starving,** shaky and lightheaded
2	**Very hungry,** you have to eat soon
3	**Moderately hungry,** you feel you could eat a meal
4	**Neutral,** neither hungry nor full
5	**Moderately full,** comfortable
6	**Somewhat uncomfortable,** your stomach feels overfull
7	**Stuffed,** you can't take another bite

STEP 2 Hours Since Last Meal

1 hour or less since last meal	1.5 hours since last meal	2 hours since last meal	2.5 hours since last meal	3 hours since last meal	3.5 hours since last meal	4 hours or more since last meal
7	6	5	4	3	2	1

Black: Your ghrelin level is high. You should begin eating within 10 minutes.
White: Your ghrelin level is rising. Eat a ghrelin-suppressing snack within 30 minutes or a meal within 60 minutes.
Gray: Your ghrelin level is low. Wait 30 minutes and check again.

Use this scale to determine your ghrelin level so you can eat when your body signals that it's time.

It's simple. Consider the G-Scale a quick hunger quiz that helps you determine your ghrelin level as it correlates to your *feeling* of hunger. Your quiz score will lead you to the next step—what you choose to eat. It'll help you determine when and what to eat based on the timing of ghrelin secretions in your body.

It's a fast, easy, three-step process. Let's jump in.

1. Go to the left side of the Ghrelin Hunger Scale. Ask yourself, "On a scale of 1 to 7, how hungry am I"? Pick the number that seems most accurate.

2. Go to the bottom of the scale and determine how many hours it's been since your last meal.

3. Find the place on the graph where those two answers meet. *That's* your personal hunger quotient.

How do you determine which number most closely corresponds to your state of hunger at the present time? Here's an easy key:

Step 1: What's your hunger/fullness level?

   1 = Starving; shaky and lightheaded

   2 = Very hungry; you have to eat soon

   3 = Moderately hungry; you feel you could eat a meal

   4 = Neutral; you're neither hungry nor full

   5 = Moderately full; you're feeling comfortable

   6 = Somewhat uncomfortable; your stomach feels overfull

   7 = So stuffed that you couldn't take another bite

Step 2: Choose the number that best represents the number of hours since your last meal.

   7 = 1 hour or less since your last meal

   6 = 1.5 hours since your last meal

   5 = 2 hours since your last meal

   4 = 2.5 hours since your last meal

3 = 3 hours since your last meal

2 = 3.5 hours since your last meal

1 = 4 hours or more since your last meal

Now trace across the chart to see where your personal hunger number meets up with the number that most closely corresponds to how long ago you ate.

Suppose, for example, your hunger level is at a 1, and it's been 4 hours since you've last eaten. Look on the chart to see where the 1 from the left-hand side intersects with the 1 from the scale's bottom. That would put you into that first black box.

Notice, now, the black, white, and gray on the scale. Once you find your number, consider the color. If your box is black, that means that your ghrelin level is high and you should begin eating quickly. Find a G-List ghrelin-suppressing snack immediately or select a G-List ghrelin-suppressing meal within 10 minutes. This is important: At this point, every 10 minutes counts. The longer you wait, the higher your ghrelin levels rise and the more likely that you'll feel so hungry that you'll override what you know you should eat, reaching for high-calorie choices and over-eating instead.

Where's My G?

Not sure if you're truly hungry or psychologically hungry? Use this checklist. If you check three or more statements, you're truly ghrelin hungry.

☐ It's been 3 or more hours since my last meal.

☐ My hunger has crept up slowly over a 30-minute (or longer) period.

☐ I want to eat a meal with protein, carbs, and fat.

☐ I've had all my water so far today.

☐ I got at least 7 hours of sleep each of the past 2 nights.

☐ I don't feel stressed right now.

☐ There's no food within my sight, and I haven't smelled food within the past 10 minutes.

If your box is in the white zone, your ghrelin level is rising, so eat a G-List ghrelin-suppressing snack within 30 minutes or have a G-List ghrelin-suppressing meal within the hour.

If your box is in the gray zone, your ghrelin level is low. Wait 30 minutes and check again. If you're still hungry, have a G-List snack.

GHRELIN AND THE BODY CLOCK: PHYSIOLOGICAL HUNGER

As you begin to track your appetite, you're likely to find that it follows distinct patterns related to time. If it's true physiological hunger, it arises on a fairly predictable schedule that's related to your body's own master clock. Your body's clock is itself influenced by the cycles of light and dark, day and night.

The term "master clock" refers to the internal circadian clock buried deep in the back of our hypothalamus. Just as old-fashioned mechanical clocks depend on gears, the body's master clock depends on specific intelligent proteins. (Similar "clocks" have been found in peripheral tissues, such as in the liver and intestine, another site of ghrelin production. The master clock synchronizes them all.)

The master clock is called *circadian* after the Latin words meaning "around a day." Many biological processes exhibit a circadian rhythm. Appetite is one of them. The processes by which the body creates fat cells and stores energy in the form of fat are also linked to the core clock mechanism. Here's why this matters: *When* you eat appears to determine how fat you get from *what* you eat. In theory, same calories, different time of day, different *effect* on body composition.

How can that be? Well, it's complicated. But the answer lies partly in the fact that the DNA codes in white fat (white adipose tissue) follow a diurnal, or day-night, rhythm, raising the possibility that the actual time that a fat cell is exposed to nutrients in the process of digestion has a "profound impact on the rate of [fat] accumulation."[8] If this proves true, it means exactly what you think it does: You can eat more and maintain your weight—*if* you eat at the right times.

What *are* the right times? Well, to figure that out, let's look at ghrelin's ebbs and flows throughout the day.

Even when people fast, ghrelin has a pattern that correlates with three meals a day. On the first day of a fast, ghrelin levels rise at four points during the day—at 8:00 a.m., between noon and 1:00 p.m., between 5:00 and 7:00 p.m., and then again at midnight—although by just a little at that late hour. On day 2, they rise again at 8:00 a.m.

This was shown in a study conducted at the Medical University of Vienna, Austria, which looked at ghrelin levels over a 24-hour fasting period. The study took ghrelin profiles every 20 minutes for a full 24 hours to evaluate the pattern of ghrelin without food. And guess what? When people fasted under conditions in which they were not exposed to food, "fasting ghrelin levels display a circadian pattern similar to that described in people eating three times per day."[9] Basically, ghrelin peaked three times a day at times that coincide with the peaks that occur when people are eating at regular mealtimes.

Your ghrelin naturally rises and falls three times a day, even when you don't eat. So eating three meals a day, plus a snack, is the best way to support your body. When you work with your body instead of against it, it rewards you with good health and weight loss. The Belly Fat Fix is undoubtedly the best way to keep your ghrelin balanced and your hunger in check.

After rising, ghrelin levels fall spontaneously about 2 hours after these peaks, provided you haven't eaten anything in that time.[10] This explains why hunger eventually subsides when you wait too long to respond. You'd think this would be a *good*

What's Your BMI?

Body mass index (BMI) is a measure of your height-to-weight ratio, not your actual body fat. BMI is important because it helps determine overall health risk. If your BMI is 18 to 24.9, you're considered "healthy" and at a low risk of disease. A BMI of 25 to 29.9 is considered "overweight," putting you at a moderate risk of disease. And a BMI of 30 or more is considered "obese," with a high risk of disease. Pull out your calculator and figure out your BMI. Here's how:

1. Multiply your weight in pounds by 703.

2. Divide that number by your height in inches.

3. Divide that number by your height in inches again.

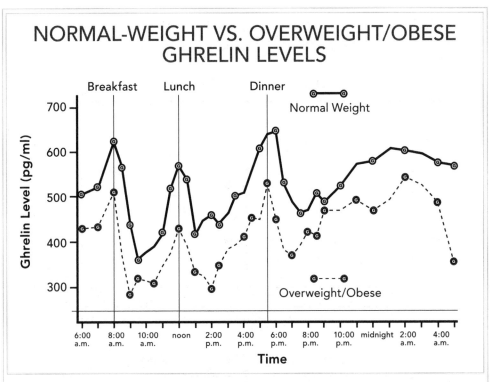

NORMAL-WEIGHT VS. OVERWEIGHT/OBESE GHRELIN LEVELS

This graph shows the difference in ghrelin levels between normal-weight and obese individuals. Normal-weight people have higher overall ghrelin levels, and the rise and fall before and after meals is more dramatic compared with rhythms experienced by overweight or obese people.

thing, but it's not. Your body may give up on you for the time being, but it *will* push back. That's because when you ignore the hunger signal for too long, ghrelin levels become extra-elevated and stay that way. And that gives you trouble at the scale.

Researchers who studied ghrelin activity in people who are fasting found that the lower the person's body mass index (BMI)—their weight-to-height ratio—the higher the ghrelin peaks during appetite surges. The higher someone's BMI, the lower the ghrelin peak during appetite surges. In plain English, this means that slender to normal-weight people feel the rise and fall of ghrelin more sharply. Such vivid contrast is a good thing because it makes physiological or true hunger much easier to distinguish from nonphysiological hunger.

Telling the difference between true and false hunger is really important—that way, you can tell when to eat and when to fill your hunger another way. As you

OBESE GHRELIN AND HUNGER VS. NORMAL-WEIGHT GHRELIN AND HUNGER

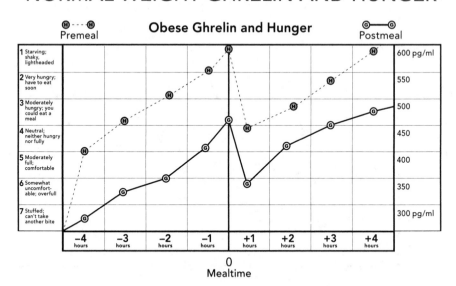

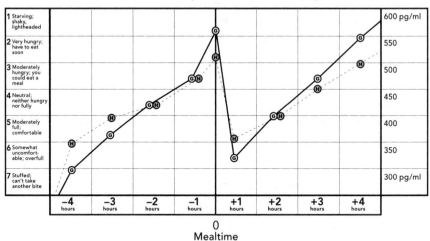

These graphs compare the difference in hunger and ghrelin level before and after meals in a healthy-weight and an obese person.

practice, you'll *experience* the difference in the way various kinds of hungers *feel*. And when ghrelin rises to normal heights and then diminishes, you'll know the difference between hungry and full. Some people eat all the time in the absence of such cues—those are people who are likely to be obese and have low blood levels of ghrelin.

Fortunately, if your ghrelin levels are low, you can reset them and nudge them up toward normal so you can discern when you're really hungry. That's what the 3-Day Fast-Track (see Chapter 5) will help you do. Losing weight the right way will help, too. When the pounds drop off, ghrelin levels will also drop—they'll be lower after meals and rise higher before meals.[11] This is a good thing.

Snack Time!

Remember how ghrelin levels zoom in the afternoon, rising higher between 1 and 3 o'clock? That's why—regardless of whether you think you should snack or not, regardless of when you plan to eat dinner—you *need* that afternoon snack.

Here's the rationale: Ghrelin starts to rise about an hour after a meal and continues to rise about every 30 minutes until you hit the 4-hour mark. That's when ghrelin kicks into overdrive, rising every 10 minutes. Ghrelin, after all, doesn't have an off switch. With no other hormone to counteract it, ghrelin simply continues to rise—until you eat.

That's why your afternoon snack is so important. My clients find that snack is a real help. Here's what one of them, Lisa N., has to say about it:

Whenever I went on a diet, I'd try to avoid all snacking. The problem was I'd be so hungry I'd start munching while I was cooking, then eat dinner—and then eat the leftovers on my kids' plates.

Now I realize after all was said and done, I'd eaten a lot more than I would have if I'd had a midafternoon snack. I didn't understand that my ghrelin was so high I couldn't make healthy decisions and when the food was in front of me I had to eat it. Now I have my snack every day!

Think about this: If Lisa had eaten a snack a half hour before making dinner, she wouldn't have munched or finished her kids' plates—and that would've saved her a lot of calories and loads of guilt.

GUMMING UP THE GHRELIN WORKS

When ghrelin is working optimally, it rises a bit even while you're eating. Not long after you start eating, though, your cells stop making more. Within an hour, the level of ghrelin in your body drops back down to its baseline levels. But the falling ghrelin levels don't make you feel full—they only suppress the pressure to eat. It's ghrelin's sidekick, leptin, that gives you that full, satisfied feeling. Let's take a look at leptin here.

G-Scale Q&A

The Belly Fat Fix is simple: Eat three meals a day, plus a snack, timing your eating around your ghrelin signals according to the G-Scale. But chances are, you've got some questions. Here are the most common ones, followed by my answers:

Q *I hate eating breakfast right away. Can I wait until I get into work?*

A. No. Your metabolism really does kick-start in the morning, and ghrelin drives it. Without fuel (food) in your tank (stomach), your body can't drive. After you eat and begin to digest your food, your ghrelin drops and other systems in your body rev up. We call this process thermogenesis: the process of creating heat. One way your body creates heat is through the digestive process. So when you create heat, you burn calories; when you burn calories through digestion on a regulated schedule (such as that of the meal plans in Chapters 5 and 6), your body goes from a clunky old Chevy stick shift to a brand-new Ferrari with all the bells and whistles.

Q *Why do I get hungry earlier for lunch when I eat breakfast?*

A. Because your ghrelin cycle has been stimulated. That's a good thing, because hunger means your body's metabolism is working. When you eat in the morning, you're setting in motion a cascade of stabilization. Stabilization means getting hungry. I tell my clients, "Stop being afraid of your hunger. That's a losing battle, because you'll get hungry every day for the rest of your life." So instead of fighting it, learn to work with your hunger.

LEPTIN: THE "I FEEL FULL" HORMONE

Leptin—the word means "full" in Greek—is produced in the fat cells and sends its signals to the hypothalamus in your brain. When it floods your cells, you feel full. So as ghrelin enhances your appetite, leptin suppresses it.

Remember that leptin works to maintain long-term energy balance. Ghrelin, on the other hand, is a fast-acting hormone that stimulates appetite and induces you to

Q *Drinking coffee fills me up. Do I still need to eat?*

A. Coffee is a stimulant that will curb your hunger for a short time. Once the caffeine (even decaf works this way) wears off, your ghrelin sensors kick into high gear. Coffee doesn't fill you up— it simply masks hunger the same way makeup covers a huge zit on your nose. If you drink coffee all day, at some point in the evening after you stop drinking it, your hunger will resurface—the same way that huge zit reappears when you wash off your makeup.

Q *Do I have to drink water? I really don't like plain water.*

A. Hunger and thirst are easily confused. Your body is over 70 percent water, and on a cellular level, water conducts every metabolic process that sustains your life. When you don't drink enough water every day, your body becomes chronically dehydrated, compromising your cellular activity. This means your cells work at a slower rate and your overall metabolism slows down. How do you feel when this is happening inside the billions of cells in your body? You feel slow and sleepy; your muscles feel heavy; you may develop a headache. You also feel hungry—after all, the side effects of dehydration are exactly the same as those of hunger, so it's really hard to tell the difference between hunger and thirst. You must drink water to get your metabolism working at full speed and to enjoy a great added benefit: Staying hydrated will help you distinguish more efficiently between the various kinds of hunger. So drink your water. It's a win-win.

eat. In normal-weight people, leptin and ghrelin function independently to maintain equilibrium, keeping your weight pretty stable over time. But it's different in people who are obese or overweight. For them, there are disturbances in the expression of each hormone that make it harder for them to take the weight off.

Scientists are just beginning to understand why this is so. We know that weight gain—and simply being overweight—increases leptin production. When you think about it, this makes sense—after all, if you're overweight, you've got more fat cells, and that's where leptin is made. But if your body's producing more leptin, shouldn't you be feeling more full? Unfortunately, despite the extra leptin, if you're overweight, you find yourself feeling hungry all the time. How come?

That's because obesity causes *leptin resistance* in much the same way that insulin resistance causes type 2 diabetes. The high and sustained concentration of leptin produced by fat cells results in overall leptin desensitization. To make matters

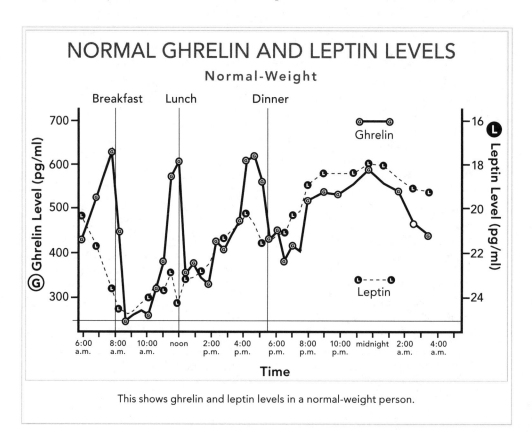

This shows ghrelin and leptin levels in a normal-weight person.

worse, in overweight and obese people, ghrelin levels are *lower*. This causes a reverse interplay between leptin and ghrelin. People who are obese feel hungrier, have lower ghrelin levels, *and* feel less full—all while eating more food.

The fact that leptin resistance occurs in obese people suggests—as some scientists suspect—that leptin's primary role isn't to signal fullness and stop people from eating. Instead, it may function primarily as a "starvation signal" to maintain adequate fat to help your body survive during lean times. In the obese, leptin resistance—turning off the feeling of fullness—is the standard physiological response. The body's ability to become resistant to leptin was meant to give our ancestors a survival advantage.

Here's how: During times of plenty, resistance to leptin gave our ancestors the ability to maintain their appetites, driving them to continue to accumulate and store excess fat. In ancient times, after all, a little extra fat could make the difference between life and death. The genetic codes our ancestors passed down to us were designed with one fundamental purpose—to keep us alive—and leptin resistance is built right into that genetic code. Problem is, in Western society in the 21st century, there's not much threat of starvation. So for most of us, leptin resistance is more of a problem than a solution. It no longer confers protection.

But what about ghrelin resistance? Seems like that'd be a handy weight-loss tool. Well, maybe good in theory—but not so much in practice. Human beings, it turns out, are genetically incapable of developing resistance to ghrelin. If that were possible, the human race wouldn't have survived. Ghrelin, after all, is designed to keep us alive in times of famine, revving up our appetites and impelling us to eat.

But wait! The leptin-ghrelin relationship gets more complicated: Chronic sleep deprivation (as in shift work) decreases leptin levels and increases ghrelin levels. (It's a bit like a seesaw; if one hormone drops precipitously, the other rises precipitously.) And that snares us into the Hunger Trap, the feedback loop that leads to weight gain. Once a shift worker—or any sleep-deprived person—puts on some pounds, the opposite happens. Leptin rises and ghrelin drops. As leptin levels rise and ghrelin levels drop, over time the chronically high leptin levels create leptin resistance. The leptin resistance causes a spike in appetite, while the drop in ghrelin prevents that overweight individual from feeling truly full and satisfied, even after a hearty meal.

OBESE, HEALTHY, SLEEP-DEPRIVED GHRELIN AND LEPTIN LEVELS

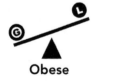
Obese

Healthy

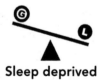
Sleep deprived

These seesaws represent the balance of ghrelin and leptin levels in situations of obesity, healthy weight, and sleep deprivation.

One of the key points to keep in mind is that ghrelin and leptin function in a dynamic way, affected by any number of variables. The more you heed what your body needs, the better these hormones function. Let's look now at how dieting affects ghrelin.

YOUR DIET ON GHRELIN

Dieting—especially restrictive plans that don't provide enough calories in the form of protein and carbohydrates—actually increases levels of ghrelin. Reducing food intake, skipping meals, and losing weight rapidly (as in the beginning of a fad diet) all increase the amount of ghrelin circulating in the blood. Have you ever tried a quick weight-loss diet or simply cut out too much food during the day? Then you know what happens next. You feel deliriously hungry, make poor food choices, and ultimately you fall off the wagon, gaining back more weight than you ever lost.

This self-imposed hunger is ghrelin deregulation, and it affects your entire system. It throws your body into a hormonal nightmare of increasing stress hormones and lowered leptin. Way back when, this was our ancestors' survival mechanism; now it's a major contributor to obesity. Remember The Survival Effect loop in Chapter 1? Well, that's exactly the effect dieting has on ghrelin. It causes you to get fatter, especially in your belly, which in turn causes stress eating. (Refer to the Stress

Hunger loop on page 21.) This leads to depression and cravings for high-calorie, high-fat foods. In short, dieting sets the ghrelin Hunger Trap in motion.

But there's a solution: Following the Belly Fat Fix and eating according to your body's natural ghrelin cycle will break the Hunger Trap and take off those extra pounds for good.

TUNING IN TO GHRELIN

I've said it before and I'll say it again: It's crucial to become familiar with ghrelin's signals. This way, you eat when your body tells you that it needs more nutrients. You must learn to heed the hunger cue immediately to avoid the Hunger Trap, which creates the biological pressure to binge.

You also need to learn which foods to eat to satisfy your appetite, depending on how hungry you are. In Chapter 3, you'll learn all about ghrelin-suppressing foods. I'll show you how to eat so you'll feel so full you can't possibly eat more than you should.

But let's start slowly. I want you to focus first on becoming aware of your hunger. Then let's take the next step and determine what kind of hunger you're experiencing.

Use this checklist to figure out if you are *truly hungry* or just wanting to nosh because you had a stressful day or you feel tired or you need comfort:

True Hunger

☐ Your hunger "craving" has been creeping up for a while.

☐ The "craving" doesn't go away if you wait it out.

☐ Your stomach is growling, feels hollow, and is making noises.

☐ You could eat a variety of foods.

☐ If you eat something, you'll stop eating when you feel full.

False Hunger

☐ The "craving" comes on quickly, coupled with a negative emotion.

☐ You feel you *have* to eat right now.

☐ You're craving a particular food—probably something unhealthy.

☐ If you started to eat now, you might not be able to stop at an appropriate portion.

☐ You feel embarrassed or guilty for wanting to eat.

If you chose mostly "True Hunger," refer to your G-Scale and have a snack or your next meal. If you chose mostly "False Hunger," set an alarm for 15 minutes and distract yourself. Chances are, your craving will subside. As time goes on, you'll get better at this. Later, in Chapter 11, I'll explain how to use a food tracker, which will help you become more aware of what it feels like when your body truly needs more food. For the moment, though, let's look at the other kind of hunger—the kind that no food will *ever* permanently satisfy.

THE MANY FLAVORS OF HUNGER

Until now, we've focused primarily on genuine physical hunger. Now let's consider the full spectrum of hunger—because there are many different kinds.

First is real, physical hunger—the hunger you feel when your body needs nutrients. Next is the hunger you feel when you're stressed—that has a physiologic component, too. Then there's the hunger you feel when you smell steak cooking on your neighbor's grill or see dessert delivered to the table next to you in a restaurant. There's also the hunger you feel when you're stuck in a cubicle, in front of your computer, bored sense- less. There's the hunger you feel when habit kicks in and you hanker for that sweet taste at the end of a meal that has driven you to seek out dessert night after night.

Remember, only one of these kinds of hungers comes from the body's genuine need for more fuel. With the rest, some other aspect of you is likely asking to get "fed." You need to find a way to feed those other hungers—with sleep, or at least rest; stress reduction or creativity practices; or by distracting yourself.

Let's look at each of these in turn so you can become expert at teasing out genu- ine physical hunger—which you want to address quickly so ghrelin levels don't sky- rocket and cause you to sabotage your diet—from the other kinds of hunger.

Sensory Hunger

Akin to true physical hunger is sensory hunger, which also has a physical compo- nent. Back in Chapter 1, we talked about ghrelin's relationship to the brain's pleasure and reward centers. We learned how ghrelin can enhance our sensory appreciation of the enticing sight and smell of food—and how those sensory abilities sharpen the longer we put off eating, fueling our appetite all the more.

Sensory hunger is what causes us to go into a restaurant, get a whiff of the foods we've promised we'd avoid, and—as if we're puppets controlled by our sensory organs—order them anyway. And in case you were wondering, ghrelin is also involved in sensory hunger. It stimulates gastric motility and acid secretion, both of which increase *anticipation* of meals. In fact, if we anticipate food at specific times, ghrelin rises.

Why Did I Order That?

You're at your favorite restaurant sitting in front of an empty plate— not just empty, but licked-clean empty—and wondering . . . "Why did I order that?!"

In human brain imaging studies,[12] ghrelin administered intravenously to healthy volunteers increased the neural response to food pictures in several regions of the brain, including the amygdala, orbitofrontal cortex, anterior insula, and striatum—all parts of the brain that are sensitive to food cues. The amygdala in particular lights up in response to the taste, sight, smell, and descriptions of food—like those you might see on a menu. The anterior (back part) of the insula is also a key player in the anticipation and taste reward of food. And guess what? The amygdala and insula are ghrelin responsive. That's why, despite every intention of ordering the healthiest, most low-calorie option on the

menu, or choosing the most wholesome offerings from the all-you-can-eat buffet, you inevitably go for the double bacon cheeseburger and french fries. Or you get through a lovely, nutritious meal—only to be derailed by that "one bite" of dessert that turns into a giant serving of pie à la mode.

Here's the kicker: Your insula is as responsive as your ghrelin is high. So when you "save room," you become even *more* susceptible to making the wrong choice.

The takeaway: Don't get to the restaurant starving and expect to stick to your diet. It won't happen. Here's what you can expect instead from your ghrelin-flooded brain when decision time rolls around at the restaurant: Your ghrelin genetic coding takes over and you're left sitting in front of your licked-clean plate, wondering, *"Why did I order that?"*

Stress Hunger

Does it feel like the universe is conspiring against your diet? Well it is, sort of. Scientists have discovered that psychosocial stress not only boosts the body's level of the stress hormone corticosterone but also ups your production of ghrelin. When stress kicks in, so does your preference for high-fat foods, which causes you to strengthen that nasty habit of soothing yourself with a cheeseburger and fries. Stressed out? Take another glance at the "Are You a Stress Eater"? on pages 22–23.

Stress is the most identifiable false hunger I encounter with my weight-loss clients. Stress eating is a type of instinctive emotional eating. It occurs when stress stimulates the part of your brain that gets pleasure from food—and it happens to be the part that sits right on top of the area that gets pleasure from sex and drugs. What's going on? Scientists call it reverse receptor stimulation. In other words, when you're stressed, ghrelin doesn't circulate and make its way to your body's pleasure receptors. Instead, the pleasure receptors send out a signal that loops back to your ghrelin-producing cells in the stomach. Those cells then start to produce ghrelin even when you don't need to eat. Know what happens next? Ghrelin loops back to your brain and stimulates the same receptors even more.

That's exactly what happens when you eat a huge bowl of ice cream when you're already full to brim, then ask yourself in exasperation, "What was I *thinking*?" You *know* you should dump that dish of Rocky Road, but you can't seem to do it. Your body goes into protective mode, and the ancient area of your brain—the part that's trying to protect you from starvation—shifts to autopilot.

But there's hope! The goal of the Belly Fat Fix is to help you 1) recognize this kind of situation when it happens so you can stop yourself from getting sucked into this cycle, and 2) learn how to prevent this situation in the first place.

How? By the process of ghrelin stabilization. This is the way it works: When your ghrelin is stable, those brain receptors that are inevitably triggered by stress are less sensitive to the *"Time to eat for comfort!"* message. And when that happens, you're not functioning within the stress-eating feedback loop. So the message being sent by the receptors in your pleasure center won't affect you as much. In short, you may feel some stress, but you won't immediately go for the chips and dip.

Have you ever noticed how parents of toddlers don't jump every time their kids make a loud noise? I notice this with my sister, who has two children—a 2-year-old girl and a 5-year-old boy. Those kids never stop, and they are *loud*, yet my sister doesn't blink an eye when they scream, stamp their feet, or throw toy cars against the wall. But when one of them whimpers in pain, my sister hears the cry from a hundred yards away.

Her "mom receptors" have become desensitized to the nonthreatening noises and are tuned in to the true needs of her kids. Your ghrelin receptors function in much the same way once you're balanced and tuned in to your different hungers. When you're balanced, you can ignore false (nonthreatening) hunger and respond appropriately to true hunger.

Mindful Eating 101

In our fast-food culture, meals have become just another task to squeeze into an already-too-busy day. It's common to grab breakfast on the run or attend a lunch meeting where business is front and center and food is an afterthought.

But mindless eating—eating without awareness—can have a huge impact on your weight and how full you feel. A University of California, San Francisco study showed that participants who engaged in mindful eating practices experienced significant abdominal fat loss. In fact, those who reported the greatest improvements in mindfulness had the largest reductions in weight and abdominal fat. The connection seems clear: Improvements in mindfulness lead to changes in body weight.[13]

Here's why: Once you begin to eat, ghrelin production drops off, which lowers the concentration level of ghrelin in your blood. That means the weaker ghrelin signal to your brain has less impact than before, allowing competing thoughts, activities, and signals to "hijack" your brain. If your body/mind is multitasking as you eat, the decreasing concentration of ghrelin doesn't register in the hypothalamus. And if the brain doesn't receive the message—such as the sensation of taste and satisfaction—it may fail to register the event as "eating" at all. So your brain may continue sending out additional hunger signals, increasing your risk of overeating. Eating mindfully, though—savoring every mouthful—enhances the experience of eating, increases awareness of how much you eat, and makes you feel fuller on less food.

Psychological Hunger

We took a look at psychological hunger in Chapter 1. Now let's consider some ways to respond to this kind of hunger. Journaling can help. So can a bit of self-reflection: Walk away from the cookies and ask yourself what you *really* need in the moment. Your response might be to call a friend, take a walk, get some exercise—whatever it takes to truly meet the psychological need rather than mask it with chocolate chips.

Even when you do decide to address psychological hunger by eating, it helps to be mindful of what you're doing and why, what you're eating, and what kinds of feelings you're experiencing as you practice being more attentive to yourself.

Sleep-Deprivation Hunger

Americans get nearly an hour less sleep a night than they did 40 years ago, according to the National Academy of Sciences. And too little sleep is associated with weight gain and obesity. Shift work is also problematic because it puts workers out of sync with natural cycles of time.

Working the Graveyard Shift

In a 2010 report, the US Bureau of Labor and Statistics said that more than 21 million workers, almost 20 percent of the labor force, work alternative shifts outside daytime hours.[14] And shift work, studies show, is a risk factor for obesity. This isn't just an American problem—global studies looking at widely diverse ethnicities, dietary and lifestyle patterns, and socioeconomic, educational, and occupational backgrounds

Is Your TV Making You Fat?

Studies show that Americans average about an hour of television watching before bed. So if you're among the 20 to 40 percent who get less than 7 hours of sleep a day—and you watch an hour or more of television each weeknight—consider trading that TV time for sleep time. Your scale will thank you.

have turned up pretty much the same results. This collective data suggests that about 74 percent of shift workers are obese.[15] Worldwide, there are lots of reasons for this link between shift work and weight, including alterations in eating and exercise and disruption of the circadian clock, which causes hormone and metabolism imbalances.[16]

Work the night shift? Don't worry—you're not doomed to being overweight forever. Though weight loss is a bigger struggle for you than for your 9-to-5 neighbor, it's still possible to lose weight. For maximum success, try these strategies in conjunction with your Belly Fat Fix:

- **Reverse your meals.** Instead of the standard breakfast, lunch, and dinner sequence, have your lunch at the beginning of your "day," dinner in the middle, and breakfast last. Fit your snack in between whatever meals are farthest apart. You'll still be balancing meals in a way that maximizes your metabolic rate—and balancing your ghrelin, too.

- **Eat your meals at the same time when you're working a late shift.** Your body adapts to specific mealtimes, so keeping to a routine will program your system to release ghrelin at specific times, helping you feel full after meals.

- **Drink extra ice water with lemon.** Shift workers tend to drink more coffee, which can lead to dehydration, making you feel fatigued and hungry. Water, though, enables your body to function better, and the cold temperature will help keep you awake and alert. Plus, lemon is a natural diuretic, and the tart taste cuts cravings for sweets. If you must have coffee, be sure to drink an extra glass of water.

- **Go to bed earlier every other night.** Studies show that we can make up for lost sleep for about 2 or 3 nights. After that, lost sleep is lost for good. If you're so busy that you find it hard to get to bed early enough, try an earlier bedtime every other night instead.

- **Exercise for 10 to 15 minutes during your shift.** Movement energizes your body and works to reset your clock—and your hunger.

- **Create a nighttime bedroom environment.** If you must sleep during the day, make sure your sleep is peaceful. Invest in room-darkening window shades, turn off your phone, shut down your computer, and wear some earplugs and an eye mask.

Hormonal Hunger

Food cravings, bloating, insatiable hunger—PMS is famously hard on your diet. If you're like many women, the week before—and the week of—your period can make you feel miserable and throw your diet completely off track. You're starving, you feel bloated from water retention, and now you want to eat chocolate brownies, ice cream, and salty chips.

But don't add guilt to the list of PMS miseries. Your body genuinely uses more calories during the time right before your period, and that makes you feel hungrier. In fact, you burn between 100 and 300 extra calories a day during the time leading up to menstruation. Even worse, the hormones make you crave particular foods, most often simple sugars and starches.

Ghrelin levels during the menstrual cycle have not been well researched, but if you've ever been in the throes of PMS, you can attest that your hunger definitely rises. Actually, there are several PMS symptoms we know increase ghrelin: fatigue, stress/sadness, and hormonal shifts. The correlation is hard to ignore.

Regardless of the reasons you're hungrier before your period—whether it's true hunger, psychological hunger, stress hunger, or sleep-deprivation hunger—when you come right down to it, hunger is hunger. So how can you deal? Try these techniques:

▶ **Drink extra water with lemon.** Aim for additional water the week before and during your period—at least two extra 16-ounce glasses per day. Proper hydration will help you determine your level of true hunger more easily because, on a cellular level, thirst feels a lot like hunger, so drinking extra water lets your body release the water you're retaining and hydrates your cells. (And don't forget: Lemon, a natural diuretic, will help reduce bloating, while its tart taste will help cut your crazy cravings for sweets.)

▶ **Get more shut-eye.** Make it a point to give up Letterman or Leno during "that time of the month" and get an extra hour of sleep each night. Being well rested will reduce premenstrual stress to a minimum, keeping ghrelin at bay.

▶ **Amp up your lean protein.** Ward off risky hunger swings before they occur by adding an ounce or two of lean protein at lunch and/or dinner. Protein is jam-packed with B vitamins and iron, both of which are needed to keep energy levels up. Plus, lean protein takes longer to digest (you'll learn more about protein digestion in Chapter 3). The longer the digestion time, the longer you feel full.

Ghrelin and Sleep

Remember ghrelin's relationship to the natural cycles of rest and activity, light and dark? Well, there's emerging evidence that ghrelin may not only help regulate sleep but also promote slow-wave sleep. Studies show that ghrelin mediates the functions of two sleep-regulating hormones: growth-hormone-releasing hormone (GHRH) and corticotrophin-releasing hormone (CRH).[17] Ghrelin influences sleep by affecting nighttime hormone secretions. We don't know the exact mechanism, but scientists believe that ghrelin may act as an interconnection between GHRH and CRH. A decrease of 2 hours of sleep from an individual's average nightly routine increases circulating ghrelin by 12 percent and decreases leptin by 15 percent. Too little sleep causes high ghrelin levels and low leptin levels. It's easy to see how that can add up to extra pounds.

Ghrelin's role in promoting sleep is interesting, given what we know about the link between increased obesity and higher risk of early death in those who sleep less than 7 hours a day. And this trend toward too little sleep is itself a symptom of lifestyles far removed from nature. Once upon a time, the sun went down and people went to sleep. There was no late-night Letterman, no Internet chat rooms.

The takeaway: If you want the Belly Fat Fix to be optimally effective, get yourself in balance by eating when you're supposed to—as you've learned here in Chapter 2—and getting plenty of sleep.

DON'T BE AFRAID OF HUNGER

My clients seem to have one common fear when they embark on a diet: "I'm afraid I'll be hungry," they lament. My response? Get over it. You *will* get hungry every day, several times a day, until the day you die. Hunger is a function of living. Learn how to accept it as a part of your daily routine. If not, you'll continue to struggle with your weight for the rest of your life. But still, there *is* a difference between normal, healthy, predictable hunger and *starving*.

Most of my clients have had the experience when dieting of feeling deprived and fighting hunger all day—until their hunger gets the better of them in the evening. By that time, they often find that they'll put anything—and a lot of it—into their mouths. With the Belly Fat Fix, you've got the tools and knowledge you need to understand your hunger so that it never intimidates you again. That's an important step on your weight-loss journey. Let's climb to the next step—choosing the right foods with your handy G-List—in Chapter 3.

CHAPTER 3

Fill Up, Slim Down

When it comes to meal planning, timing is—almost—everything. In Chapter 2, we learned that *when* you eat can make a big difference at the scale. But you'll get better weight-loss results if you eat the *right foods* in the *right combination* at the *right time*. In fact, if you choose the right foods—meals and snacks that are nutritious and ghrelin suppressing—you can load up your plate with more than you'd think you can eat on a diet and *still* lose weight. Seriously.

To do this right, you need to know a bit about the science behind the foods I recommend. Use that science, commit to memory the practical tips in this chapter, and say good-bye to hunger. You'll see how easy it is to fill up while sticking to your diet—and what a breeze it is to pass up all the foods you know aren't good for you.

Let's begin with a little lesson in digestion to see just how our bodies take food and turn it into fuel. Then we'll learn which foods help suppress ghrelin (giving you biological control of appetite), which increase ghrelin (whipping up your appetite), and which have little to no effect. By the time you're done with this chapter, you'll know what to shop for (and why) and how to combine foods on your plate so that you're eating nutritious, delicious meals that not only fill you up but also slim you down.

A CALORIE IS *NOT* JUST A CALORIE

A lot of diets get you to count calories. Weight loss comes down to a simple equation: Burn more calories (or units of food energy) than you take in and you'll lose pounds. (A pound is roughly equivalent to 3,500 calories.) There's truth to that, but it's not the whole story. In fact, the saying that "a calorie is a calorie is a calorie" is *not true*. Different foods with the same calorie counts fill you up more or less and can keep you full for longer or shorter amounts of time. On the Belly Fat Fix, you'll forget about calories and focus on portion size instead. And you'll eat nutritious foods that keep you full longer, sparing you the pain of hunger and the temptation to eat between meals.

Calories, of course, come from different sources. There are carbohydrate calories, protein calories, and fat calories. (You can throw in some alcohol calories on occasion, too.) Carbohydrates have 4 calories per gram, proteins have 4 calories per gram, and fats have 9 calories per gram. Alcohol weighs in at 7 calories per gram.

Now think of your typical meal—usually a combination of carbohydrates, proteins, and fats. The combinations you create determine how long it takes to digest your food and what happens to your blood sugar as that food is digested. (We'll talk about how to best combine foods in Chapter 4.)

In short, you influence your metabolism by your decisions about what, when, and how much to eat. (The word *metabolism* refers to the set of biochemical processes that convert what you eat and drink into calories your body can use for fuel. These calories are joined with oxygen so that energy can be distributed.) Typically, between 5 and 10 percent of the calories you eat are used to actually digest and absorb the food. Here's how it breaks down: If you're eating a 200-calorie snack, somewhere between 10 and 20 calories are burned simply by the process of digestion. And the more high-quality and nutritious the food, the harder your body works to digest it. So 200 calories' worth of baby carrots with hummus will require closer to 10 percent of their calories to digest, while potato chips, which glide effortlessly through your digestive tract, will need only about 5 percent. This is digestive thermogenesis. (*Thermo* means heat, and *genesis* means creation.) Digesting food creates heat, increasing your metabolism and using up more of the calories you've consumed. If your body's using those calories in the process of digestion, it won't be storing them on your hips!

Later on in this chapter, I'll introduce you to a list of foods that suppress ghrelin—some do it so well that I call them *superfoods*. These foods take longer to digest, creating more digestive thermogenesis. *This* is why you can eat so much more food on this plan. The amount of digestive thermogenesis you spur through your food selections helps determine the speed of your metabolism. (Yes, it *is* within your power to boost or slow down your metabolism.) The right choices help you burn more calories and keep you full longer. It's a win-win!

Think about this: What will fill you up more? A third of a large bag—about 4 ounces—of pretzels, or a meal made up of 4 ounces of chicken breast, ⅔ cup of brown rice, and a cup of veggies drizzled with your favorite dressing? Both are about 400 calories, but the way your body uses those calories is vastly different. You digest the pretzels easily and quickly, without creating much thermogenesis. And that pretzel snack makes your ghrelin levels drop right away—but then rise quickly after you're done eating. If you choose the chicken meal, though, your body needs a lot more time *and* uses a lot more energy to transform the food into energy your body can use. This creates thermogenesis, which is your metabolism rising. Because it takes more time and energy to digest the chicken meal, you feel full longer and burn more calories in the process.

Here's another useful tidbit about the body's digestive process. The minute you taste something is the very minute your body starts secreting digestive fluids. So if you shovel in "empty calories"—food with little to no nutritional value—you're setting yourself up for a "lose-lose." Here's why.

Say you decide to snack on a "low-cal" cream-filled snack cake mostly made of food chemicals rather than real food. It's okay because it's a "diet food" and you're on a diet, right? Perhaps this little treat contains 300 calories. Here's what happens in your body: Your taste buds can't distinguish between real and "fake" food, so they send a signal to other parts of your digestive system to secrete the usual digestive enzymes and hormones. Once those digestive juices encounter substances that aren't exactly food, your empty digestive tract sends a signal to the hypothalamus, telling it that you need food. Before you know it, your body secretes more ghrelin,[1] making you hungry again. So now you feel like you have to eat something else, adding even more calories on top of that so-called diet dessert. Maybe you reach for those pretzels and scarf down a third of the package—another 400 calories. You now have 700 calories to burn. Five days of eating like this and you've added a pound—thanks, in part, to that "diet" dessert. Not a good move.

But there's a much smarter way to eat: Work *with* your body and temper the rise of ghrelin—and the timing by which it rises—to gain biological control of your appetite.

SMART EATING THE BELLY FAT FIX WAY

The type of food you eat has a major impact on ghrelin. There are many factors that determine whether a specific kind of food suppresses ghrelin, increases it, or has no effect. These factors include the timing of your meals (as you've already learned), the specific category of food you choose (is it a protein, carbohydrate, or fat?), the way you combine food to put together a meal, and the amount or volume you eat. (Remember that ghrelin secretion stops when your stomach is full.)

All these variables have been taken into account on the Belly Fat Fix and in the G-List, so you don't have to think about it—it couldn't be easier. What's unique about the foods on the G-List is that they're *wholesome* and *filling*. You'll find the list beginning on page 77. In short, the foods on the G-List are the ones that suppress your ghrelin to the max. The G-List was specifically designed with ghrelin in mind. It takes the guesswork out of what to eat to suppress ghrelin by dividing food groups into three categories:

- Ghrelin suppressing
- Ghrelin neutral
- Ghrelin increasing

To understand the food science behind the G-List, we'll first look at each of the major food groups. Then we'll look at ways to combine those foods and learn about their effects on the body. When you understand the ghrelin-suppressing power of different foods and apply that knowledge to putting together the right food combinations, you'll be able to plan and/or choose meals that'll keep your belly full and your weight down.

Let's look now at the three main food groups featured in the G-List: protein, carbohydrates, and fats.

PROTEIN

There are two classes of protein: complete protein and incomplete protein. The terms *complete* and *incomplete* refer to the amino acid makeup of the protein. Amino acids are the "building blocks" of protein. There are 20 different amino acid compounds that make up all proteins in the human body. Amino acids are needed to replenish tissue, generate red blood cells, make enzymes for digestion, and build muscle. They can be further broken down into "essential" or "nonessential." Of the 20 amino acids, the body can manufacture 11—those are the *nonessential amino acids*, because they don't have to be consumed in the diet. Your body is capable of making them from the remaining nine "essential" amino acids. The *essential amino acids* can't be made by the body and must be obtained from the foods we eat.

Animal products (such as meat, fish, poultry, and dairy products) are complete proteins because they contain all the essential amino acids and so are considered high-quality. Plants like vegetables, nuts, seeds, and some grains—with the exception of soybeans and quinoa—are incomplete proteins, considered lower-quality because they don't contain every essential amino acid.

When it comes to ghrelin suppression, high-quality, animal-based proteins make a huge difference. Studies show that animal proteins work best to suppress ghrelin. Hands down, the most filling food you can put on your plate is animal-based protein. This was shown in a study, published in the *American Journal of Clinical Nutrition*, designed to investigate the difference in ghrelin level and hunger scores after a high-protein breakfast versus a high-carbohydrate breakfast. Blood samples and fullness scores of 15 healthy men were assessed for 3 hours after they had finished eating. Results proved the high-protein breakfast slowed digestion and decreased ghrelin more strongly over time than did the high-carbohydrate breakfast.[2]

What if you're a vegetarian? Don't worry—you can still make effective use of the Belly Fat Fix. You'll just have to work a little harder to combine foods in a way

(continued on page 70)

Lisa N.

AGE: 55

POUNDS LOST:

FAST-TRACK: 5

TOTAL: **37 in 4 months; 42 to date**

OVERALL INCHES LOST: **28**

Lisa N. has been obese her *entire* life—she was even a hefty baby at birth. "I went from being a heavy baby to an overweight kid," says Lisa, a nursing professor. "That's been my identity my whole life."

Now, for the first time in years, Lisa feels comfortable wearing a swimsuit without a cover-up. And resplendent in her mother-of-the-bride finery, she's walked her youngest daughter down the aisle on her wedding day.

But let's flash back a few years. No other diet—and Lisa has tried many—worked for her. Years ago, when her oldest daughter married, Lisa, wanting to look her best, tried the Atkins diet. She lost 40 pounds in time for the wedding but gained 5 pounds during the wedding festivities and put on another 5 within the next 10 days—and it was all downhill from there. The Belly Fat Fix, though, gave her the "kick in the butt" she needed to try once more.

On the Fast-Track, Lisa lost 5 pounds immediately as she began to see how much better she felt eating nutritious meals on a regular schedule. Setting up that schedule required a change in her daily habits.

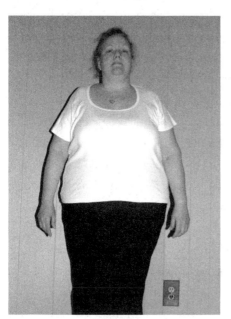

BEFORE

AFTER

What made the biggest difference for her, however, was learning to distinguish between her true hunger and non-hunger-based cravings. "Before, I used to feel that the ice cream in the refrigerator was literally calling to me. I was convinced I wouldn't have any peace until I answered that call." Now she's come to learn that she *can* control her cravings—she knows she has the power to decide what she will eat and what she won't eat.

Using the food tracker daily helped her become more aware of her cravings to gain more control over them. Learning how her body actually felt when she was full, and how the "physical" feeling differed from the "psychological" feeling of a craving, also helped. Making this distinction put her back in the driver's seat with appetite control. Now she can keep her eating within healthy limits whether she's preparing meals at home or enjoying a dinner out with family and friends.

She's also healthier. During her 4-month weight-loss journey, she improved on several measures: Her LDL cholesterol and HgbA1c (which measures blood glucose concentration) dropped from high into the normal range; the value associated with her thyroid stimulating hormone (TSH) went up, indicating improved functioning in her metabolism; and her blood pressure improved so much that her doctor cut Lisa's medication by half. After a recent visit to her physician, Lisa reported that the whole office staff cheered her success. "They've tried to get me to lose weight and get my blood pressure under control for quite some time now. Everyone is anxiously waiting for my next checkup to see how much more I've lost!"

But some of the most positive changes can't be measured by numbers. Lisa is feeling more energetic and experiencing less joint pain and swelling. "At the end of a typical day, my feet would be twice their normal size, and my knees ached so much I took pain relievers three or four times a day. Now my feet are much less puffy than before, and my knee pain is so much better now, I only need ibuprofen a few times a week."

The other thing she enjoys? Her new body shape. "I'm not a skinny minny," she says, "but after losing so many pounds, I'm definitely lighter. The first month, I lost 11 inches from my gut. Now I can bend over and tie my shoes comfortably. The last thing to go was the extra padding on my butt."

Because Lisa's work requires her to be on the go a lot—traveling from one teaching venue to another on different days—she's mastered planning ahead so that she always has what she needs on hand. And to be ready for healthy, quick weekday meals, she cooks ahead on weekends, so workday dinners are a breeze.

The best part of the plan, though, was the fact that it was her daughter—author Marjorie Nolan Cohn—who developed it. And Lisa had extra reason to be proud of her daughter—and herself—when she slipped into that mother-of-the-bride dress. "My weight now is within a few pounds of what it was 9 years ago, when my first daughter got married," she says. "And you know how hard it is to lose weight when you're in your fifties. I feel more in control of my own destiny than I ever have. I know I'll be on this plan for life."

that fully suppresses ghrelin. In most cases, vegetarian proteins—complete, although not high-quality, proteins—are ghrelin neutral. So if you're vegetarian, choose ghrelin-suppressing carbohydrates and fats to assure that you fully suppress your ghrelin.

There are two reasons high-quality protein keeps you full longer than choices from other food groups. First there's the "thermic" or heat-producing effect of high-quality protein digestion, which we will examine in a moment. Second, there's the fact that when you eat high-quality proteins, your stomach empties more slowly. These two factors combine to suppress ghrelin more—and for a longer time.

Protein and Your Digestive Thermometer

The digestion of proteins produces more heat than the digestion of carbohydrates and fats. This heat quotient is called protein's "thermic" effect. The higher the thermic effect, the more calories your body has to use to digest and absorb food. The thermic effect may be higher in protein digestion because high-quality protein can't be stored in the body in its original form, so your body has to work harder—and create more heat—to break it down and use it.

There are many steps the body must take to make the nutrients in high-quality protein usable. Protein must be digested, absorbed, and then metabolized. When a protein is metabolized, it's broken down into individual amino acids, rearranged, then used for muscle preservation and tissue building. The digestion of high-quality protein requires much more effort from the body than, say, the digestion of simple sugars. That's why protein is so highly thermogenic compared with other kinds of foods. High thermogenesis means high metabolism, which contributes to weight loss and better body composition.

A study published in the *Journal of Nutrition* compared changes in body weight and muscle mass after a 4-month weight-loss diet that was then followed by an 8-month weight-maintenance period. Participants were put on one of two diets. One was higher in protein; the other, higher in carbohydrates. At 4 months, those in the protein group had lost 22 percent more fat mass than those in the carb group. At 12 months, those in the protein group had greater improvement in overall muscle mass. The high-protein diet proved to be more effective for fat loss and muscle preservation during initial weight loss *and* long-term weight maintenance.[3]

Slow and Steady Ghrelin Suppression

Animal protein has staying power. To be fully digested, it needs to be in the stomach longer. Those proteins begin chemical digestion in the stomach, where stomach acids (gastric juices) start to chemically break down the animal proteins—not carbs or fats—into smaller parts. Quite simply, your stomach houses protein longer to make sure it's adequately digested before moving it into the small intestine. Remember that we learned in Chapter 1 that ghrelin is suppressed when food is in the stomach? (See the True Hunger loop on page 14.) Well, if you eat foods that stay in your stomach longer, you naturally help your body suppress ghrelin for a longer period of time—you won't get hungry as quickly and you'll probably eat less.

Even before ghrelin was discovered, a groundbreaking study published in the *European Journal of Clinical Nutrition* looked at how different foods affect fullness levels. Guess what? It confirmed that lean protein is the most filling. This study verified that protein takes longer to digest, affecting how full you feel—and for how long.[4]

CARBOHYDRATES

Carbohydrates are classified into two categories, simple and complex. And all carbohydrates, both simple and complex, are broken down further into simple sugars (such as glucose, the most well known in this category), which circulate in the blood. The classification of a specific carbohydrate depends on its chemical structure and how quickly it's digested and absorbed. Just as protein is "built" from amino acids, carbohydrates are "built" from sugar units. Simple carbs have only one (single) or two (double) sugar units. Complex carbohydrates have three or more sugar units combined. Another description of carbohydrates you may have heard of is "refined carbohydrates." This isn't a formal classification but an important description of carbohydrates in the food supply.

Simple carbohydrates are found in fruit, milk, candy, syrup, honey, soda, and table sugar. Complex carbohydrates are found in starch-based foods such as bread, cereal, potatoes, pasta, starchy vegetables (mainly corn and peas), legumes/beans, and grains. It may surprise you to learn that refined carbohydrates such as white bread and pasta are technically complex carbohydrates.

When it comes to ghrelin suppression, the difference between "simple," "refined," and "complex" is extremely important. Eating simple or refined carbohydrates is like filling your brand-new car with a low-grade gasoline. Your car will still run and get you where you need to go, but not nearly as smoothly and efficiently as it would on high-octane gas.

Complex carbs are high in fiber and have higher protein content than refined carbohydrates. The combination of fiber and protein slows digestion and suppresses ghrelin longer than simple or refined carbohydrates do.

Carbohydrate digestion, in contrast to protein digestion, begins the moment you put the food in your mouth. Saliva contains digestive enzymes that start to break apart the sugar chains that form carbohydrates. Carbohydrate digestion—unlike protein digestion—comes to a halt in the stomach. What does all this mean? The predigested carbohydrates from your mouth quickly move through your stomach and into your intestines, with no need for your body to house them for long in your stomach.

But even though they don't hang around in your tummy, complex carbs are *very* important in suppressing ghrelin. The Belly Fat Fix won't work if you don't eat

An Apple a Day Keeps Ghrelin at Bay?

Apples are an excellent source of fiber, water, and lots of important vitamins and minerals. But an apple alone isn't a ghrelin-suppressing snack. Think about the last time you had an apple for a snack when you were hungry between meals. How long did the apple keep you full?

Did you say about 30 minutes? That's about right. The reason you got hungry 30 minutes later is that an apple is a carbohydrate and will only suppress ghrelin for a short time. Remember from Chapter 1 how ghrelin rises every 30 minutes? Well, the carbs in an apple are just enough to reduce your ghrelin for one cycle of secretion. After that, your ghrelin levels surge back up and you feel hungry all over again.

enough carbohydrates. No-carb or low-carb diets do not work. If they did, everyone who ever went on one would have lost weight and kept it off. Cutting carbs is an enemy to weight loss. That's because carbohydrates are our first defense in terms of suppressing ghrelin. But their effect on ghrelin is short term. They slow ghrelin secretion right away—but not for long.

A study from the University of Naples in Italy looked at ghrelin levels after a higher-fat meal compared with a higher-carbohydrate meal. Circulating ghrelin dropped after both meals, but it dropped *significantly more* right after the carbohydrate meal. In addition, the higher-carb meal suppressed hunger levels more than the higher-fat meal. That's because the higher-carb meal suppressed ghrelin more— and did so more quickly.[5]

FIBER

Most everybody's heard of fiber. You may know that it fills you up, slows digestion, and doesn't have calories. It's not exactly a food group, but it *is* a food nutrient that you need to include for optimal results on the Belly Fat Fix. A nutrient is a substance that provides nourishment essential for growth and the maintenance of life. Here's the lowdown on fiber:

People don't have the ability to break down fiber in the digestive tract, so fiber moves though the tract nearly intact, binding to cholesterol and filling up space along the way. There are two classes of fiber, soluble and insoluble. Soluble fiber reduces cholesterol; insoluble fiber fills you up. A third type called "resistant starch" isn't actually fiber at all but functions like it in your body. Resistant starch is unique in its dual capacity to function as both a soluble and insoluble fiber.

Soluble Fiber

If you were to stir soluble fiber into hot water, it would dissolve. In your stomach, it does the same thing, dissolving in the water from your food and digestive juices and creating a gel called pectin. Pectin traps some food components, making it less available for absorption and significantly slowing digestion.

Pectin, a type of soluble fiber, interferes somewhat with the absorption of fats and sugars. It doesn't keep you from absorbing calories—at least, not in any meaningful way. But its fat-binding action can help reduce cholesterol. And by slowing down the absorption of sugar, it helps keep blood sugar levels steadier. When blood sugar is steady, ghrelin secretion is balanced.

Insoluble Fiber

If you were to stir some insoluble fiber into hot water, it wouldn't dissolve. In fact, as soon as you stopped stirring, it would sink to the bottom. But it *would* soak up a bunch of the water and puff up like a sponge.

Now imagine this puffed-up sponge moving through your stomach, then through your intestines, and you'll begin to get an idea what insoluble fiber does for you. It puffs up and fills your digestive tract with volume, slowing down digestion. When digestion is slowed, you feel full longer and ghrelin is suppressed.

Resistant Starch

Resistant starch isn't technically fiber, but because it delivers some of the benefits of both soluble fiber and insoluble fiber, it's often categorized as a type of fiber. Most starchy foods contain some resistant starch. Ghrelin-suppressing carbohydrate superfoods (we'll learn about these special foods later in this chapter) are particularly high in resistant starch.

Carbohydrate-based foods, such as sugars and starches, are quickly digested and absorbed as glucose into circulating blood. Glucose in the blood is used for immediate energy or stored for later use in the form of fat. Resistant starch, on the other hand, resists digestion, passing through to the large intestine, where it functions like dietary fiber. It has more water-holding capacity, so it soaks up more water in your digestive tract, fills up space—and makes your body feel more full and work harder to complete digestion. In fact, studies have shown that higher consumption of resistant starch increases the use of fat stores.[6] This may be because your body is working harder to move the resistant starch through your digestive tract, creating thermogenesis.

Resistant starch does contain calories, but only about half the amount of regular starches. That's because when resistant starch reaches the colon, it's used for fuel by the bacteria there in a process called bacterial fermentation, which slows digestion, increases overall metabolic rate, promotes a healthy colon and bowel regularity, and may also protect against cancer.[7]

Resistant starch, because of its fiberlike qualities, has been shown to be much more filling than other starch-containing foods. A study at the University of Minnesota evaluated the effect of four different forms of fiber on satiety. Twenty healthy volunteers on five separate visits were fed breakfast of either a low-fat muffin with 1.6 grams of fiber or one of four high-fiber muffins with 8.0 to 9.6 grams of fiber. Researchers concluded that the resistant-starch muffins consistently had a much higher fullness effect than other forms of fiber.[8]

Another study published in the *American Journal of Clinical Nutrition* looked at the effect of resistant starch on postmeal blood sugar level and satiety. In two different visits, 10 healthy adults were fed one of two meals made with equal amounts of starch. Meal 1, given to half the study participants, contained no resistant starch. Meal 2, given to the other participants, contained 54 percent resistant starch. The resistant-starch group showed lower blood glucose and insulin levels.[9] When resistant starch is eaten in combination with other G-List food groups, it will slow digestion and prevent a spike in blood sugar and insulin. This in turn keeps your hunger at bay.[10]

FAT

Fat may not be filling—and it may not suppress ghrelin secretion[11]—but it's really important for a healthy body and mind. Plus, it tastes great! And that increases your feeling of fullness because your brain's food pleasure center registers that you've eaten.

Just because fat won't suppress ghrelin, though, doesn't mean you shouldn't eat it on the Belly Fat Fix. Remember that dietary fat is essential—it's a critical component of cells, especially cell membranes. Cell membranes are the skin of your cells, protecting the inside of a cell from the outside environment. You have billions of cells in your body, and fat is a component of every single one of them. Without fat, your body couldn't function at its best. Remember high school biology lab? You may have done an experiment in which you mixed water with oil. The oil and water—even after vigorous shaking—would always separate. That's because oil (fat) is water resistant, which makes it such an important component of cell membranes (or skin). Fat provides cell membrane structure, preserving cell integrity and keeping it intact.

Think about those billions and billions of cells in your body. If you don't eat enough fat, every single one of your cell membranes can't function properly. Without healthy cell membranes, you're more prone to illness, infection, cancer, slowed metabolism, and weight gain. You have to eat fat to lose weight and keep your body healthy, regardless of the fact that it does *not* fill you up.

And don't forget that the fat you eat does *not* immediately turn into the fat on your thighs—as long as you eat the right kinds and amounts. There are three major categories of fat:

▶ Saturated fats, also known as "bad fats"

▶ Unsaturated fats, known as "good fats"

▶ Trans fats, a type of artificial fat

Most saturated fats, such as butter and lard, come from animal sources, though there are also a few plant-based saturated fat sources, including palm oil, coconut oil, and cocoa oil. You can tell a fat is saturated when it becomes solid at room temperature. When choosing foods from the G-List ghrelin-suppressing category, you'll naturally minimize saturated fat, but you won't completely avoid it, no matter how you try. Saturated fat is even found in several "good fats," such as olive oil, which contains about 2 grams of saturated fat per tablespoon.

Unsaturated fats, on the other hand, are plant-based fats that are liquid at room temperature. These fats are broken down into monounsaturated and polyunsaturated. Both are "good fats" and are listed in the G-List ghrelin-suppressing category. In fact, you'll see in the meal-planning chapter that fat is an essential component of this plan. The G-List (opposite) prioritizes which fats are best to support a healthy body and metabolism. Unsaturated fats may not fill you up, but they do provide your body with a host of benefits, including cell membrane protection; removal of bad cholesterol; transportation of vitamins A, D, E, and K; joint lubrication; and healthy skin and hair. Plus, unsaturated fats are essential for brain development and function. In fact, fat is a major component of your central nervous system and spinal cord and an outstanding conductor of electricity—it functions as the key component of your brain and spinal cord, allowing electrical impulses and messages to be sent throughout your body.

Most trans fats are human-made (there is only a very small amount of naturally occurring trans fats in high-fat cuts of beef and lamb and in some dairy products). Trans fats are neither saturated nor unsaturated, but they started out as unsaturated fats that were chemically altered, turning them from a liquid at room temperature to a solid at room temperature. Trans fats are ghrelin increasing—but the negative effects don't stop there. They raise bad cholesterol and decrease good cholesterol, and they can't be used within our body for cell membrane structure or vitamin transport. Trans fats are metabolically useless; they provide lots of calories but no functional benefit.

Now that you understand how your body digests and uses food from different food groups differently, let's look more closely at which foods suppress ghrelin, which increase it, and which have no effect at all. Then we'll look at the Ghrelin superfoods, which I hope you'll eat often.

THE G-LIST

The G-List (starting on page 78) has three main food groups: protein, carbohydrates, and fat. Within these groups are the subgroups: ghrelin-suppressing foods (+), ghrelin-neutral foods (=), and ghrelin-increasing foods (–). All fruits and vegetables are neutral (=) and must be paired with a ghrelin-suppressing food for optimal ghrelin balance.

I've included the symbols (+), (=), and (–) for a quick reference with the G-List. I also encourage you to write these symbols in your food tracker in Chapter 11. That way, you'll further ingrain the ghrelin-suppressing foods into your memory. Those ghrelin-suppressing foods are "+" or positive, so you'll remember that you want to eat them most. Neutral foods are simply "=", and ghrelin-increasing foods are "–" or negative, so you remember to avoid them. I've also included the calorie count on the G-List, so you can understand how many calories are in the foods you'll be eating. You'll learn in Chapter 6 how you can use the calories as a reference when switching your G-List foods.

Your objective: Make all meals/snacks ghrelin suppressing by choosing one or more foods from the ghrelin-suppressing food list.

Note: The Ghrelin menus are based on cooked portions unless otherwise stated.

G-List Ghrelin-Neutral Foods (=)

Fruit (=) 60 calories	Nonstarchy Veggies (=) 25 calories
• 4 ounces—whole piece fruit (1 small fruit) • 1 cup cut fruit • ½ cup pureed fruit • 2 tablespoons 100% unsweetened dried fruit	• 1 cup raw • ½ cup cooked

While all fruits and veggies are neutral, some have a higher ghrelin-suppressing effect when combined with ghrelin-suppressing foods.

Fruit (=)	Nonstarchy Veggies (=)
• Granny Smith apple • Grapefruit	• Kale • Raw carrots

G-List Ghrelin-Suppressing Foods (+)

Ghrelin-suppressing foods* are whole foods that are high-quality proteins, high in fiber, complex carbohydrates and heart-healthy fats. These ghrelin-suppressing foods take a long time to digest.

Proteins 75 calories	Carbohydrates 75 calories	Fats 50 calories
One cooked serving equals:	One cooked serving equals:	One serving equals:
• 2 ounces chicken/turkey breast (no skin)	• 3-ounce baked potato	• *1 tablespoon pine nuts/pine nut oil*
• *2 ounces 95% lean ground beef*	• *⅓ cup lentils/beans*	• 1 teaspoon 100% pure oils (olive, walnut, canola, coconut)
• *2 ounces beef, 95% lean cuts*	• ⅓ cup brown rice	• 1 tablespoon chia seeds/flaxseeds
• 2 ounces ground turkey breast	• ⅓ cup whole wheat couscous	• 1 tablespoon raw nuts/seeds
• 2 ounces veal/pork (lean cuts)	• *⅓ cup quinoa*	• 2 tablespoons avocado
• 2 ounces bison/elk meat	• ⅓ cup faro	• 5 large olives
• *3 ounces white fish*	• ⅓ cup barley	
• 3 ounces shrimp/shellfish	• ⅓ cup corn/peas	
• ½ (5-ounce) can tuna in water, drained	• ⅓ cup cooked whole wheat pasta	
• 4 egg whites or 1 medium egg	• *½ cup rolled oats* (¼ cup uncooked)	
• *⅔ cup fat-free Greek yogurt*	• 2 tablespoons hummus	
• ½ cup fat-free cottage cheese	• ⅔ cup unsweetened cereal with 5 grams or more of fiber	
	• 1-ounce slice 100% whole grain bread with 3 grams or more of fiber	

*Ghrelin-suppressing superfoods are in **bold** type; you'll learn about these special foods later in this chapter.*

G-List Ghrelin-Neutral Foods (=)

Ghrelin-neutral foods are somewhat refined and processed. They're generally whole-food ingredients with some processing for convenience. Ghrelin-neutral foods contain less fiber and less high-quality protein than ghrelin-suppressing foods. They are digested faster than ghrelin-suppressing foods, and they won't suppress ghrelin for very long.

Proteins 75 calories	Carbohydrates 75 calories	Fats 50 calories
One cooked serving equals: • 2 ounces tempeh/tofu/seitan • 2 ounces imitation crab • ⅓ cup edamame • 1½ ounces low-fat cheese • ½ veggie burger • 2 ounces low-fat deli meats (turkey, chicken, ham, etc.) • ⅔ cup low-fat/fat-free liquid milk • ⅔ cup fat-free yogurt (non-Greek) • ⅓ cup 2% cottage cheese • ¼ cup part-skim ricotta cheese	One cooked serving equals: • ⅓ cup white rice • ⅓ cup white pasta • 3 popped cups popcorn • 1 ounce whole wheat crackers/pretzels • 1 cup premade organic soup • 3 tablespoons bread crumbs • ⅔ cup unsweetened cereal with less than 5 grams of fiber • 1-ounce slice bread with fewer than 5 grams of fiber	One serving equals: • 1½ teaspoons nut butter (peanut, almond, cashew) • 1 teaspoon pure unsalted butter • 1 tablespoon oil-based dressing • 1 tablespoon mayo (regular or light) • 2 tablespoons shredded coconut • 1 tablespoon regular sour cream • 2 tablespoons half-and-half • 2 tablespoons cream cheese • 1 tablespoon 72% chocolate/cocoa powder

G-List Ghrelin-Increasing Foods (−)

Ghrelin-increasing foods are highly refined or processed. They are often marketed as healthy "diet" foods with fortified (added) vitamins, minerals, and fiber. They contain little to no natural fiber; they have low-quality protein; they are digested very quickly. Reading food ingredient labels is key to determining if a food is ghrelin increasing. Refer to the "Top Five Ingredients to Avoid" section of Chapter 4 (page 99) to determine if a food is ghrelin increasing or not.

Proteins	Carbohydrates	Fats
• Processed high-fat meats (salami, pepperoni, hot dogs, etc.) • Fat-free flavored yogurt and cottage cheeses (such as 60-calorie Light & Fit yogurt) • High-fat cheeses	• Sweetened breads/pastries • Diet/light breads • 100-calorie snack packs • Sweetened cereals • Refined white bread/pasta • Muffins/dough-nuts/waffles • Breakfast cereal bars • Potato chips/pretzels • Graham crackers/butter crackers • Fruit drinks/soda	• Vegetable oil • Margarine • Bacon • Low-fat/fat-free salad dressings • Bottled meat marinades • Candy bars, milk chocolate

Did you notice the food items in bold type in the ghrelin-suppressing list? Those are *very* important foods. They'll suppress your ghrelin in a major way, and here we'll learn why.

The G-List tells you which foods are ghrelin suppressing (+), ghrelin neutral (=), and ghrelin increasing (–). If you stick with ghrelin-suppressing G-List foods for 75 percent or more of your meals, your ghrelin levels will be balanced and you won't have to fight hunger to lose weight.

But food science tells us that even within the ghrelin-suppressing food list, there are a few items that stand out. I call these *ghrelin-suppressing superfoods.*

YOUR PROTEIN SUPERFOODS
Fat-Free Plain Greek Yogurt

This kind of yogurt was virtually unknown in the United States until a few years ago but is rapidly gaining popularity. Its availability is a real boon to anyone making the effort to use ghrelin in the war on weight. That's because fat-free plain Greek yogurt has roughly the same number of calories as regular yogurt yet double the protein and half the sugar. In fact, the only sugar in plain Greek yogurt is naturally occurring and can't be removed. Plus, this yogurt is high in calcium and promotes healthy digestion. Its nutritional punch—and its thick, satisfying consistency—make Greek yogurt a ghrelin-suppressing superfood.

One serving of Greek yogurt provides about 20 percent of daily calcium needs and 12 percent of the Daily Value of pantothenic acid (vitamin B5), plus 9 percent of the Daily Value for thiamine (vitamin B1). According to the Institute of Medi-

It's Greek to Me!

In the West, successful marketing campaigns have made the term "Greek yogurt" synonymous with strained yogurt. But strained yogurt isn't a staple in Greece. In fact, most yogurts in Greece don't resemble the yogurt known in America as Greek yogurt.

cine, pantothenic acid promotes fat metabolism, and thiamine aids in the metabolism of carbohydrates.[12]

Be sure to choose fat-free *plain* Greek yogurt to get the full ghrelin-suppressing benefits. Some of the volume in flavored yogurt comes from the sugary fruit topping, not the yogurt itself, but if you don't like the tartness of plain Greek yogurt, you can easily sweeten it with fruit or honey. I enjoy my Greek yogurt with a drop or two of vanilla extract and stevia, a healthy sugar substitute derived from the leaves of the South American stevia plant. In the recipe chapter, you'll see Greek yogurt as a stand-in for many other ingredients. It's a versatile ingredient that you can use in almost any meal and in lots of sweet treats and snacks.

Lean Beef

Lean beef is highly ghrelin suppressing. That's because, due to its complex protein structure, beef is digested slowly. Think about how many times you have to chew a piece of steak compared with a piece of chicken. Quite simply, your body has to work harder to digest the beef. That difficulty starts with chewing and continues through all the other digestive processes as the meat is propelled through your digestive tract. All this effort takes time, keeping ghrelin at bay for a longer period. Lean beef does have a few more calories than chicken breast, but it's well worth it when you consider beef's iron, zinc, and vitamin B12 content.

Beef supplies the body with more than 15 percent of daily iron needs. There are two different types of iron: heme iron and nonheme iron. Heme iron is found in animal protein and is highly bioavailable—that means that the body absorbs it quickly and efficiently. Nonheme iron is found in vegetables and in some dried fruits and beans. While plant sources may have a significant amount of nonheme iron, it's not as easily absorbed as heme iron is. So when it comes to iron, beef is the clear winner.

That's because iron is necessary for hemoglobin, which carries oxygen to the muscles. Without enough iron, you become anemic, feel tired or dizzy, get headaches, bruise easily, and experience muscle aches. Plus, when your muscles don't get enough oxygen, your metabolism slows down. According to the Centers for Disease Control and Prevention's *National Health and Nutrition Examination Survey*, at least 10 percent of US adult women are anemic,[13] and it's likely that many more women have low iron levels without a diagnosis. Low iron compromises oxygen transport to muscles—and to every other tissue in the body. When this occurs, your muscles become weak and fatigued, and they can bruise easily. This iron-deficiency bruising—one of the classic signs of anemia—is due to weak muscle fibers that lack oxygen and injure more easily. And when muscle fibers are weak and lack oxygen, your overall metabolic rate is lower. The bottom line: Eat beef. The iron it provides will support and improve your metabolic rate.

Four ounces of lean beef delivers 40 percent of your zinc needs and 40 percent of your need for vitamin B12. Both support your metabolism, keep your energy levels up, and maintain your muscles when you lose weight. That's *exactly* what you want to happen—and that's why lean beef is a superfood. In fact, this was shown in a study published in the *Journal of Nutrition* that looked at lean beef's ability to maintain muscle tissue and prevent muscle loss during weight loss. It showed that a diet with higher amounts of beef protein—combined with moderate exercise—improves body composition during weight loss.[14] Improved body composition means more muscles, which increases metabolism and helps keep your ghrelin balanced.

White Fish

White fish includes tilapia, cod, haddock, whiting, and pollock. All white fish are low in fat and high in protein, and they tend to have fewer calories than other meat

Does Red Meat Cause Heart Disease?

No. There's no need to avoid red meat—but do choose the right kind. Consider this: New research from Pennsylvania State University has shown that when lean beef is part of a healthy daily diet, it can actually lower bad cholesterol (LDL) by 10 percent. It can be as effective in lowering bad cholesterol as the well-known DASH (Dietary Approach to Stop Hypertension) diet.[15]

proteins. The G-List allows for 3 ounces of white fish, as opposed to 2 ounces of beef or poultry.

White fish isn't just an excellent, lower-calorie source of protein; it's also rich in vitamins and minerals. It provides 16 percent of the body's daily niacin (vitamin B3), which promotes healthy cells and eliminates toxins from the body. White fish supplies the body with over 25 percent of the Daily Value of pyridoxine (vitamin B6), which keeps the nervous system and red blood cells healthy. White fish also delivers about 75 percent of the Daily Value of vitamin B12, important in brain function and metabolism.

White fish is rich in several essential minerals, such as iron, selenium, and iodine. Selenium and iodine are important for proper thyroid function and for the immune system. Deficiency of these minerals leads to a higher risk of infection and to certain forms of cancer.

So why is white fish a ghrelin superfood? Easy. You get to eat a few more ounces of white fish—roughly a third more volume compared with other meat proteins—because of the fish's lower calorie content. It takes you longer to eat and digest, both of which decrease ghrelin. Plus, how can you not like seeing more food on your plate while you're dieting?

And there's no need to worry about mercury in white fish. Mercury is oil soluble, which means it accumulates in the oily part of fish. Since white fish are low in oil and fat, mercury (and other toxins) are not a concern.

CARBOHYDRATE SUPERFOODS

Carbohydrates that contain high amounts of fiber, particularly pectin and resistant starch, are super ghrelin suppressing.

100 Percent Rolled Oats

This is my top pick of traditional breakfast foods. One serving (¼ cup of raw oats) has 3 grams of protein and almost 3 grams of fiber. The fiber in oats is a mixture of soluble and insoluble fibers *plus* resistant starch.

You may have heard that oatmeal reduces cholesterol. That's because oats contain pectin, the cholesterol-lowering soluble fiber. Remember how pectin forms a gel that traps some the cholesterol along the digestive tract? (Refer to the Fiber section beginning on page 73.)

Sweet Potatoes

All potatoes are ghrelin suppressing, but sweet potatoes stand out above the rest. You may have heard sweet potatoes are better than white potatoes, and when it comes to ghrelin suppression, that's spot-on. Sweet potatoes, true to their name, are sweet and can be easily prepared for filling meals and delicious sweet treats or desserts.

Sweet potatoes are a good source of vitamin C, iron, and potassium. Vitamin C fights off colds and flu viruses; it's also important in cell membrane formation and wound healing. You may remember that iron is important for blood functioning and for the transport of oxygen throughout the body. And potassium is an important electrolyte that helps regulate your heartbeat and nerve function.

Sweet potatoes are high in fiber, particularly in pectin. They also contain lots of resistant starch, which delivers some of the benefits of insoluble fiber and some of the benefits of soluble fiber. Studies have shown that higher consumption of resistant starch increases the use of the fat stores,[16] known as "lipid oxidation." *Lipid* means fat and *oxidation* refers to the process of breaking down. This is probably due to the higher thermogenesis and because when resistant starch reaches the colon, it's used for fuel by the bacteria there. This process is called bacterial fermentation (see the Fiber section earlier in this chapter).

The Oats Ate My Homework

Oats are better suited than wheat to Scotland's short, wet growing season and thus quickly became the staple grain of the country. Ancient universities of Scotland had a holiday called Meal Monday, when students were permitted to stay home from school to help collect oats.

Potato Power

French fries and potato chips are much less filling than whole potatoes, despite the significant increases in calories. Boiling potatoes and allowing them to cool increase how full they make you feel—probably because boiling increases a potato's soluble fiber content by 3 percent, which increases pectin, forming the viscous pectin gel and slowing digestion.[17]

- ☐ Potatoes were the first crop to be grown in outer space.
- ☐ Potatoes have long been considered an aphrodisiac in Europe.

Quinoa (Pronounced Keen-Wah)

Quinoa is native to the Andes mountains in South America, where it's been cultivated since 3000 BC. Some people consider quinoa a grain because of its shape and cooking qualities. But it's actually a seed, with more than 120 different varieties, though only three kinds—red, black, and white—are cultivated and sold. Quinoa seeds have a nutty, mild flavor and are roughly the size of sesame seeds.

Quinoa is very high in protein; in fact, up to 18 percent of the calories in quinoa are protein. Just one G-List serving of quinoa (⅓ cup cooked) has 6 grams of protein, much more than most other carbohydrates. It's high in fiber, too, containing about 12 percent of the daily requirement in total, with over 60 percent of that being insoluble fiber (the kind that expands and fills you up). Quinoa's high protein and fiber content make it about twice as filling as white rice for an equal portion. It's also high in key vitamins and minerals, such as folate, iron, magnesium, and phosphorus, which all support metabolism and overall health.

The Incas considered the quinoa crop sacred and referred to the *plantas*, the "mother of all grains." During the European conquest of South America in the 16th century, the Spanish colonists scorned quinoa as "food for Indians" and actively suppressed its cultivation. In fact, quinoa cultivation was forbidden for a time, and the Incas were forced to grow wheat and corn instead.

Archaeological evidence suggests that some of the wilder forms of quinoa were cultivated as long ago as 7000 BC.

Lentils

Lentils are considered a vegetarian protein because of their high protein content. In fact, one G-List serving (⅓ cup) of lentils has 6 grams of protein. Compare that to 1 ounce of meat, with 7 grams, and you can understand why lentils are so highly regarded. Plus, they're a plant-based food, so they're high in fiber and complex carbs, which lands them a place on the G-List ghrelin-suppressing carbohydrate category. In ancient Greece, Hippocrates prescribed lentils to cure liver ailments.

Lentils have a whopping 5 grams of fiber per ⅓ cup serving, and their fiber is close to 20 percent pectin. Lentils also contain resistant starch—and cooking them will actually increase that amount. The pectin-and-resistant-starch combination in lentils significantly slows digestion—that's what makes them a ghrelin superfood.

Think about the ghrelin suppression that will come from combining a super protein, such as beef or white fish, with lentils. The more superfoods in your meal, the more ghrelin suppressing it will be.

FATS

There is only one ghrelin-suppressing superfood in the fat group.

Pine Nuts/Pine Nut Oil

Pine nuts are exactly what they sound like—the crunchy and delicious edible seeds of a pine tree. Two species of pine trees are most known for their edible kernels: Korean and chilgoza. Pine kernels are an excellent source of essential minerals, vitamins, and heart-friendly monounsaturated fatty acids that help reduce cholesterol.

Pine nuts are rich in vitamins, antioxidants, and minerals, plus they're loaded with monounsaturated fatty acids, which work to lower LDL (or "bad cholesterol") and increase HDL (or "good cholesterol") in the blood. Pine nuts are high in vitamin E, an antioxidant that helps protect cellular membranes from damage.

The Power of Phytochemicals

Phytochemicals are plant compounds that have antioxidant or hormonelike actions; they can prevent or treat lots of health conditions, including cancer, heart disease, diabetes, and high blood pressure. There's some evidence that certain phytochemicals may help prevent the formation of potential carcinogens (substances that cause cancer), block the action of carcinogens on their target organs or tissue, or act on cells to suppress cancer development. Many experts suggest that you can significantly reduce your cancer risk by eating foods from plants that contain phytochemicals.

They're also an excellent source of B-complex vitamins, which aid metabolism.

The standout nutrient in pine nuts is the essential fatty acid and phytochemical called pinolenic acid. One ounce of pine nuts contains 15 percent of daily pinolenic acid needs. Research has shown that pinolenic acid increases the release of the hormones cholecystokinin and glucagon-like peptide, which can slow gastric emptying. One study demonstrated a significant increase in these hormones over a 4-hour period after participants consumed pinolenic acid. Ghrelin levels were not meaningfully different, but participants' "desire to eat" scores were 36 percent lower in those who consumed pinolenic acid than in those who did not.[18] This demonstrates the acid's potential as a powerful appetite suppressant. Now imagine how ghrelin suppressing a meal with pine nuts and other ghrelin-suppressing superfoods can be.

Pine nuts are most often associated with pesto sauce, but they can be used in desserts, too. Italian biscotti are traditionally topped with pine nuts.

FRUIT AND VEGGIE SUPERFOODS

While all fruits and veggies are basically neutral, some will have a higher ghrelin-suppressing effect when combined with ghrelin-suppressing foods.

Granny Smith Apples

Granny Smith apples are filled with water, soluble fiber, and pectin, all of which give you the feeling of being full. Granny Smiths have more pectin than other apples and work well on the Belly Fat Fix because they're tart and crisp. The combination of pectin, crispy texture, and tartness when combined with a full ghrelin-suppressing meal will help to keep sugar cravings at bay.

Grapefruit

The history of grapefruit as an ideal diet food dates back decades to several popular diets that called for eating grapefruit with every meal. The premise of the grapefruit diet is an urban legend; it was said that grapefruit contains enzymes that burn fat and/or speed metabolism. But it's not *all* urban legend. There *is* something about grapefruit that helps with weight loss.

In a study done by the Department of Nutrition and Metabolic Research at the Scripps Clinic in San Diego, California, researchers found that half a fresh grapefruit eaten before meals was associated with significant weight loss. They concluded that it made sense to include grapefruit in a weight reduction diet.[19]

Another study published in *Nutrition and Metabolism* looked at the efficacy of adding grapefruit to meals for weight loss. Researchers found that eating a grapefruit with meals not only aids in weight loss but also increases the ability to stick with a diet.[20]

Grapefruit can aid in ghrelin suppression in several ways. First, grapefruit is high in water; therefore, a dieter can get a lot of volume for fewer calories. Second, grapefruit is a citrus fruit, and thus cuts the desire for sweets. And third, grapefruit is a good source of pectin.

A bit of salt can make a grapefruit taste sweeter.

Kale

Kale is a super ghrelin-suppressing standout among vegetables. It's high in fiber—3 grams per serving, in fact. When combined with other ghrelin-suppressing foods, the fiber in kale creates bulk that fills you up and keeps you full for a long time. Kale is denser than other greens, so it takes more energy to digest and longer to move through the digestive tract.

Kale is rich in calcium, vitamin C, folic acid, vitamin B6, manganese, and potassium. With its combination of vitamins, minerals, and phytonutrients, kale is a dieter's dream food. Though greens in general are nutritious, kale stands out as an excellent source of beta-carotene, one of the antioxidants that fight cancer, heart disease, and certain age-related chronic diseases. It also provides other important nutrients called carotenoids, which help keep UV rays from damaging the eyes and forming cataracts.

Raw Carrots

I love raw carrots because they have a high chew factor and they take a long time to eat. Carrots fight ghrelin because they have few calories compared with their bulk and the effort it takes to eat them. So, when your body is digesting carrots, a lot more calories are used to break them down. That not only helps suppress ghrelin but also trips your volume switch. Ghrelin, you may recall, has a volume trigger, so by combining a fiber-filled veggie like carrots that take lots of chewing with other ghrelin-suppressing foods, you're maximizing your sense of fullness.

WATER

We've been talking about filling foods, but now let's take a look at water, another essential on this plan. Sometimes when you *feel* hungry, you're actually thirsty.

About 85 percent of the clients who come to my office are chronically dehydrated. Funny thing is, they have no clue. When you're dehydrated, your thirst sensors shut off. It's only when you *do* drink enough water that your thirst sensors kick back on and you actually *feel* thirsty. The point? You need to drink in order to feel thirsty. Strange—but true.

Drinking water keeps your metabolism working at its best and helps you distinguish between different types of hunger. But did you know different beverages affect your hydration differently? Some beverages leach water from your cells, and some help keep your cells hydrated. Think of your cells on water this way: Fully hydrated cells are like a ripe blueberry—soft, plump, and supple. Cells that aren't fully hydrated are like old blueberries—hard, small, and wrinkly.

What Not to Drink

Diet soda, regular soda, coffee, tea, and alcohol don't contribute to hydration. Your body is made up of 75 percent water, so water is the best way to stay hydrated—period. Just because soda, coffee, tea, and alcohol are liquids doesn't mean they contribute to hydration. Actually, they dehydrate you. And the only way to make up for the dehydration effect is to drink double the amount of water. So for every 8 ounces of diet soda, coffee, tea, or alcohol you drink, make it a point to drink 16 ounces of water.

Consider this: If you're a coffee drinker, or if you put away a liter of diet soda a day, your cells are the equivalent of an old blueberry. Not to worry, though. Your wrinkly cells can and will be plumped back to normal within a couple of days if you simply drink enough water.

How Much Is Enough?

For optimal ghrelin stabilization, drink 75 ounces or more of water daily. Sound impossible? Let me break it down for you. Using a standard 16.9-ounce water bottle as your reference, you need to drink about four and a half bottles a day. With 24 hours in a day—and subtracting 8 for sleep—that leaves you with 16 hours of potential water-drinking time. This means you need to drink just over one water bottle every 4 hours, or about 5.5 ounces of water per hour. It's not much if you sip throughout the day. The key is to not wait until the end of the day. If you can drink a teacup (literally) full of water once per hour, you'll be fully hydrated.

> NOW THAT YOU KNOW the best foods to eat and the best beverages to drink on the ghrelin diet—and why—let's look next at how to combine all of this to create belly-filling, nutritious meals that will help you take the weight off.

CHAPTER 4

Practical Matters: Plan. Prepare. Shop. Portion.

Back in Chapter 1, we looked at how ghrelin—the hunger hormone—
can help or hurt your efforts to keep your eating in check and your weight where
you want it to be. We also looked at why it's important to follow your body's lead
and eat only on cue. In Chapter 3, you learned about the ghrelin-friendly foods that
can keep you full longer and the not-so-friendly foods that will set you up for a diet
disaster. But that's still not enough.

*All the knowledge in the world won't help you if you don't put the right combination
of food, in the right amount, on your plate.* Please read that sentence again. That's the
key to success. Most everything else I tell you will help you choose the right foods in
the right amounts—and steer you away from the temptation to do otherwise.

In this chapter, we'll look at how to combine foods to fill you up—in the healthiest way possible—so you don't need to supersize your portions. We'll also talk

about portioning your meals the ghrelin way and ridding your refrigerator and cupboards of the hidden diet saboteurs that could prevent you from reaching your target weight.

You're probably thinking, *Here it comes—all the bad news about the stuff I can't have.* You may even be about to superimpose your experience of other diets on this one. But wait! Give yourself a chance to see how different your experience will be on the Belly Fat Fix.

This might help. If you follow the 3-Day Fast-Track (see Chapter 5) *to the letter,* adhering to my instructions 100 percent, you'll see changes you like a lot. But you don't have to be quite that strict following the Belly Fat Fix plan, which I lay out for you in Chapter 6. Life happens. If you follow the meal plan 90 percent—and I mean an honest 90 percent—you'll get excellent results. That gives you a 10 percent buffer.

And when you "cheat," be smart about it. In fact—and I'll bet you never heard this in any other diet book—I'll even tell you the smart way to cheat. That's right: Occasional cheating is okay, as long as you cheat the Belly Fat Fix way. (See Exceptions to the Rule on page 108.)

So let's get the bad news out of the way. I'll identify foods (and quasi-foods that are more food science concoctions than actual food) that are diet *enemies.* They provide empty calories, make you hungrier, and cause you to eat more and then—most likely—get down on yourself for blowing it. The best way to head off these saboteurs is to avoid them like the plague.

I'm not here to bash the food industry or tell you that you can't eat foods containing additives. Stabilizing ghrelin is about balancing all foods, even processed foods, if that's what you choose to eat. Whole foods are ideal but not always affordable, convenient, or palatable given your taste preferences. But as your weight-loss coach, I want to tell you this: The less you eat of these processed foods, the easier it'll be to lose the weight and the quicker you'll see results.

TOP FIVE GHRELIN-INCREASING FOOD ADDITIVES

Avoid these five diet enemies as completely as you can. Don't buy foods that contain these ingredients for your home, and when you're eating out, don't order foods that contain them. Follow this advice and you'll do yourself a huge favor in the long run. These products are so injurious to your diet that it's worth getting into the habit of studying ingredient labels carefully, even if that means you have to pull out your reading glasses to make out the fine print.

When you choose to avoid one of these additives, you'll probably be avoiding most—if not all—of the others. That's because these ghrelin-increasing additives frequently show up together within the same foods. For example, diet fruit-flavored yogurts seem like such a great idea—low calorie and "healthy," right? But did you know most varieties of diet fruit-flavored yogurts contain high-fructose corn syrup, artificial flavors, and artificial sweeteners? That's three out of the five top ghrelin-increasing ingredients, all in one little cup of yogurt.

Let's look at these ingredients one by one:

1. HIGH-FRUCTOSE CORN SYRUP (HFCS)

HFCS is a sweetener derived from corn syrup. It was approved in 1983 by the Food and Drug Administration, and was immediately embraced by food manufacturers for it stability, texture, color, and ability to enhance flavor. It's also cheap to make, giving convenience-food manufacturers the ability to inexpensively create tastier foods that last a long time. Have you ever had a 2-month-old loaf of bread without a single spot of mold on it? If you answered yes, HFCS is probably the reason.

Current research on HFCS is conflicting. Studies don't prove that it affects you any differently than any other type of sugar. But excessive sugar in the diet works against ghrelin suppression. It also adds excess calories and causes weight gain. And weight gain most definitely affects long-term ghrelin levels. Some research says HFCS doesn't stimulate the release of insulin the way other sugars do.[1] When insulin isn't released, blood sugar remains high, and when blood sugar is high due to a lack of insulin, your gut secretes more ghrelin, causing ghrelin levels to increase.[2] And you know what happens when your ghrelin is high.

The bottom line: When you eat high amounts of HFCS—perhaps without even being aware of it—you're likely to negatively affect your ghrelin levels. The lack of insulin secretion will drive ghrelin levels up, which will whip up your appetite. And that means you'll probably eat more and put on weight. Do you remember what happens when someone becomes obese? Ghrelin levels drop and stay lower than normal—and this makes it almost impossible to distinguish between hunger and fullness. And that, by the way, makes you eat more.

2. HYDROGENATED OILS/ TRANS FATTY ACIDS (TFA)

Hydrogenated oils are made by forcing hydrogen gas molecules into unsaturated oil at a high pressure and temperature. This process makes oil, a liquid at room temperature, into a solid at room temperature. These oils take the place of butter in many baked items, because, like HFCS, they offer food manufacturers a relatively inexpensive way to extend shelf life and add flavor.

Studies show that trans fats may decrease the insulin sensitivity of fat cells,[3] making insulin less effective, an outcome you definitely *do not want*. Insulin's job is to attach to sugar in the blood and shuttle it into cells, where it's used for energy. When this process doesn't work effectively, the lack of sugar in the cells triggers a starvation signal within those cells. The starvation signal is then sent to your brain and eventually loops back to ghrelin-secreting cells in your stomach. Ghrelin is secreted and hunger increases, which causes you to eat more and gain weight. Can you see the negative cycle that gets initiated when you eat foods that contain trans fats (hydrogenated oils)?

Trans Fats Free? Maybe Not!

The "trans fats free" label is deceptive! A food that has less than half a gram of trans fats per serving can be labeled as "trans fats free." This means you may be consuming trans fats without knowing it. You need to carefully read product labels.

Look for "hydrogenated oil" or "partially hydrogenated oil" to determine if the product is truly trans fats free. If it contains either ingredient, then it *does* have trans fats, even if it's just in tiny amounts. It all adds up!

3. ARTIFICIAL SWEETENERS

There are three primary artificial sweeteners: saccharin, aspartame, and sucralose:

- **Aspartame,** which is found in the little blue packets of Equal, NutraSweet, and about 6,000 common foods and beverages, including diet sodas
- **Sucralose,** more commonly recognized as Splenda (in the yellow packet), which is generally believed to be a natural sugar substitute
- **Saccharin,** which is found in the pink Sweet'N Low packets and is about 300 times sweeter than table sugar

Artificial sweeteners are chemicals mainly found in diet food products. The problem: They can trick your body into thinking you've eaten real food. Your taste buds can't distinguish between diet food filled with artificial sweeteners and *real* food.[4] And the minute your digestive enzymes encounter substances that aren't exactly food and contain no calories or nutrition, your empty digestive tract sends a signal to the hypothalamus, telling it that you need food. Before you know it, your body secretes more ghrelin[5] and you get hungry again. In short, artificial sweeteners are *not* diet friendly.

Artificial sweeteners can be disastrous when you consume a lot of them frequently. If you're a diet-food junkie—or if you've been one in the past—you might be able to see a correlation. In my practice, I see this all the time. Most dieters eat "diet" foods that leave them hungrier and wanting more, and after a few hours, they eventually binge. Right about the period artificial sweeteners hit the big time—making their way into any and every food product so manufacturers could put a "diet" or "lite" label on it—Americans started gaining lots of weight.

Diet foods don't fill you up. In fact, they often leave you hungrier than before. Fortunately, the ghrelin-increasing effects of artificial sweeteners can be blunted when consumed in small amounts and balanced with *real* food. Check out the dessert recipes in Chapter 7 to learn how you can incorporate some artificial sweeteners, in small amounts, without hindering your ghrelin-balancing efforts.

4. MONOSODIUM GLUTAMATE (MSG)

When you hear MSG, you probably think of Chinese takeout—but this additive is widely used in many processed foods. MSG is a food manufacturer's dream because it can reduce the amount of whole food ingredients and still create "big" taste. MSG works by stimulating taste buds and changing the perception of how a food tastes, intensifying and enhancing flavors and odors. It can lessen acidity, suppress bitterness and sourness, and enhance the flavor of bland low-fat foods. Plus, it has excellent storage properties, and it's a useful blending agent for mixed spices. MSG stretches the flavor of ingredients, lowering production costs.

A study evaluating the appetite-stimulating effect of MSG found that participants who consumed soup (beef consommé) containing higher concentrations of MSG rated the soup as more "pleasant," "savory," and "satisfying" than soup with no added MSG. The study results show that the desire to eat occurred more rapidly after a lunchtime meal in which MSG-supplemented soup was served than after a meal of soup without MSG. The study concluded that MSG, through its stimulation of the food pleasure pathway and/or by improving the palatability of the soup, may influence how quickly a meal is digested and how strongly a person desires to eat more.[6] And let's not forget that there are ghrelin receptors on that same pathway. See the connection?

5. ARTIFICIAL FLAVORS

Artificial flavors are chemical mixtures that mimic a natural flavor in some way. They're typically not harmful, but in the body they work in much the same way as artificial sweeteners. Artificial flavors taste good, enhancing the taste of food without adding extra calories. They're most often found in diet foods that don't contain many calories or other valuable nutrients (like vitamins or minerals). When you eat foods that contain artificial flavors, just like artificial sweeteners, digestive secretions are stimulated. Then, when no actual food is delivered to the gut, a signal is sent that you need more food. So you're left feeling hungry—and wanting more.

Cut the Culprits

It's a big task to cut out food additives, but I'm here to make it as easy as possible. Now that you have some knowledge of the top five ghrelin-increasing food additives, I hope you're inspired to remove them from your diet. Most additives have several names and are found in multiple foods. For your convenience, I've provided this chart. Make a copy and take it with you when you grocery shop. Compare the

Top Five Ingredients to Avoid

Additive	Common Names	Products to Check
High-fructose corn syrup (HFCS)	Corn sugar, corn syrup, high-fructose corn syrup, high-fructose maize syrup	Breads, breakfast bars, breakfast cereals, candies, desserts, low-calorie snacks, low-fat dressings, soda, yogurt
Hydrogenated oils/ trans fats	Hydrogenated oil or partially hydrogenated oil	Baked goods, bread crumbs, breakfast cereals, cakes, candies, chips, cookies, crackers, margarine, peanut butter, popcorn
Artificial sweeteners	Acesulfame potassium, aspartame (Equal and NutraSweet), saccharin (Sweet'N Low), sucralose (Splenda), sorbitol	Chewing gum, diet beverages, diet soda, sugar-free baked goods, sugar-free candies, sugar-free desserts, yogurt
Monosodium glutamate (MSG)	Calcium caseinate, glutamic acid, hydrolyzed protein, MSG, sodium caseinate, yeast extract	Canned foods, chips, frozen entrees, processed meats, salad dressings, seasoning packets
Artificial flavors	Artificial flavoring, natural flavoring	Breakfast cereals, desserts, light ice cream, light mayonnaise, salsa, seasoning packets, soda

Make a copy of this chart and keep it with you when you go grocery shopping. Refer to it whenever you're considering a questionable food to figure out if it's ghrelin increasing or not.

ingredient list on the food label to the list of alternative names on this chart to determine if it is a ghrelin-increasing food or not.

Now I'd like you to set aside time this week to go through your cupboards and refrigerator (and maybe even that stash of snacks you keep at work) and toss the foods that contain these ingredients. This is not being wasteful. This could potentially save you much more in medical bills later. Please put the date you plan to do this on the calendar. This is an important step to take in preparing to succeed on the 3-Day Fast-Track and on the Belly Fat Fix plan.

Here's the other thing I'd like you to do: Make two copies of the page with the "Top Five Ingredients to Avoid" list on page 99. Put one in your wallet and affix the other to your refrigerator.

Now that the bad news is out of the way, let's look at what you can put on your plate and in what portion size. Remember, to suppress ghrelin—and get biological control of appetite—you need to eat three meals a day, plus a reasonable snack, when your body gives you the signal by stimulating your appetite. In this next sec-

COACHING TIP

Beware of Obesogens

Never heard of obesogens? Listen up. Scientists have identified them as a big contributor to America's obesity epidemic. Studies show that obesogens promote insulin resistance, increase hunger in the appetite center of your brain, and increase the number and size of your fat cells.

Obesogens are hormone-disrupting chemicals that interfere with your body's ability to maintain normal weight. They're *everywhere!* They're in the food supply, in household items such as shampoo and deodorant, and even in the plastic lining of baby bottles.

Unfortunately, it's pretty much impossible to completely avoid obeso-

gens. You can, however, minimize eating foods that contain them by staying away from the top five ghrelin-increasing food additives. High-fructose corn syrup (HFCS), which I've already warned you about, is considered one of the primary obesogens in the food supply. In fact, all of the top five ghrelin-increasing food additives is considered an obesogen. Avoid them, and you minimize your consumption of obesogens. This, in turn, helps your efforts to lose weight. The big problem with obesogens is that they gum up the body's weight regulatory system and make it even more difficult to lose.

tion, I'll explain exactly how to combine ghrelin-friendly foods to create nutritious, filling meals that will stabilize your ghrelin and keep you healthy.

FOOD COMBOS TO FILL YOU UP AND SLIM YOU DOWN

Here's the secret to winning the war on hunger: Combine carbohydrates (which suppress ghrelin right away) with protein (which suppresses ghrelin longer) *and* fat (which keeps your body healthy). When you choose foods from all three groups and put them on your plate—in the right proportions—your ghrelin level drops and you lose weight without having to put up with constant, gnawing hunger.

This is one of the keys to success, but I often shake my head at all the diet myths that drive people's behavior. Here's just one example. Many of my weight-loss clients tell me they have a "salad" for lunch. A salad can be great, mediocre, or terribly unhealthy when trying to lose weight. In fact, salads are one of the most deceiving meals. A salad is typically a setup for a ghrelin disaster.

When I tell dieting clients to describe their salad, the litany often goes something like this: "Lettuce, tomatoes, peppers, mushrooms, and grilled chicken with lemon juice." My response? "Where are the carbohydrates, fat, and fruit?" It may surprise you to learn that this salad is just as unhealthy for your weight-loss efforts as the "Southwest Crispy Chicken Salad" from the local fast-food joint. The takeaway message: If your meal isn't balanced, regardless of total calories and fat, you'll impede your weight-loss efforts.

All the food groups must be accounted for at every meal, *period*. I advise clients to try this balanced alternative to the salad I've just described. Have greens with your choice of three or four fresh veggies, grilled chicken breast, chickpeas, a small wheat roll, olive oil dressing, avocado, and fruit. But whenever I make that suggestion, I'm greeted with a look of shock, as though I were blaspheming against the diet gods. The usual reply: "If I eat all that, I'll gain weight!"

But a meal like that will *not* make you gain weight. In fact, you will *lose* weight if you eat this way.

You will lose weight because when you combine all the food groups, your digestive system works harder and longer. Earlier, you learned about digestive thermogenesis, the process by which heat is created during digestion. When you combine multiple food groups, you challenge your digestive system to work a bit harder. The carbohydrates (in this example, it's the wheat roll and chickpeas) are digested and absorbed quickly, where they work to raise your blood sugar, causing ghrelin levels to quickly drop. The protein (grilled chicken) takes the longest to digest, and it suppresses ghrelin for a longer period of time. The importance of having carbohydrates and protein as part of a meal is that they *balance* each other. Carbohydrates suppress ghrelin quickly and for a short amount of time. By the time ghrelin suppression from carbs wears off, protein is kicking into high ghrelin-suppressing gear.

Where does the fat fit in? Fat won't help suppress ghrelin, but it tastes great, stimulating the pleasure and reward centers in your brain and indirectly helping you feel more satisfied. Fat is also necessary to transport certain vitamins, and it's part of every single one of your cell membranes. Healthy cell membranes keep your metabolism working at its best. Simply stated, your body needs fat, and you have to eat it no matter how it affects ghrelin.

For *maximum* ghrelin suppression, have two or more ghrelin-suppressing foods at each meal. This could be two servings of the same food or—even better—two or more different foods that are ghrelin suppressing.

Look at these three meals. All are sandwiches, equal in calories and portioned according to the G-List. But each has a very different ghrelin-suppressing effect.

Ghrelin-Suppressing Meal	Ghrelin-Neutral Meal	Ghrelin-Increasing Meal
• 2 slices 100% whole grain, high-fiber bread • 4 ounces sliced chicken breast • 1 tablespoon pine nut pesto • Spinach, tomato, and onion • 1 small grapefruit	• 2 slices wheat bread • 4 ounces turkey deli meat • 1 tablespoon mayonnaise • Spinach, tomato, and onion • 1 cup strawberries	• 2 slices "light" white bread • 4 ounces low-fat salami • 1 tablespoon fat-free Thousand Island dressing • Large pickle • 4 ounces fruit juice drink

Ghrelin Balancing Act

Dying for a Sunday-morning jelly doughnut or some other forbidden treat? There's a way to balance your off-plan eating so your diet won't be thrown completely off track.

First, be mindful of the portion. One small or medium-size jelly doughnut is okay. Three jelly doughnuts will do you in. These same principles apply to other treats, of course.

Second, balance ghrelin-increasing foods with at least one ghrelin-suppressing food each. So if you decide to have a doughnut on Sunday morning, balance it with a ghrelin-suppressing protein such as an egg white veggie omelet.

Third, for the rest of the day (or the next day, if you ended your night with a ghrelin-increasing dessert), have two ghrelin-suppressing foods (even better, choose *superfoods*) at each meal. This will help stabilize your ghrelin level.

Take a careful look at the chart (opposite). If you understand the principles behind it, you'll find it easy to make healthy choices—especially when you're at a restaurant and you're faced with *lots* of decisions.

Review the list of ghrelin-suppressing foods and superfoods from Chapter 3, and reread the section on combining foods starting on page 101 until you feel you really "get" it. You'll start to soak this information in when you're on the Fast-Track program and, after that, on the Belly Fat Fix plan. When this knowledge becomes second nature, it'll be easy to make healthier choices. That's what my clients have found.

Uma J., a New York education consultant who lost about 8 pounds on this plan the month before her wedding, says she makes very different food choices now for herself and her husband, thanks to what she learned while she was on the plan. "Before, I made my food choices in the moment, based on what was around me," she says. "I didn't stop to think about what would work for me and help me reach my weight goals. In the past, when I was working late, I'd stop work for just a few minutes and order something online. When the food arrived, I'd just scarf it down. But now I keep my refrigerator stocked with the right foods, like carrots and hummus." She learned to do that on the program, and now she's become a Ghrelin Master. (You'll find her story on pages 266–267.)

Making smart, consistent choices about which foods to eat—and combine—will speed you toward your weight-loss target. But even that's not enough. Let's look at one more critical strategy for success.

PORTION CONTROL—THE NEXT PIECE OF THE PUZZLE

There's a difference between "portion size" and "serving size." A portion is the amount you put on your plate. A serving is a standard measurement of food, such as a cup or an ounce. Often the "portion" that you should eat is two or more "servings." For example, when you see your Belly Fat Fix plan in Chapter 6, you'll notice that lunch and dinner have a minimum of two protein servings. When you add up the "servings," you have a "portion."

The best way to determine the amount of food in a serving is to measure it out. Of course, measuring and portioning food can be a real hassle, and sometimes it's not even possible. But give it a try. You need to be somewhat exacting about your portions because if you eat too much, you ingest too many calories. And if you take in more calories than your body can use, you eventually put on weight.

To help you succeed on the Belly Fat Fix, I created the guide on the next page that you can use when you're dining out or you find yourself in situations where you can't measure your food. It will help you get the portions right so you don't undereat or overeat. Both will trip you up, so avoid either extreme.

Start getting used to these portion sizes now, before you begin the 3-Day Fast-Track program.

So far, I've given you a lot to learn. But relax and take your time—you'll get the hang of it.

Easy Ghrelin Portion Guide

A single serving of . . .	Is about the size of . . .
1 cup raw vegetables	fist
¼ cup cooked vegetables	top of a lightbulb
1 cup chopped fruit	fist
4 ounces whole fruit	baseball
fruit juice	teacup
¼ cup dried fruit	large egg
1 ounce hard cheese	pair of dice
2 ounces meat protein	table tennis ball
sliced cheese	1 individual wrapped piece
½ can tuna or salmon	½ tennis ball
⅔ cup yogurt	baseball
⅔ cup milk	coffee mug
3-ounce potato	computer mouse
1-ounce slice of bread	audiocassette
1 pancake, waffle	compact disc
⅓ cup rice, couscous, quinoa	cupcake wrapper
½ cup cooked pasta	ice-cream scoop
⅔ cup unsweetened cereal	coffee mug
1 ounce snacks (pretzels, chips)	teacup
½ cup mashed potatoes	ice-cream scoop
1 teaspoon oil/butter	fingertip
1 tablespoon nuts/seeds	thumb

CLEAN AND SIMPLE PORTIONING BASICS

If you're new to the whole idea of getting the portion size just right, this section can really help. In fact, if you dread the clutter and dirty dishes that accumulate when divvying out meals, I have good news for you! There's a way to set up your kitchen

Are You Portion Savvy?

Restaurant portions have grown in the past 20 years. You may be surprised to learn how much. Take this pop quiz to see how portion savvy you are:

1. A typical spaghetti-and-meatball dinner 20 years ago had about 500 calories. How many calories are in today's typical portion?

   a. 600 calories

   b. 800 calories

   c. 1,100 calories

2. A muffin 20 years ago was 1.5 ounces and had 210 calories. How many calories are in a muffin today?

   a. 320 calories

   b. 605 calories

   c. 500 calories

3. A chicken Caesar salad had 390 calories 20 years ago. How many calories are in today's chicken Caesar salad?

   a. 520 calories

   b. 790 calories

   c. 920 calories

4. A bagel 20 years ago was 3 inches in diameter and had 140 calories. How many calories are in today's bagel?

   a. 150 calories

   b. 620 calories

   c. 350 calories

5. Two slices of pepperoni pizza 20 years ago had 500 calories. How many calories are in two slices today?

   a. 850 calories

   b. 1,000 calories

   c. 1,200 calories

ANSWERS: 1.C 2.C 3.B 4.C 5.A

efficiently so that portioning doesn't create more of a mess. Here are two great tricks that will reinforce your healthy dieting habits, help you maintain your weight loss, *and* keep your kitchen clean:

1. **Buy three (or more) sets of measuring spoons and cups.** Having multiple measuring utensils allows you to leave specific measuring cups directly in food containers. For example, my cereal box has a ⅓-cup utensil in it at all times. When I go to measure my morning portion of cereal, I don't have to rifle through my cabinets to find a measuring cup, and I always know that I'm eating the right amount. I even do this with my leftovers in the refrigerator. (I keep a ⅔-cup measuring cup in the yogurt container, for instance.)

   If you store a measuring spoon or cup directly in your food container, you'll eliminate your excuse for eating too much. You'll also save time. You'll never have to scrounge around your kitchen, only to find a dirty cup that you have to clean before you assemble your meal. You can simply wash and rotate the measuring tools as you finish the food items they were in.

2. **Invest in a digital scale.** A digital scale is your wingman on the Belly Fat Fix. Protein needs to be measured according to weight. You can put your plate or other serving dish directly on the digital scale and set it to zero, voiding the weight of the plate. That's your starting point. From there, portion your protein onto the plate on the scale, which will read the weight of your protein, not your plate. No mess, no fuss—and you'll have the perfect amount on your plate.

   Be sure to leave your digital scale out on your counter at all times to remind you to measure every time you put food on your plate.

THREE SQUARES AND A SNACK: THE OTHER KEY TO YOUR SUCCESS

This one should come as no secret. In Chapter 2, we spoke of ghrelin's peaks and valleys. Typically, ghrelin levels are highest at 8:00 a.m., noon, and 6:00 p.m. If you eat at—or close to—the times when your ghrelin peaks, and your ghrelin is functioning normally, the levels in your blood will drop within one hour of eating.

Your ghrelin-suppressing snack is best eaten between lunch and dinner, somewhere between 1:00 and 3:00 in the afternoon. That's because ghrelin peaks slightly between these hours, just enough to cause hunger. This makes sense. In my practice, I've seen that late afternoon is the time of the day dieters are most susceptible to overeating. I tell clients that their ghrelin-suppressing snack is just as important as their full meals. Think about it this way: If your ghrelin is slightly high, it's better to suppress it now rather than wait until it's too late and you become so hungry that you binge.

Given those peaks, three meals and one snack is ideal for ghrelin balance. That's why the Belly Fat Fix has you eating three full meals a day plus a snack, so that you work with your body, not against it.

Studies show that three meals per day will quell ghrelin more than small, frequent meals. You simply need a larger meal to fully suppress ghrelin. The way you combine foods and the portion sizes you select determine how long ghrelin will be suppressed. (See Portion Control—The Next Piece of the Puzzle on page 104.) If you don't fill your stomach enough at any one time, digestion will happen quickly and you'll get hungry faster. If you eat a larger meal at one sitting, however, you can suppress your ghrelin for hours at a time, making you much less likely to feel the need for a snack.

A study published in the *American Journal of Physiology–Endocrinology and Metabolism* looked at the rise of ghrelin in people who were kept from knowing the time of day and weren't given any cues that it was mealtime. Study participants could eat whenever they felt like it. It's probably no surprise that researchers found a correlation between rising ghrelin levels and the times people decided to eat a meal. The study brought further proof of the connection between ghrelin levels and reported hunger. In short, the daily pattern and level of circulating ghrelin correlated with when, and how much, participants ate.[7]

As we saw in Chapter 1, higher ghrelin levels correlate with higher hunger ratings and food intake. Higher food intake is followed by a drop in circulating ghrelin for a longer amount of time, supporting the theory that larger meals—rather than small, frequent snacks—suppress ghrelin more and for longer.[8]

EXCEPTIONS TO THE RULE

Being on the Belly Fat Fix doesn't mean you have to give up all the foods you like every day of the week. You know from experience—that doesn't work. You just have to be smart about how you treat yourself. You can indulge in an occasional ghrelin-increasing meal in a way that will keep your ghrelin stable. It comes down to the order and timing of how you eat.

So if you're feeling deprived because you haven't had your favorite pizza for a while, and you feel ready to indulge *without* reckless abandon, here's how. (I chose pizza for this example because that's the meal clients ask me about most frequently.)

1. **Ordering basics:** First, order by the slice—generally, you should order two small/medium slices (if only large slices are available, order just one). If you have more than that, you're setting yourself up, and leftover pizza is way too tempting. So do yourself a favor and order only enough for one meal. Second, hold the extras—no sides of garlic sticks and no extra toppings, except veggies.

2. **Set the dining scene:** Every Friday night, my family would order pizza, and that treat represented so much more than food. It was an event; it was our time to relax into the weekend. We'd eat it in front of the TV, watching a favorite movie. Sounds good? Go for it. In a perfect world, we'd all eat mindfully at the dining table. But that's not always fun. If you want to enjoy your pizza while watching the latest action flick or romantic comedy, do it—but do it intentionally.

3. **Have protein first:** Pizza is a delicious ghrelin-increasing food without enough protein to suppress ghrelin levels fully. That's why you can eat three to five slices without batting an eye. The key to enjoying your favorite pizza without turning it into a ghrelin disaster is to eat your ghrelin-suppressing meat protein first. Then wait 15 minutes to allow some ghrelin suppression to begin before you dig into your pizza. That way, by the time you finish eating your pizza, your ghrelin has started to diminish and you're not setting yourself up to continue eating. You may still *want* to eat more pizza—but your drive to continue eating will be under control.

NEXT STEPS

There you have it—all the keys to losing weight on the Belly Fat Fix. The right timing of meals. The right food choices. Avoiding ghrelin-increasing food additives. The right portion sizes. Now you're ready to take the next step—preparing yourself to put this information to work. A little prep beforehand can ensure success on the 3-Day Fast-Track, detailed in the next chapter, and the Belly Fat Fix plan, which comes in the chapter after that.

Here's what I'd like you to do next. Decide whether you're a candidate for the 3-Day Fast-Track program, which is a 3-day ghrelin-stabilizing plan to get a quick 3 to 5 pounds off and get your ghrelin balanced. It's also a great way to make a break with your past bad habits and start fresh, as my clients have found. I encourage you to start out on the 3-Day Fast-Track. But it's not for everyone: Your work and family obligations, schedule, food preferences, and state of health may rule it out. That's okay. If that's the case, skip the Fast-Track and start right on your Belly Fat Fix plan in Chapter 6.

A FAMILY AFFAIR

I designed the Belly Fat Fix for grown-ups, not for kids. But America's obesity epidemic reaches right down to school-age children. According to the Centers for Disease Control and Prevention, childhood obesity has more than tripled in the past 30 years.[9] Studies have shown that children with overweight or obese parents have a significantly higher risk of becoming overweight or obese as adults.[10] So if you're struggling with your weight, chances are that one or more of your children may be as well.

What to do? Follow the plan yourself and be a good role model for your children. Studies also show that parents' food choices are the number-one influencer of a child's food choices, and that families who eat together are healthier and weigh less.[11] Just make sure kids are eating the kind of foods—in the right amounts—that are appropriate for their developmental needs.

Some hints for making healthy eating a family affair—and making the Belly Fat Fix family friendly:

- **Ask your kids to help choose some foods from the grocery list.** The earlier you get them involved, the more likely they'll want to participate throughout your entire weight-loss journey.
- **Include your kids in meal planning and preparation.** Have your kids look through the Chapter 7 recipes with you. You can choose meals that use the foods they picked out from the grocery list. They'll be more likely to help prepare *and* eat the healthy meals that you're eating.
- **Teach your kids how to portion food.** Have your kids help portion your meals

according to your meal plan from Chapter 6. This is good modeling behavior and invites kids to be active partners in a new, healthier lifestyle. Chances are, they'll want to follow in your footsteps.

▶ **Play the G-Scale Magnet Game.** Post your G-Scale chart on the fridge and invite your kids to stick their favorite magnet on the block that identifies their hunger level before meals. It's a fun way to teach kids what healthy hunger is!

Each of the Ghrelin Masters whose stories you'll learn started out with the 3-Day Fast-Track. They've told me that it helped them turn the corner and start fresh—exactly what it's designed to do. So if you're still not sure you want to follow the Fast-Track—or you're debating whether to start this week or next—take this quiz to find out if you're Fast-Track ready.

Are You Fast-Track Ready?

1. I want to stabilize my ghrelin and learn how to lose weight without hunger.

   a. Yes

   b. No

2. I often can't tell the difference between hunger and fullness.

   a. Yes

   b. No

3. I like having structured menus when I'm on a diet.

   a. Yes

   b. No

4. I reviewed my calendar, and I'll have at least 3 days free from social eating plans.

   a. Yes

   b. No

5. I'm willing to throw out tempting foods that are ghrelin increasing.

   a. Yes

   b. No

6. I feel motivated when I lose weight quickly.

   a. Yes

   b. No

Answer key: If you answered yes to three or more of these statements, you're Fast-Track ready. If you didn't answer yes to at least three, skip ahead to Chapter 6 and begin your weight-loss meal plan immediately.

STOCKING YOUR FRIDGE FOR THE FAST-TRACK

In Chapter 5, I'll explain how to get your kitchen prepped for success on this accelerated diet program. But here I'll list the foods you'll need to stock up on so that you can set aside time to shop before you begin the plan. Of course, if you don't intend to go on the Fast-Track, skip ahead to Stocking Your Kitchen for the 7-Day Plan on page 114. The foods on that list are for the Belly Fat Fix plan outlined in Chapter 6.

Produce

6 small Granny Smith apples

3 small grapefruit

3 lemons

1 avocado

1 red bell pepper

1 yellow bell pepper

1 small tomato

1 package cherry tomatoes

1 large onion

1 medium sweet potato

1 head of broccoli

10 ounces raw spinach

10 ounces raw kale

8 ounces packaged mushrooms

10-ounce bag baby carrots

Deli

6 ounces fat-free turkey breast

7-ounce container hummus

Dry Goods

1 small package pine nuts

1 small container 100% rolled oats

6-ounce box high-fiber cereal

6-ounce can low-sodium large black olives

15-ounce can black beans

8-ounce bottle olive oil

8-ounce box whole wheat couscous

12-ounce box quinoa

12-ounce box whole wheat pasta

1 loaf Arnold Healthfull 10-Grain Bread

Dry Goods (cont.)

1 package La Tortilla Low Carb
Original Tortillas

1 package Thomas' Sahara Whole
Wheat Pita Pocket

Protein

9 ounces tilapia or shrimp

7 ounces 95% lean beef

12 ounces chicken breast

7 ounces fat-free ground turkey
breast

1 quart fat-free milk

1 dozen eggs

6 ounces plain 0% Greek yogurt

8 ounces light sour cream

2 low-fat cheese sticks

Frozen Food

16-ounce bag frozen stir-fry veggies

10-ounce bag frozen shelled edamame

10-ounce bag frozen lima beans

Vegetarian Alternatives (noted in meal plans with **)

12-ounce package Boca Ground
Crumbles

10-ounce package Amy's California
Veggie Burgers

8-ounce package veggie chicken strips

8-ounce package tempeh

4 ounces part-skim ricotta cheese

6 ounces firm tofu

COACHING TIP

Choosing meat? Look for color. The more vibrant crimson, the fresher is the meat.
As oxygen hits the meat it begins to deteriorate, discolor, and dry out, turning an
unpleasant gray hue that tells you it was cut a while ago. Always go for the vibrant red!

If you plan to skip the Fast-Track and go straight to the Belly Fat Fix plan, purchase the foods from the following list and have them on hand in time to get started. Keep an eye on local supermarket ads to determine where the best deals are, so you can buy what you need without blowing your budget. You'll use these foods in conjunction with the meal plans described in Chapter 6.

STOCKING YOUR KITCHEN FOR THE 7-DAY PLAN

It's hard to plan meals for a new diet. Grocery shopping alone can be overwhelming. The list that follows, based on the G-List, tells you exactly how much to purchase from each category to get you started. You'll even see what brands to buy that

Your Grocery Guide to Lean Beef

Under USDA regulations, five cuts out of 29 are considered extra-lean. These are the recommended cuts:

- Eye of round roast or steak
- Sirloin tip side steak
- Top round roast or steak
- Bottom round roast or steak
- Top sirloin

Generally, meats with *loin* or *round* in the name have the least fat. But sometimes, cuts of beef are called by other names—a top loin steak, for instance, may also be called strip steak or club sirloin steak. Confused? Ask the butcher for a lower-fat option.

I like to use cuts graded as

choice or select instead of prime, which normally have more fat. If you see lots of fat when shopping, the meat is probably marbled and contains even more fat. Marbling is small streaks of fat within the muscle that can be seen in the cut of meat. The less fat you see, the leaner the cut.

When choosing any ground meat, first look for a number. For example, 92/08 in ground beef or other ground meats is the lean-to-fat ratio. This designation tells you that 92 percent of the meat is lean and 8 percent is fat. Always opt for the lowest percentage of fat.

fit the Belly Fat Fix way of eating—this will make grocery shopping a cinch. This list will provide about 1 week of ghrelin-suppressing meals.

Another option for your first grocery-shopping trip is to skip ahead to Chapter 6 and look over your prebuilt meal plan. Pick two breakfasts, three or four lunches, three or four dinners, and three or four snacks that you like best. When you go to the grocery store, purchase the foods you need based on your top picks. Then you can rotate these meals and snacks for your first week.

Fruit
(Choose five different fruits, and purchase five of each, for a total of 25 pieces of fruit.)

1 pint strawberries

½ pint blueberries

2 small grapefruit

1 medium orange

4 small apples

½ pound grapes

2 small kiwifruits

1 small banana

1 cantaloupe

1 peach

1 mango

1 small pear

1 ounce dried cranberries

2 ounces raisins

8-ounce can pineapple chunks

24 ounces mixed-fruit cups (packed in water)

8-ounce bag frozen blueberries

Vegetables
(Choose four different vegetables. Then purchase four of each, for a total of 20 portions.)

10-ounce bag mixed salad greens

10-ounce bag baby spinach

1 small cucumber

2 medium carrots

1 bunch celery

1 red bell pepper

1 yellow bell pepper

3 tomatoes

1 bunch cilantro

1 medium potato

1 medium sweet potato

1 medium yellow onion

1 small red onion

2 heads broccoli

1 bunch kale

12-ounce steamer bag veggie mix

Fats

(Purchase four different types.)

8-ounce bag ground flaxseed

8-ounce bag almonds

8-ounce bag pine nuts

8-ounce bottle olive oil

8-ounce bottle canola oil

15-ounce jar low-fat mayonnaise

8-ounce bottle low-fat dressing

8-ounce bottle low-fat Caesar dressing

16-ounce jar peanut butter

6-ounce can low-sodium large black olives

8-ounce container light sour cream

Carbohydrates

(Purchase eight types.)

1 large box whole grain Cheerios

16-ounce box Fiber One cereal

16-ounce box steel-cut oats

16-ounce box 100% rolled oats

9-ounce box Wasa Sourdough Crispbread

15-ounce can black beans

15-ounce can chickpeas

12-ounce box quinoa

7.6-ounce box whole wheat couscous

1 pound brown rice

1 box whole wheat pasta

1 box buckwheat pasta

1 loaf Arnold Healthfull 10 Grain Bread

COACHING TIP

Just Add Water

If you really don't like drinking plain water, try mixing a noncalorie iced tea or flavored water with plain water. For every 8 ounces of plain water, add 1 ounce of your favorite noncalorie beverage, such as flavored water or diet iced tea. This way, you get enough fluid to keep you hydrated, and you minimize the artificial sweeteners. You will get used to it. Most of my clients say after a week or two they stop craving flavored drinks and are perfectly fine with drinking plain (or almost plain) water.

Carbohydrates (cont.)

1 package La Tortilla Low Carb Original Tortillas

1 package Thomas' 100% Whole Grain English Muffins

1 package Thomas' Sahara 100% Whole Wheat Pita Pockets

1 package Thomas' Plain Mini Bagels

1 loaf Arnold Real Jewish Marble Rye Bread

1 package Thomas' Sahara 100% Whole Wheat Wraps

1.5-ounce bag Athenos Baked Pita Chips

8-ounce bag frozen corn

7-ounce tub red pepper hummus

Protein: Meat and Seafood

(Choose five different proteins. Then purchase three of each, for a total of 15 portions.)

7 ounces 95% lean ground beef

7 ounces top sirloin steak

1 pound boneless, skinless chicken breast

7 ounces ground turkey

7 ounces pork loin

10 ounces tilapia

4 ounces fat-free deli ham

4 ounce fat-free deli turkey

5 ounces canned salmon, water-packed

5 ounces canned tuna, water-packed

1-pound bag frozen shrimp

8-ounce package Applegate turkey sausage links

1 dozen eggs

Protein, Dairy

(Choose three different daily. Then purchase three of each for a total of 9 portions.)

1 quart fat-free milk

½ gallon Silk Original almond milk

8 ounces fat-free cottage cheese

12 ounces fat-free plain Greek yogurt

6-ounce package Laughing Cow Light cheese wedges

1 package low-fat shredded cheese

1 package low-fat cheese stick, any flavor

1 ounce Parmesan cheese

Protein, Vegetarian

(Choose four different vegetarian proteins. Then purchase three of each for a total of 15 portions.)

10-ounce bag frozen shelled edamame

10-ounce package Amy's California Veggie Burgers

8-ounce package firm tofu

8-ounce package tempeh

Dry Goods, Condiments

(Purchase one.)

8-ounce bottle balsamic vinegar

8-ounce jar Dijon mustard

26-ounce jar DeLallo Marinara fat-free sauce

Be Prepared for Quick Weekday Meals!

To make weeknight meals on the Belly Fat Fix plan a snap, prepare G-List proteins and carbs in bulk on your day off. They're the main components of your meals, and often the most time consuming to prepare. So if they're already cooked, you can quickly and easily assemble them to create tasty meals. When you come home starving after a long day at work, you won't regret the extra 30 minutes you spent in the kitchen on your day off making that big batch of quinoa or baked chicken breast.

Cooking a chicken breast, potato, and veggies would take a solid 45 minutes—while popping a premade chicken breast and potato into the microwave, then steaming some veggies, adds up to a total time investment of just 10 minutes— a big deal on a busy weeknight!

Some tips for getting started:

* When you prepare one meal, add two to three times as much ingredients as you need. The leftover food can be frozen or stored in your fridge for another meal or two. If you do this every time you cook, you'll build up a variety of ready-made meals or basic ingredients for other recipes.

* Have enough room in your freezer for the extra meals. Store them flat, stacking them the way you'd stack books on a bookshelf.

The Buddy System

When it comes to weight loss, the buddy system really works. A study cited in the *Journal of Consulting and Clinical Psychology* found that people who recruited three friends or family members to support and check in on them had better results losing weight and keeping it off compared with those who didn't have a buddy system.[12]

Being accountable to a supportive buddy can help you avoid mindless eating and resist temptation like cookies in the office or brownies at a family party.

Jot down the names of three people you can ask to be your buddies:

1. _____

2. _____

3. _____

- Choose the best quality bags you can find to be sure your food will be properly protected. Remember: Air is not a friend of freezing. Improperly sealed bags will result in tasteless food once it's thawed and reheated. Whether you use bags, foil, plastic wraps, or plastic containers with tight-fitting lids, make sure everything is sealed properly.

- Buy and cook a larger quantity of turkey, chicken, or other animal protein. Basics like these can be turned into lots of different meals and snacks. This will also help cut down on the prep time down the road.

- Use little to no seasoning when you cook in bulk. That way, when you reheat, you can make the meal taste different every time.

- Label and date everything you stash in the freezer or fridge—it may be difficult to identify a dish after it's frozen. Rule of thumb: If it's been in the freezer more than 6 months, throw it out.

Since protein and carbs form the foundation of your Belly Fat Fix meals, here's a quick guide to choosing the right ones—and storing them properly in your freezer or fridge.

- **Carbs:** Prepared G-List carbs will last in your fridge 4 to 6 days. Try preparing oatmeal, rice, baked potatoes, couscous, lentils/beans, or quinoa ahead.

- **Protein:** Prepared G-List proteins will last in your fridge 3 to 4 days. Try baking chicken breast, fish, or ground meat burgers. You can easily reheat, dice, or slice, then add to salads or mix with a precooked carbohydrate.

Do It

CHAPTER 5

The 3-Day Fast-Track

Why do the 3-Day Fast-Track? Three reasons: to stabilize your ghrelin levels, help you lose a quick 3 to 5 pounds, and break some unhealthy patterns. The plan is completely safe—but if you want results, you need to give it 100 percent.

The Fast-Track is a great introduction to the diet portion of the Belly Fat Fix, since you'll be eating the same foods as those found on the diet. The major difference: You'll consume fewer calories and drink more fluids during the Fast-Track. There's also a difference in the precisely prebalanced meals and snacks for each. These two differences are what make the Fast-Track so effective.

The Fast-Track sets the stage for transformation. Let's be honest—it's *very* motivating to lose a couple of pounds right off the bat. If you're like most of my clients, a drop on the scale gives you a big motivational boost. Everyone wants results, and the 3-Day Fast-Track is designed to give them to you—fast.

My clients—including my own mother—have found that the plan's a great way to kick-start their weight-loss efforts and their new way of life.

Uma J., the educational consultant you'll read about on page 266, used the Fast-Track to help her break her "bad" diet habits and start anew. (She did it before her wedding because she saw it as a way to get a fresh start on her eating habits and be at her healthiest when she starts a family.)

The Fast-Track helped ground her in making better food choices, Uma says. "It primed me to think about meals that were healthier than the ones I've been eating."

It also introduced Uma to foods she now buys regularly. "I keep olives and edamame in the house—I'd never eaten those on a regular basis before."

My mother, Lisa N., who has long struggled with her weight, lost 7 pounds her first week on the Fast-Track. The structure, she says, was especially helpful. She's gone back on the Fast-Track several times over the last few months and lost an additional 3 to 5 pounds each time, using it after she notices she's gone "overboard" with her eating.

"I feel more in control and get a better handle on my cravings when I'm following this structured plan," she explains. "I appreciate knowing what my menu will be—and it's really cut down my cooking time." Since she's careful to choose the 3 days when she has the fewest commitments, she doesn't have to worry about packing food for herself to take along, and she never has to think about cooking ahead.

As this book went to press, Lisa had lost 42 pounds.

YES, 3 DAYS CAN MAKE A DIFFERENCE

While the 3-Day Fast-Track may not be for everyone, I strongly encourage you to consider starting your new eating regime with this transitional program. (Be sure to take the quiz "Are You Fast-Track Ready?" on page 111 in Chapter 4.)

If you don't like strict programs, and/or you peeked ahead and most of the Fast-Track foods don't appeal to you, just skip ahead to Chapter 6 and start in on the full-fledged Belly Fat Fix plan. Remember: You *can* and will lose weight without completing the 3-Day Fast-Track. However, your first-week weight loss won't be as fast, and you'll need to follow the weight-loss meal plan for a bit longer to stabilize ghrelin.

But if you're excited about losing a quick 3 to 5 pounds and resetting your ghrelin immediately, here's more good news: You can repeat the 3-Day Fast-Track as often as once a month. Use it to stabilize ghrelin, take off a few pounds, and keep yourself motivated. Also use it when you reach an occasional weight plateau. (I'll talk more about how to break plateaus in Chapter 10.) Another reason to use the Fast-Track: to reset ghrelin after a vacation, a holiday, or a weekend of indulgence.

I know it works because I've used it, too. When I moved into my new home, my ghrelin was thrown way off. After several weeks of packing, stressing out, losing sleep, and eating takeout at odd times, I knew I needed to follow the Fast-Track to get back to a healthy working balance.

Are you a skeptic? You may be thinking, "How can 3 days make that much of a difference?" My advice: Let your reservations go. I went on the plan many times as I perfected the food balance, and I can assure you, 3 days really *can* make a difference. I can also tell you with confidence that you won't feel overly hungry, as long as you follow the 3-Day Fast-Track rules to the letter.

Here's what two of my clients, who have successfully lost weight on this program, have to say about the Fast-Track:

"It took some time for me to prepare the foods, but it was totally worth it," says Lisa N., who lost 5 pounds on the Fast-Track. "It was easy because the preparation was already done. I lost 5 pounds and wasn't even hungry!"

"It took a bit of getting used to," says Dave H., who lost 6 pounds on the Fast-Track. "I didn't love all the foods, but it worked. I felt good, and by the time I was hungry, it was time for the next meal. I started to understand how my ghrelin works."

If you want results like these, follow the Fast-Track 100 percent.

GET YOURSELF READY: THE 3-DAY FAST-TRACK GUIDELINES

Set yourself up for success by taking these preparatory steps before you start the Fast-Track. Complete *all* of them before you begin.

1. CLEAR YOUR CALENDAR

As I tell every client before starting the 3-Day Fast-Track, **wait to start until you are fully ready and committed to following the plan 100 percent**—no matter how excited you are about jumping right in. Remember: This is a completely new way of eating. It requires planning and effort. *Do not* start the plan unless your calendar is clear of diet-busting commitments for at least the first 3 days (a full week is even better). So if this coming weekend is your birthday, or cousin Sally's wedding, wait until after the festivities. Set yourself up for success!

You may need to clear your social and work calendar or start on a certain day of the week. Mondays are the most popular day for working folks, who can use Sunday for grocery shopping and meal prep. Starting the 3-Day Fast-Track on a workday, with a predesignated schedule, can be a big advantage. The structure of your work-day may keep you organized and make it easier to eat at scheduled times. If you have a job with unpredictable hours, though, you're better off starting on a Satur-day, so you'll have 2 days of ghrelin stabilization under your belt before you're at the mercy of your hectic work schedule.

2. PREPARE YOUR KITCHEN

Getting your kitchen ready is essential to your success on the 3-Day Fast-Track. In Chapter 4, I asked you to get rid of foods with food additives. Now I'm asking you to go a few steps further to fully prepare yourself:

▶ **First, get rid of the foods you know tempt you.** I love ice cream, and when I say love, I mean *love*—I simply can't resist it. If you experience this kind of tempta-tion—and you probably do about some foods—it's best to get rid of whatever your guilty pleasure is. Throw it out, give it away, or hide it in the bottom back drawer. Whatever you need to do, *just do it*. Telling yourself "It's bad to waste food" or "I won't eat it" is, well, a lie. If this reasoning worked, you wouldn't need to lose weight in the first place. Also, be sure to get rid of all foods with ghrelin-increasing ingredients, whether they tempt you or not.

▶ **Second, clean your kitchen.** Wipe out your refrigerator, mop the floor, empty the trash, and disinfect your cabinet surfaces. Cleaning your kitchen will set the stage for the expedition you're about to embark on. A clean kitchen will make it easier to prepare your food—and you'll feel good doing it!

▶ **Third, purchase all your Fast-Track foods ahead of time.** Success is a result of preparation. Now that you've removed ghrelin-increasing foods and cleaned your kitchen, it's time to fill it back up with the best foods possible. This makes the process of choosing the right foods to eat much, much easier. In Chapter 4 starting on page 112, you'll find a Fast-Track shopping list for your convenience. Just take inventory of your cabinets. Whatever you don't have, buy. This is important, because you must not make food substitutions on the Fast-Track. Most people don't have to buy everything on the shopping list—common ingredients such as olive oil may already be a staple in your home.

3. GET IN THE ZONE

If you have a history of starting diets only to fall off the wagon soon after you begin, it's critical you get your head in the game. Tell friends and family you're starting a new diet and that you need their support and encouragement. It's a powerful motivation to share an intention you set for yourself. It creates an obligation for you to fulfill.

I practice visualization and journaling with my clients. Both techniques work well, depending on whether you're "right brained" or "left brained." Right-brain people tend to do better with visualization, while left-brain people do better with journaling. Here are two techniques for you to try—give them both a shot. The more you mentally prepare for the 3-Day Fast-Track, the better—and the easier—it will be.

▶ **Visualization.** In a quiet place, sit comfortably or lie down and close your eyes, then take 10 deep breaths, focusing on your chest rising and falling. Visualize yourself successfully completing the 3-Day Fast-Track. Think about yourself stepping on the scale the morning of day 4 and discovering that you're 3 to 5 pounds lighter. Think about how you'll feel. How do you look? Are you happy and motivated? Imagine yourself in a new body. Etch this image of yourself in your mind. By focusing on this image frequently throughout the day, you'll start to rewire your mental picture of yourself. If you can imagine yourself being who you want to be, it will encourage and support the actions you must take in order to change.

▶ **Journal writing.** If you're like most dieters, you're probably torn between unhealthy habits (along with the negative thoughts that got you where you are) and a desire for a healthy, slender existence, where food and weight aren't constant concerns. One way to distinguish between the two is to write about it. Write one journal entry focusing on the habits and thoughts that have brought you to this point. What makes you feel bad? What keeps you at the mercy of your weight? Then write a second journal entry focusing on positives. Focus on what you want to accomplish and how you'll feel when you set new, healthy habits that take the weight off. Reflect on both journal entries. Ask yourself which outcome you want. If you chose the second one, great. Now's your time—let's get started!

THE FAST-TRACK RULES

Three days. Five rules. How closely you follow them determines your results. These rules were designed with ghrelin in mind. Follow them *conscientiously* to expedite ghrelin stabilization. This will enable your ghrelin-producing gut and mind to work together. It will also allow your hormonal system, starting with ghrelin, to come into balance and work at its best.

1. **Follow the Fast-Track exactly.** Eat the meals precisely as they're laid out in the pages ahead. If you break up the meals or switch food around, it may affect your body's ability to fully stabilize ghrelin. Remember, these meals are meticulously calculated and arranged. They'll benefit you—but *only* if you follow them exactly. You can prepare the meals differently if you prefer, but you must be attentive to the spices and seasonings you use. Make sure they don't contain any of the top five ghrelin-increasing additives listed in Chapter 4. (Your ingredients to avoid list on page 99 can be a big help when you're at the supermarket.)

    The total calories in the Fast-Track are lower than they are in the regular ghrelin weight-loss meal plans found in Chapter 6. This will get your body into fat-burning/weight-loss mode. The ghrelin-suppressing superfoods we learned about in Chapter 3 are featured in many of the meals. Using them, you can consume fewer calories without extreme hunger. The superfoods keep you full longer and help stabilize ghrelin more effectively. (Men, since you need more food, even when losing weight, you're allotted more calories than women on the Fast-Track. That's why I've created different Fast-Track plans for men and women.)

2. **Eat according to the ghrelin schedule.** To balance ghrelin, you must eat when ghrelin peaks, even if you don't *feel* hungry. Remember: Ghrelin peaks three times a day, at 8:00 a.m., noon, and 6:00 p.m., so these are the ideal times to eat. Have your afternoon snack at 3:00. If your job or household responsibilities make it impossible to follow this ideal, it's critical for you to eat every 4 hours, which is the time span of ghrelin's natural peaks.

   Arrange to eat breakfast within 1 hour of waking, lunch 4 hours later, and dinner 6 hours after lunch. Your afternoon snack must be right in the middle of lunch and dinner, 3 hours after lunch and 3 hours before dinner. If you do this, ghrelin will stabilize based on your schedule.

3. **Drink 100 ounces of lemon water daily.** The Fast-Track aims to get your entire system into optimal ghrelin balance, and the water requirements aim to ensure full hydration, which can make or break your weight loss for several reasons. First, if you don't drink enough water, you might confuse thirst with hunger. It would be a shame to go through all this effort just to "feel" hungry, when in reality you're thirsty. Second, hydration has a huge impact on digestion, which plays a role in ghrelin secretion. Third, water with lemon is a natural diuretic and appetite suppressant. It will help you release any excess water you may be retaining. In addition, the tart flavor of lemon helps cut sugar cravings.

4. **Don't exercise.** There are several reasons why *not* exercising is a Fast-Track rule. First, it makes you hungry, which negates your ghrelin-stabilizing efforts. Second, it's more effective to use your time getting in touch with your hunger and eating at the times that support ghrelin balance. After you complete the Fast-Track and spend the rest of the month getting used to this way of eating, you can move on to the No-Sweat Exercise Program in Chapter 8. Until then, take it easy.

   This isn't a free pass to become a couch potato, though! Simply follow your normal routine. If you take your dog out for a 20-minute walk every morning, continue to do so—just don't jog. A no-exercise directive may sound strange, but it's critical. Not exercising for 3 days will help stabilize your ghrelin and teach you what true ghrelin hunger feels like.

5. **Track your food daily.** The first few days of a diet are never easy, and starting this plan is no exception. You'll be changing the way you eat, giving up some of the foods you love, and following a schedule that may feel completely unnatural. Trust that it will be worth the effort. In my 10 years of counseling people, I know this to be true. Until you see results, the effort is exhausting. That's why I want you to use your food trackers every single day. Keep copious notes about your thoughts, your feelings, and the challenges you face during the next 3 days. These notes will be critical to your long-term success.

Your Fast-Track food tracker will become your dieting journal. You can look back at your notes to remember what worked, what didn't work, what you liked, what you didn't like, and how you got your ghrelin stabilized. When things seem rough and you're tempted by that chocolate brownie calling out to you, it'll help to remind yourself of your weight-loss goals, right there in black and white in your Fast-Track tracker.

Note: If you're a vegetarian or choose the vegetarian option for a Fast-Track Meal, look for **. If you're not vegetarian, avoid eating the item marked with **.

WOMEN'S 3-DAY FAST-TRACK

BREAKFAST

 2 slices Arnold Healthfull 10-Grain Bread
 4 egg whites
†½ teaspoon cinnamon
†¼ cup part-skim ricotta cheese
 4 ounce Granny Smith apple
12 ounces water with lemon
 8 ounces coffee/tea (optional)

1. *In a nonstick skillet coated with cooking spray, scramble the eggs. Add salt and pepper, if desired.*
2. *Toast the bread and serve the eggs as a sandwich.*

   †Mix the cinnamon into the ricotta cheese and spread on the toast.
3. *Serve the apple on the side.*

LUNCH

⅓ cup cooked whole wheat pasta
¼ cup lima beans
 1 teaspoon olive oil
 4 ounces chicken breast
**4 ounces veggie chicken strips
 1 cup cherry tomatoes
½ cup raw baby carrots
 1 small grapefruit
12 ounces water with lemon

1. *In a skillet, heat the oil and add the chicken (or the veggie chicken strips). Add the beans and tomatoes. Season with salt and pepper, if desired.*
2. *When the chicken is cooked through, add the cooked pasta and stir until covered in a light sauce.*
3. *Serve the grapefruit and baby carrots on the side.*

Day 1

SNACK

1 low-fat cheese stick
1 La Tortilla Low Carb Original Tortilla
12 ounces water with lemon

Wrap the tortilla around the cheese stick.

DINNER

  3 ounce sweet potato
  5 ounces 95% lean ground beef
**4 ounces tempeh
  1 teaspoon 100% olive oil, divided
  1 cup broccoli
  1 cup mushrooms
  4 ounce Granny Smith apple
12 ounces water with lemon

1. *Pierce the potato a few times with a fork and wrap in foil. Bake at 350°F for about 30 minutes, or until a fork inserted in the flesh indicates that it is soft.*

2. *In a nonstick pan, heat ½ teaspoon of the oil. Add the beef (or the tempeh), brown, and remove from the pan to drain.*

3. *In the hot pan, add the remaining oil and the broccoli and mushrooms. Cook until the broccoli is just cooked. Add the beef (or the tempeh). Season as desired with salt and pepper or other favorite spices.*

4. *Serve the apple on the side.*

**Vegetarian alternative

GHRELIN HUNGER SCALE

Mark your ghrelin hunger directly on the G-scale:
B for Breakfast, L for Lunch, S for Snack, D for Dinner

STEP 1 Hunger/Fullness

1	**Starving,** shaky and lightheaded
2	**Very hungry,** you have to eat soon
3	**Moderately hungry,** you feel you could eat a meal
4	**Neutral,** neither hungry nor full
5	**Moderately full,** comfortable
6	**Somewhat uncomfortable,** your stomach feels overfull
7	**Stuffed,** you can't take another bite

STEP 2 Hours Since Last Meal

1 hour or less since last meal	1.5 hours since last meal	2 hours since last meal	2.5 hours since last meal	3 hours since last meal	3.5 hours since last meal	4 hours or more since last meal
7	6	5	4	3	2	1

Black: Your ghrelin level is high. You should begin eating within 10 minutes.
White: Your ghrelin level is rising. Eat a ghrelin-suppressing snack within 30 minutes or meal within 60 minutes.
Gray: Your ghrelin level is low. Wait 30 minutes and check again.

FOOD TRACKER
Day 1

BREAKFAST

	G-SCALE:
TIME:	gray
HUNGER BEFORE:	white
HUNGER AFTER:	black

CHALLENGES / THOUGHTS:

LUNCH

	G-SCALE:
TIME:	gray
HUNGER BEFORE:	white
HUNGER AFTER:	black

CHALLENGES / THOUGHTS:

SNACK

	G-SCALE:
TIME:	gray
HUNGER BEFORE:	white
HUNGER AFTER:	black

CHALLENGES / THOUGHTS:

DINNER

	G-SCALE:
TIME:	gray
HUNGER BEFORE:	white
HUNGER AFTER:	black

CHALLENGES / THOUGHTS:

WOMEN'S 3-DAY FAST-TRACK

BREAKFAST

½ cup uncooked oats

⅔ cup fat-free plain Greek yogurt

4 ounce Granny Smith apple, diced

12 ounces water with lemon

8 ounces coffee/tea (optional)

1. Cook the oats according to the package directions.
2. When the oats are cooked and still warm, add the yogurt and apple. Add cinnamon or other spices, as desired.

LUNCH

½ Thomas' Sahara Whole Wheat Pita Pocket

1 tablespoon hummus

4 ounces fat-free deli turkey

**1 Amy's California Veggie Burger, cooked

2 tablespoons avocado

5 spinach leaves

2 slices tomato

2 slices onion

1 small grapefruit

12 ounces water with lemon

1. Open the pita and spread the hummus over one half.
2. Layer the turkey (or the veggie burger), avocado, spinach, tomato, and onion on top of the hummus.
3. Serve the grapefruit on the side.

Day 2

SNACK

⅓ cup frozen edamame, shelled

4 medium black olives

12 ounces water with lemon

1. Heat the edamame in a microwave oven for 15 seconds to thaw.

2. Slice the olives and mix with the edamame, or serve the olives on the side.

DINNER

⅓ cup cooked quinoa

6 ounces tilapia or shrimp

**⅔ cup uncooked edamame, shelled

1 tablespoon pine nuts

½ cup bell pepper, chopped

¼ cup onion, chopped

1 cup steamed kale, ribs removed

4 ounce Granny Smith apple

12 ounces water with lemon

1. In a dry nonstick skillet, add the onion and bell pepper. Mix with 2 tablespoons water. Add black pepper, salt, and paprika to taste, if desired. Cook until the bell pepper is half cooked, then add the tilapia or shrimp (or the edamame)

2. Add the kale. Cover and heat through. Check the seasoning and adjust to taste.

3. Serve the mixture on a bed of the quinoa. Sprinkle the pine nuts on top and serve warm.

4. Serve the apple on the side.

**Vegetarian alternative

GHRELIN HUNGER SCALE

Mark your ghrelin hunger directly on the G-scale:
B for Breakfast, L for Lunch, S for Snack, D for Dinner

STEP 1
Hunger/
Fullness

	STEP 2 Hours Since Last Meal	1 hour or less since last meal	1.5 hours since last meal	2 hours since last meal	2.5 hours since last meal	3 hours since last meal	3.5 hours since last meal	4 hours or more since last meal
1	**Starving,** shaky and lightheaded							
2	**Very hungry,** you have to eat soon							
3	**Moderately hungry,** you feel you could eat a meal							
4	**Neutral,** neither hungry nor full							
5	**Moderately full,** comfortable							
6	**Somewhat uncomfortable,** your stomach feels overfull							
7	**Stuffed,** you can't take another bite							
		7	6	5	4	3	2	1

Black: Your ghrelin level is high. You should begin eating within 10 minutes.
White: Your ghrelin level is rising. Eat a ghrelin-suppressing snack within 30 minutes or meal within 60 minutes.
Gray: Your ghrelin level is low. Wait 30 minutes and check again.

FOOD TRACKER

Day 2

BREAKFAST

TIME: _____

HUNGER BEFORE: _____

HUNGER AFTER: _____

G-SCALE:
gray
white
black

CHALLENGES / THOUGHTS: _____

LUNCH

TIME: _____

HUNGER BEFORE: _____

HUNGER AFTER: _____

G-SCALE:
gray
white
black

CHALLENGES / THOUGHTS: _____

SNACK

TIME: _____

HUNGER BEFORE: _____

HUNGER AFTER: _____

G-SCALE:
gray
white
black

CHALLENGES / THOUGHTS: _____

DINNER

TIME: _____

HUNGER BEFORE: _____

HUNGER AFTER: _____

G-SCALE:
gray
white
black

CHALLENGES / THOUGHTS: _____

WOMEN'S 3-DAY FAST-TRACK

BREAKFAST

1¼ cups Fiber One cereal

⅔ cup fat-free milk

4 ounce Granny Smith apple

12 ounces water with lemon

8 ounces coffee/tea (optional)

1. Place the cereal in a bowl and pour in the milk.

2. Serve the apple on the side.

LUNCH

⅓ cup canned black beans, rinsed and drained

5 ounces fat-free ground turkey breast

**4 ounces Boca Ground Crumbles

2 tablespoons light sour cream

¼ cup bell pepper, chopped

¼ cup onion, chopped

1 cup spinach

1 small grapefruit

12 ounces water with lemon

1. In a nonstick skillet, cook the turkey with salt and black pepper to taste until browned.

2. Add the beans to the cooked turkey (or the Boca crumbles, if using). Remove from the pan and set aside.

3. In the same skillet, quickly cook the bell pepper and onion with a tablespoon of water. Add the spinach and the turkey (or Boca crumbles) mixture.

4. When all is heated through, remove the pan from the stove top and add the sour cream. Stir to incorporate and serve.

5. Serve the grapefruit on the side.

SNACK

    5 hard-cooked eggs

    1 tablespoon avocado

  12 ounces water with lemon

1. *Remove and discard the yolks from the eggs.*

2. *Chop the egg whites and mix with the avocado. Add a pinch of salt and pepper, if desired. Serve warm or cold.*

DINNER

    ⅓ cup cooked whole wheat couscous

    5 ounces boneless, skinless chicken breast, cut into 1-inch strips

**4 ounces firm tofu

    1 teaspoon olive oil

    1 teaspoon balsamic vinegar

    2 cups frozen stir-fry veggies

    4 ounce Granny Smith apple

  12 ounces water with lemon

1. *In a nonstick skillet, heat the oil on high. Add the chicken (or the tofu) in a single layer. Cook for 3 or 4 minutes on each side, turning about halfway through.*

2. *Remove the protein from the pan and set aside. Add the frozen vegetables to the pan and sauté until half cooked. Return the chicken (or the tofu) to the pan and stir until the protein has cooked through.*

3. *Serve over a bed of the couscous warmed and seasoned with the vinegar.*

4. *Serve the apple on the side.*

**Vegetarian alternative

GHRELIN HUNGER SCALE

Mark your ghrelin hunger directly on the G-scale:
B for Breakfast, L for Lunch, S for Snack, D for Dinner

STEP 1 Hunger/Fullness	1 hour or less since last meal	1.5 hours since last meal	2 hours since last meal	2.5 hours since last meal	3 hours since last meal	3.5 hours since last meal	4 hours or more since last meal
1 — Starving, shaky and lightheaded							
2 — Very hungry, you have to eat soon							
3 — Moderately hungry, you feel you could eat a meal							
4 — Neutral, neither hungry nor full							
5 — Moderately full, comfortable							
6 — Somewhat uncomfortable, your stomach feels overfull							
7 — Stuffed, you can't take another bite							
STEP 2 Hours Since Last Meal	7	6	5	4	3	2	1

Black: Your ghrelin level is high. You should begin eating within 10 minutes.

White: Your ghrelin level is rising. Eat a ghrelin-suppressing snack within 30 minutes or meal within 60 minutes.

Gray: Your ghrelin level is low. Wait 30 minutes and check again.

FOOD TRACKER

Day 3

BREAKFAST

TIME: _____

HUNGER BEFORE: _____

HUNGER AFTER: _____

CHALLENGES / THOUGHTS: _____

G-SCALE:
gray
white
black

LUNCH

TIME: _____

HUNGER BEFORE: _____

HUNGER AFTER: _____

CHALLENGES / THOUGHTS: _____

G-SCALE:
gray
white
black

SNACK

TIME: _____

HUNGER BEFORE: _____

HUNGER AFTER: _____

CHALLENGES / THOUGHTS: _____

G-SCALE:
gray
white
black

DINNER

TIME: _____

HUNGER BEFORE: _____

HUNGER AFTER: _____

CHALLENGES / THOUGHTS: _____

G-SCALE:
gray
white
black

MEN'S 3-DAY FAST-TRACK

BREAKFAST

2 slices Arnold Healthfull 10-Grain Bread

6 egg whites

†½ teaspoon cinnamon

†⅓ cup part-skim ricotta cheese

4 ounce Granny Smith apple

12 ounces water with lemon

8 ounces coffee/tea (optional)

1. In a nonstick skillet coated with cooking spray, scramble the eggs. Add salt and pepper, if desired.

2. Toast the bread and serve the eggs as a sandwich.

   †Mix the cinnamon into the ricotta cheese and spread on the toast.

3. Serve the apple on the side.

LUNCH

½ cup cooked whole wheat pasta

¼ cup lima beans

6 ounces chicken breast

**6 ounces veggie chicken strips

1 cup cherry tomatoes

1 teaspoon olive oil

½ cup raw baby carrots

1 small grapefruit

12 ounces water with lemon

1. In a skillet, heat the oil and add the chicken (or the veggie chicken strips). Add the beans and tomatoes. Season with salt and pepper, if desired.

2. When the chicken is cooked through, add the cooked pasta and stir until covered in a light sauce.

3. Serve the grapefruit and baby carrots on the side.

Day 1

SNACK

  2 low-fat cheese sticks
  1 La Tortilla Low Carb Original Tortilla
12 ounces water with lemon

Wrap the tortilla around the cheese stick.

DINNER

   6 ounces sweet potato
   6 ounces 95% cooked lean beef
**6 ounces tempeh
   1 teaspoon olive oil, divided
   1 cup broccoli
   1 cup mushrooms
   4 ounce Granny Smith apple
 12 ounces water with lemon

1. *Pierce the potato a few times with a fork and wrap in foil. Bake at 350°F for about 30 minutes, or until a fork inserted in the flesh indicates that it is soft.*

2. *In a nonstick pan, heat ½ teaspoon of the oil. Add the beef (or the tempeh), brown, and remove from the pan to drain.*

3. *In the hot pan, add the remaining oil and the broccoli and mushrooms. Cook until the broccoli is just cooked. Add the beef (or the tempeh). Season as desired with salt and pepper or other favorite spices.*

4. *Serve the apple on the side.*

**Vegetarian alternative

GHRELIN HUNGER SCALE

Mark your ghrelin hunger directly on the G-scale:
B for Breakfast, L for Lunch, S for Snack, D for Dinner

STEP 1 Hunger/Fullness		1 hour or less since last meal	1.5 hours since last meal	2 hours since last meal	2.5 hours since last meal	3 hours since last meal	3.5 hours since last meal	4 hours or more since last meal
1	Starving, shaky and lightheaded							
2	Very hungry, you have to eat soon							
3	Moderately hungry, you feel you could eat a meal							
4	Neutral, neither hungry nor full							
5	Moderately full, comfortable							
6	Somewhat uncomfortable, your stomach feels overfull							
7	Stuffed, you can't take another bite							
STEP 2 Hours Since Last Meal		7	6	5	4	3	2	1

Black: Your ghrelin level is high. You should begin eating within 10 minutes.
White: Your ghrelin level is rising. Eat a ghrelin-suppressing snack within 30 minutes or meal within 60 minutes.
Gray: Your ghrelin level is low. Wait 30 minutes and check again.

FOOD TRACKER
Day 1

BREAKFAST

TIME: _____

HUNGER BEFORE: _____

HUNGER AFTER: _____

CHALLENGES / THOUGHTS: _____

G-SCALE:
gray
white
black

LUNCH

TIME: _____

HUNGER BEFORE: _____

HUNGER AFTER: _____

CHALLENGES / THOUGHTS: _____

G-SCALE:
gray
white
black

SNACK

TIME: _____

HUNGER BEFORE: _____

HUNGER AFTER: _____

CHALLENGES / THOUGHTS: _____

G-SCALE:
gray
white
black

DINNER

TIME: _____

HUNGER BEFORE: _____

HUNGER AFTER: _____

CHALLENGES / THOUGHTS: _____

G-SCALE:
gray
white
black

MEN'S 3-DAY FAST-TRACK

BREAKFAST

    ½ cup uncooked oats
    ⅔ cup fat-free plain Greek yogurt
    6 ounce Granny Smith apple, diced
    12 ounces water with lemon
    8 ounces coffee/tea (optional)

1. Cook the oats according to the package directions.
2. When the oats are cooked and still warm, add the yogurt and apple. Add cinnamon or other spices, as desired.

LUNCH

    1 Thomas' Sahara 100% Whole Wheat Pita Pockets
    1 tablespoon hummus
    6 ounces fat-free deli turkey
    **1½ Amy's California Veggie Burgers, cooked
    2 tablespoons avocado
    5 spinach leaves
    2 slices tomato
    2 slices onion
    1 small grapefruit
    12 ounces water with lemon

1. Open the pita and spread the hummus over each half.
2. Layer the turkey (or the veggie burger), avocado, spinach, tomato, and onion on top of the hummus.
3. Serve the grapefruit on the side.

Day 2

SNACK

⅓ cup frozen edamane, shelled

4 medium black olives

12 ounces water with lemon

1. Heat the edamane in a microwave oven for 15 seconds to thaw.

2. Slice the olives and mix with the edamane, or serve the olives on the side.

DINNER

⅔ cup cooked quinoa

9 ounces tilapia or shrimp

**¾ cup edamame, shelled

1 tablespoon pine nuts

½ cup bell pepper, chopped

¼ cup onion, chopped

1 cup steamed kale, ribs removed

6 ounce Granny Smith apple

12 ounces water with lemon

1. In a dry nonstick skillet, add the onion and bell pepper. Mix with 2 tablespoons water. Add black pepper, salt, and paprika to taste, if desired. Cook until the bell pepper is half cooked, then add the tilapia or shrimp (or the edamame).

2. Add the kale. Cover and heat through. Check the seasoning and adjust to taste.

3. Serve the mixture on a bed of the quinoa. Sprinkle the pine nuts on top and serve warm.

4. Serve the apple on the side.

**Vegetarian alternative*

GHRELIN HUNGER SCALE

Mark your ghrelin hunger directly on the G-scale:
B for Breakfast, L for Lunch, S for Snack, D for Dinner

STEP 1 Hunger/Fullness	1 hour or less since last meal	1.5 hours since last meal	2 hours since last meal	2.5 hours since last meal	3 hours since last meal	3.5 hours since last meal	4 hours or more since last meal
1 Starving, shaky and lightheaded							
2 Very hungry, you have to eat soon							
3 Moderately hungry, you feel you could eat a meal							
4 Neutral, neither hungry nor full							
5 Moderately full, comfortable							
6 Somewhat uncomfortable, your stomach feels overfull							
7 Stuffed, you can't take another bite							

STEP 2
Hours Since
Last Meal

7   6   5   4   3   2   1

Black: Your ghrelin level is high. You should begin eating within 10 minutes.
White: Your ghrelin level is rising. Eat a ghrelin-suppressing snack within
    30 minutes or meal within 60 minutes.
Gray: Your ghrelin level is low. Wait 30 minutes and check again.

FOOD TRACKER

Day 2

BREAKFAST

TIME: _____

HUNGER BEFORE: _____

HUNGER AFTER: _____

CHALLENGES / THOUGHTS: _____

G-SCALE:
gray
white
black

LUNCH

TIME: _____

HUNGER BEFORE: _____

HUNGER AFTER: _____

CHALLENGES / THOUGHTS: _____

G-SCALE:
gray
white
black

SNACK

TIME: _____

HUNGER BEFORE: _____

HUNGER AFTER: _____

CHALLENGES / THOUGHTS: _____

G-SCALE:
gray
white
black

DINNER

TIME: _____

HUNGER BEFORE: _____

HUNGER AFTER: _____

CHALLENGES / THOUGHTS: _____

G-SCALE:
gray
white
black

MEN'S 3-DAY FAST-TRACK

1½ cups Fiber One cereal

1 cup fat-free milk

6 ounce Granny Smith apple

12 ounces water with lemon

8 ounces coffee/tea (optional)

1. *Place the cereal in a bowl and pour in the milk.*

2. *Serve the apple on the side.*

LUNCH

½ cup black beans, rinsed and drained

7 ounces fat-free ground turkey breast

**6 ounces Boca Ground Crumbles

2 tablespoons light sour cream

¼ cup bell pepper, chopped

¼ cup onion, chopped

1 cup spinach

1 small grapefruit

12 ounces water with lemon

1. *In a nonstick skillet, cook the turkey with salt and black pepper until browned.*

2. *Add the beans to the cooked turkey (or the Boca crumbles, if using). Remove from the pan and set aside.*

3. *In the same skillet, quickly cook the bell pepper and onion with a tablespoon of water. Add the spinach and the turkey (or Boca crumble) mixture.*

4. *When all is heated through, remove the pan from the stove top and add the sour cream. Stir to incorporate and serve.*

5. *Serve the grapefruit on the side.*

Day 3

SNACK

    6 hard-cooked eggs

    2 tablespoons avocado

  12 ounces water with lemon

1. *Remove and discard the yolks from the eggs.*

2. *Chop the egg whites and mix with the avocado. Add a pinch of salt and pepper, if desired. Serve warm or cold.*

DINNER

  ⅔ cup cooked whole wheat couscous

    7 ounces boneless, skinless chicken breast, cut into 1-inch strips

**6 ounces firm tofu

    1 teaspoon olive oil

    1 teaspoon balsamic vinegar

    2 cups frozen stir-fry veggies

    6 ounce Granny Smith apple

  12 ounces water with lemon

1. *In a nonstick skillet, heat the oil on high. Add the chicken (or the tofu) in a single layer. Cook for 3 or 4 minutes on each side, turning about halfway through.*

2. *Remove the protein from the pan and set aside. Add the frozen vegetables to the pan and sauté until half cooked. Return the chicken (or the tofu) to the pan and stir until the protein has cooked through.*

3. *Serve over a bed of the couscous warmed and seasoned with the vinegar.*

4. *Serve the apple on the side.*

**Vegetarian alternative

GHRELIN HUNGER SCALE

Mark your ghrelin hunger directly on the G-scale:
B for Breakfast, L for Lunch, S for Snack, D for Dinner

STEP 1 Hunger/Fullness	1 hour or less since last meal	1.5 hours since last meal	2 hours since last meal	2.5 hours since last meal	3 hours since last meal	3.5 hours since last meal	4 hours or more since last meal
1 **Starving,** shaky and lightheaded							
2 **Very hungry,** you have to eat soon							
3 **Moderately hungry,** you feel you could eat a meal							
4 **Neutral,** neither hungry nor full							
5 **Moderately full,** comfortable							
6 **Somewhat uncomfortable,** your stomach feels overfull							
7 **Stuffed,** you can't take another bite							
STEP 2 Hours Since Last Meal	7	6	5	4	3	2	1

Black: Your ghrelin level is high. You should begin eating within 10 minutes.
White: Your ghrelin level is rising. Eat a ghrelin-suppressing snack within 30 minutes or meal within 60 minutes.
Gray: Your ghrelin level is low. Wait 30 minutes and check again.

FOOD TRACKER

Day 3

BREAKFAST

TIME:

HUNGER BEFORE:

HUNGER AFTER:

G-SCALE:
gray
white
black

CHALLENGES / THOUGHTS:

LUNCH

TIME:

HUNGER BEFORE:

HUNGER AFTER:

G-SCALE:
gray
white
black

CHALLENGES / THOUGHTS:

SNACK

TIME:

HUNGER BEFORE:

HUNGER AFTER:

G-SCALE:
gray
white
black

CHALLENGES / THOUGHTS:

DINNER

TIME:

HUNGER BEFORE:

HUNGER AFTER:

G-SCALE:
gray
white
black

CHALLENGES / THOUGHTS:

SUCCESS!

You've completed the 3-Day Fast-Track—congratulations! My highest compliments on embarking on this plan and starting a new life! Now's the time to weigh yourself and find out how much your hard work has paid off.

Before you charge headfirst into the regular weight-loss phase of the Belly Fat Fix, reflect on your experience. Remember, your tracker records and reflections are your dieting journal. Your answers to the following questions will provide you with a wealth of information that sets the stage for long-term weight-loss success.

What Goes In Must Come Out

This may be an uncomfortable subject, but as a registered dietitian, I often talk to my clients about their bowel habits. That's because the way you eat determines what comes out. And it should! Your gastrointestinal tract is a processing unit that metabolizes all the nutrition you take in and eliminates all your body's waste. What passes through your digestive system is a primary indicator of your overall heath.

You probably feel better when you're going regularly. Most clients notice how regular they are on the Belly Fat Fix. It's normal for some people to experience more frequent bathroom trips the first few days on the plan. This is a good thing—it means your digestive tract is working properly and eliminating waste efficiently.

Have you ever experienced not going to the bathroom for several days in a row? Wonder what happened to the food you ate? Well, it hung out in your colon for a while, and your body had to strain to get it out. When you eat poor-quality, low-fiber foods, your bowels don't function at their peak, so you have a difficult time eliminating. The more high-quality foods you eat, the better your body digests them and removes the waste. When you start the 3-Day Fast-Track, it takes up to a week for your digestive tract to get into full working order. If this happens to you, don't be alarmed. Just wait it out. If you revert to old habits and eat poor-quality foods, you won't gain the healthy digestive benefits the Belly Fat Fix provides.

▶ Was there any aspect of the 3-Day Fast-Track that was easier than you expected? Harder than you expected?

_____

_____

▶ Describe one situation where you could discern true ghrelin hunger.

_____

_____

▶ What was your favorite meal? Least favorite?

_____

_____

▶ What time(s) of the day did you feel most full? What times did you feel most hungry?

_____

_____

▶ What will you do differently next time on the Fast-Track?

_____

_____

Are you ready now to begin the long-term Belly Fat Fix plan? That's what you'll find in the next chapter. It will help you take the gains you experience on the Fast-Track, keep the momentum going, and lead to even more success.

Pia B.

AGE: 28

POUNDS LOST:

FAST-TRACK: 3.6

TOTAL: 7.2 in 30 days

OVERALL INCHES LOST: 7

Pia B. was a self-confessed sugar addict. As an events coordinator with a hectic schedule, she'd grab half a dozen cookies and gobble them on the go. But by the end of the day, she'd feel tired and worn out. Then along came the Belly Fat Fix.

"It's made me feel so much better," she says with enthusiasm. "That first week was tough—I think my body was going through sugar withdrawal—but by the end of the week, I noticed

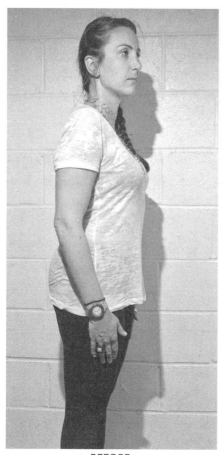

BEFORE

AFTER

that I had a lot more energy."

With an unpredictable schedule that changes from day to day, Pia is always on the run, and in the past she rarely slowed down for regular meals. But that's all changed. Now she's learned to listen to her body and eat when her appetite tells her she should. She's strict about sticking to three meals within 4 hours of each other. It's a whole new approach for her. These days, she starts her day with a good breakfast—most mornings it's oatmeal with Greek yogurt and an apple—and she even packs a healthy lunch so her diet won't be hijacked by fast-food temptation as she rushes from appointment to appointment.

"Eating this way is definitely healthier," she says. "This whole program has been a fascinating way to learn more about how my body really works."

But the changes she's made haven't been that arduous—thanks, mostly, to the plan's flexibility. She's been able to adjust her meal plan to move her afternoon snack to the evening—the only time she can relax and really enjoy her meals.

On a typical workday, Pia—who didn't have many pounds to lose—logs a lot of miles on foot, so she's focused more on the diet portion of the Belly Fat Fix than the No-Sweat Exercise Program, and she's put lots of Marjorie's diet strategies to work to ensure her success.

One of the best was drinking as much water as the plan requires. "I really think *that* was the catalyst," she insists. "It may sound strange, but the more I drank, the more I realized how thirsty I was."

Another strategy was raiding her spice cabinet to make the foods on the plan even more flavorful without adding calories. Pia says she often added cumin, cinnamon, and curry powder to her dishes, alone or in combination with other seasonings. Herbs like rosemary, sage, and parsley also helped her adjust the flavors of her meals to allow her to enjoy a greater variety of tastes. Some days, she switched ingredients around to add even more variety. The food preparation was "tedious" at first, she says, but she's gotten used to it—and now she's liking what she sees at the scale.

Another happy result: The program was a great way for Pia and her fiancé to explore new recipes and healthy nutrition together. "He didn't need to lose weight," she says, "but he learned along with me, and that was fun."

The payoff? Not only has Pia—who's never been obese but has always felt self-conscious about her weight—dropped some pounds, but now she says she feels "much more comfortable in my own skin. Even when the first pound came off, I felt like a 'better' person. This is definitely empowering."

CHAPTER 6

The Belly Fat Fix Plan for Weight Loss

You've learned how ghrelin works—how this one powerful hormone drives your true hunger. You've learned about the types of ghrelin hunger—and how to tell the difference between them. You've learned how to choose foods that suppress ghrelin and keep you full longer. Now it's time to put all these pieces together. In this chapter, you'll find the meal plan that will get you to a slimmer, trimmer you.

Maybe you've given the Belly Fat Fix a test-drive by trying the 3-Day Fast-Track. If so, you know what a difference it can make. If not, I urge you to give it a go. Just 3 days on the Fast-Track will stabilize your ghrelin, help you lose a quick 3 to 5 pounds, and break old, unhealthy patterns. The Fast-Track was designed to boost your confidence in the program and rev up your motivation. Now the Belly Fat Fix plan will help you to keep losing weight.

To make it as easy as possible to follow the diet portion of the Belly Fat Fix, I've put together 7 days of menus featuring easy-to-prepare foods, plus an additional 30 snack options. Just choose the meals and snacks that most appeal to you. Later on in the chapter, I'll explain how to exchange foods of nearly equal value. Let's say the meal you want calls for couscous, but you only have potatoes in your pantry. All you have to do is switch the couscous for an equal portion of potatoes—and the rest of the meal stays the same.

The prebuilt 7-day meal plan takes the guesswork out of menu planning. All you have to do is follow it. To make the whole experience enjoyable, we've crafted meals so delicious it won't even feel like you're on a diet. (See recipes in Chapter 7.) You *won't* feel deprived, you *will* feel full, and you'll have little reason to cheat.

You probably think, "No way." You've been on diets before, and you don't believe it can be this satisfying or this easy. *Yes, it can.* The Belly Fat Fix gives you biological control of your appetite so you don't have to rely on willpower alone, which is what makes this diet so simple and easy. Some other great things about this plan:

- It's based on the latest science. Every single aspect of this program has been thoroughly researched, then tested by my clients and by me.

- It features a Fast-Track plan that can be used over and over to restabilize your ghrelin or to take off the few pounds you may gain while you're on vacation, say, or going to holiday parties.

- It offers customizable Belly Fat Fix plans based on *your* goals—it's *not* one-size-fits-all.

- It addresses your long-term nutritional needs. These meal plans can be used for the rest of your life. They were created to take and keep the weight off and provide healthy, nutritious food. In Chapter 10, you'll learn the skills you need to stay slim forever using the menus and meal plans in this chapter.

- It achieves nutritional balance. The foods and portions were created with your health as the priority. Vitamins, minerals, fiber, and calories have all been meticulously calculated to ensure weight loss and long-term health. Consistently eating the Belly Fat Fix way can prevent disease and may help reverse degenerative diseases, such as diabetes and heart disease. Check out Lisa N.'s weight-loss experience on page 68. She not only lost weight but also significantly improved her cholesterol, blood pressure, and thyroid function.

- The dishes taste great.

It can easily be adapted for every person and for different situations—even for the times you may get off track. That's because I'll teach you how to recover quickly so that 1 or 2 days of eating fast food on the road, or binges during stress or a crisis, won't lead to prolonged unbalanced ghrelin, which *will* pack on the pounds.

For maximum success on the Belly Fat Fix, follow these three simple rules:

Rule 1: Use your G-Scale to determine your ghrelin level. Practicing this first rule will set you up for long-term success. If you don't use the G-Scale, you run the risk of eating when you're not truly hungry (maybe when you're bored or stressed) and/or eating at the wrong times in ways that don't support ghrelin balance. Remember, the G-Scale corresponds to the natural peaks and valleys of ghrelin, so you'll eat every 4 hours. Using the G-Scale also helps you become aware of true hunger and distinguish between that and the kind of hunger that needs to be addressed *without* food.

If you use the G-Scale daily for 30 days, you'll notice that you'll be in tune with your ghrelin hunger. Then you'll be better able to pick and choose the meals and snacks that best feed your hunger. I practice listening to my body in this way all the time. I've learned how to feed myself based on my hunger level and schedule, and I plan accordingly. For instance, on days when I have clients scheduled for 4 hours straight, and I know that I won't have time to eat in between, I make sure to eat a meal with at least two ghrelin superfoods. That keeps my ghrelin levels stable—and it keeps me comfortable and focused.

Rule 2: Balance meals and snacks using the G-List. The G-List (see page 77 in Chapter 3) shows you what foods suppress, increase, or have no effect on ghrelin. Memorize it so it becomes second nature to choose foods mainly from the *ghrelin-suppressing* and *ghrelin-neutral* categories. The list gives you maximum flexibility. Once you know it, you can choose between building your own ghrelin-smart meals or using the prebuilt meal plans I've created for you. Here's the real beauty of using the G-List: If there's a food you don't like (or don't have on hand), refer to the G-List and switch it for another food within the same group.

Let's say you're making lunch for work tomorrow, using the prebuilt meal plan starting on page 176. The plan calls for pita, but you're fresh out. You have two options. First, you can refer to another meal on your prebuilt menu and switch the pita for a different carb. The beauty of the prebuilt meal plans is that everything is interchangeable *within the same category and meal*. A lunch protein can be switched for a different lunch protein; a breakfast carb for a breakfast carb; a dinner fat for a dinner fat; a fruit for a fruit; a vegetable for a vegetable. Get it? Even if the food you want to switch is on another day's meal plan, the portions balance out as long as you stick within the same meal category.

The second thing you can do is switch the food for another from the same G-List category. In this situation, it's your job to measure the food according to your meal plan. It's easy: Your meal plan tells you exactly how many servings you get at each meal. So if your meal plan says you get two carb servings, simply refer to the G-List, choose a different carb, and measure two servings. You're just switching one carb for the other.

You'll get the hang of it soon. The easiest thing to do is to mix and match meals from the prebuilt menus. And remember: You don't have to eat different meals every day. If you really like a particular meal choice, feel free to have it again and again—just watch out for boredom! I eat practically the same breakfast all the time. I like it, it's quick to prepare, and it's the one that, for me, suppresses my ghrelin best throughout the morning. I vary my dinners and use the leftovers for lunch. This streamlines my life and keeps my ghrelin balanced.

With some experimenting, you'll learn what meals and food combinations work best for you. If you find something you like, prepare it in larger quantities and eat it a few days in a row. Your body works on averages. As long as you're averaging the right number of calories, vitamins, and minerals each week, you'll lose the weight. You don't have to follow the Belly Fat Fix plan perfectly all the time.

Rule 3: Exercise within your ghrelin-suppressing limits. Take a month to get used to the diet part of the plan. Learn your meal plan and use the food trackers in

Chapter 11. Using the tracker will make you aware of your eating patterns, your level of hunger, and your level of energy after eating specific kinds of foods. This will help you find the best choices for you within the program.

If you're a regular gym-goer, keep up with your routine. But if you don't already exercise, now isn't the time to start. Wait a month. Sound crazy? You're anxious to get the weight off, and exercise seems like a good way to speed up the process. But trust me on this one. Heading to the gym for an hour of sweaty elliptical training will *not* help. Over and over again, I see people try to do too much too quickly, which leads them to feeling overwhelmed and giving up entirely. Doing too much too soon just won't work.

Instead, focus only on food for at least 1 month before you start exercising. If you haven't already done so, clear the wrong foods from your cabinets and refrigerator and replace them with the right foods. Try the recipes. Take time to learn how to plan and assemble balanced, nutritious, ghrelin-suppressing meals. Write in your food tracker. Discover your habits associated with eating. Become more aware of your hunger and the differences between true hunger and the kinds that don't require food. This will be plenty for you to do. You can take long walks if you feel the need to get moving.

After a month on the Belly Fat Fix plan, you'll start the No-Sweat Exercise Program in Chapter 8. Until then, focus on changing your diet. That's a big enough job for now.

WHAT MEAL PLAN SHOULD I FOLLOW?

Now that you understand your focus for the first month, let's look at how much you can eat. To make it easier for you to reach your target weight, I've determined how many calories you can safely consume and still lose the weight. As you'll see in the charts that follow, I've created different prebuilt meal plans for different weight-loss goals, and I've made these different for men and women. Men get to eat a bit more because they have higher metabolic rates than women.

Locate your weight-loss goal on the following chart. A little farther down in this chapter, I'll provide the prebuilt meal plans that match these calorie levels.

(These start on page 176.) Then follow the plan that matches the number corresponding to your target weight-loss goal/calorie level. If you're a woman and want to lose 30 pounds, for instance, you'd follow the 1,600-calorie meal plan, which you'll find on page 168.

As you progress toward your goal, you'll have to adjust the plan you're following. You should drop down to the next-lower-calorie meal plan when the number of pounds you have left to lose matches the goal for that lower-calorie meal plan. So if you're a woman with 50 pounds to lose initially, begin by following the 1,800-calorie meal plan. Once you've lost 15 pounds and have just 35 pounds to go, drop down to the 1,600-calorie plan, which has a weight-loss goal of 16 to 35 pounds. Here's why: As you lose weight, your metabolism adjusts to your new lower weight, so you need fewer calories to keep losing. But don't drop lower than the next-level meal plan, thinking that'll speed up your weight loss. Eat too little and your ghrelin levels will soar, and you won't be able to stop overeating. Yo-yo weight loss and gain often result from an overly restrictive diet. So stick with the guide, unless you fit one of the exceptions to the rules. You'll find these listed in the Q&A section beginning on page 164.

Now, find your Belly Fat Fix calorie level.

Women

Weight-Loss Goal	15 pounds or less	16–35 pounds	36–65 pounds	66–95 pounds	95+ pounds
Meal Plan	1,400	1,600	1,800	2,000	2,200

Men

Weight-Loss Goal	15 pounds or less	16–35 pounds	36–65 pounds	66–95 pounds	95+ pounds
Meal Plan	1,600	1,800	2,000	2,200	2,400

The Skinny on the Meal Plans

My clients have raised lots of questions as they've gone through the Belly Fat Fix plan. Here are some of the questions that come up again and again—they may come up for you, too. Check out the Q&A that follows to get up to speed on the meal plan.

Q. *If I need to lose more weight, why is my calorie count higher?*

The more weight you need to lose, the more you have to eat. Counterintuitive but true—especially when you're eating to balance ghrelin. In Chapter 2, you learned that ghrelin levels tend to be lower in overweight and obese individuals. You may remember that when you're overweight, ghrelin rises less before meals and falls less afterward than it does for people of normal weight (see Normal-Weight vs. Overweight/Obese Ghrelin Levels graph on page 45.) You've also learned that when you're overweight, your levels of leptin—the fullness hormone—are higher, causing leptin resistance (see Leptin: The "I Feel Full" Hormone on page 49). The interaction of too-low ghrelin and too-high leptin is the reason you have to eat more.

Your task on the plan is to fully suppress ghrelin. There are two good reasons for this. First, to avoid getting so hungry that you binge. Second, to allow leptin, the hormone that triggers fullness, to do its job. If you can eat enough to suppress ghrelin and trigger leptin, you'll be able to take the weight off without constantly struggling with hunger.

Q. *Why do men get to eat more?*

Men have higher metabolic rates than women. That's because men have a higher percentage of lean body mass (LBM). LBM is a combination of nonfat tissues such as organs, bone, and muscle. Even an obese man with very little muscle has a lot more LBM than a woman of equal size. LBM burns more calories than fat. So men need to eat more to keep ghrelin balanced.

Q. *If my weight goal is right on the cusp of two meal plans, which one should I follow?*

Always start out by following the higher meal plan. You've already learned that eating too little elevates ghrelin and hunger, so if you jump into a meal plan that's too low, you put yourself at a higher risk of experiencing elevated ghrelin levels, extreme hunger, and overeating.

Q. *What if I'm losing weight on a higher meal plan?*

When you reach a weight-loss level that takes you down a meal plan, but you're still losing weight, stay on the current meal plan—there's no reason to cut out more calories if the plan you're on is doing the trick. Keep on the current meal plan until you go 2 consecutive weeks without weight loss, then drop down a meal plan.

Q. *What if I'm not losing weight on my meal plan?*

If you don't lose weight for 2 weeks in a row, drop down to the next meal plan. You *must* wait 2 weeks to make sure you don't cut out too many calories too quickly. Some of my clients are able to lose weight on a meal plan higher than assigned, and some need to be on a lower plan. The meal plan assignment chart is

an estimate. For 95 percent of readers, the assignment will work, but a small percentage must be on the lower meal plan to lose weight.

Sometimes, clients call, telling me they aren't losing weight. I always tell them to wait 2 weeks before adjusting. You may simply be experiencing what I call the Neanderthal effect. This means that for a couple of days to 2 weeks, your body won't let the fat go—that is, until your hormonal system is ghrelin balanced. After that, your body's ready to let go of fat. Often this is followed by a higher weight loss. My clients see this often. Let me share the experience of just one of them, Nichole D., one of the Ghrelin Masters whose story is featured on page 199.

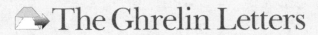# The Ghrelin Letters

I'm so disappointed this morning. I weighed myself, and I was up 0.4 pound from the last weigh-in. I feel like I've been doing really well. I feel thinner. I didn't think I would plateau this fast.

Help!
Nichole

My response:

You need to keep at it for a few more days. Your "plateau" is not unusual and probably just your body readjusting to the food and weight loss.

Humans are meant to conserve calories for times of starvation and famine—it's part of our genetic code that ensures the survival of the species. Think about how Neanderthals needed to store fat for the winter when food was scarce. Human genetics isn't much different now, although our food supply is. When you start to lose weight, there's a time when your body is confused and trying to conserve energy stores (meaning fat).

The same thing happens to me. When I gain a few pounds and then get back on track to return to my preferred weight, I usually hang out at the higher weight for a while. I get frustrated, but it never fails—after a week, I get on the scale and bam! I'm down a couple of pounds.

Let's see what happens in the next few days before we assume the worst. I want you to focus on the fact that you feel thinner and better. Allow some time to let your body sort out "the Neanderthal effect" and get back to fat burning.

Here's the e-mail I received from Nichole 3 days later:

This morning, I was down 2 pounds—that's 7.6 pounds total in 3 weeks! Yay! You were right. I waited a few days, and that nasty 0.4 pound was gone, plus some. I'm finding the plan very easy to stick to. I always feel satisfied, and I enjoy the food. I'm surprised that I don't need to add all the extra fat and calories for taste. It's really going well. I just need to work on patience. Thanks for everything!

YOUR G-LIST MEAL PLAN

Let's get started! Here's your official meal plan. Think of it as your ghrelin-suppressing road map designed to keep your ghrelin balanced. It's in chart form for easy reference—you'll be able to tell at a glance exactly which—and how many—G-List foods to eat at each meal. Just follow the meal plan and head toward your weight-loss goal.

All the foods are based on G-List *cooked* portions. This is *very* important. Some foods are significantly higher in calories when they're not cooked. For example, ⅓ cup of uncooked brown rice is 225 calories; that same rice, once cooked, is only 75 calories. **So be sure to measure cooked food, unless I state otherwise.** If you don't do this, you could actually gain weight on this plan.

Let's look at the meal plan chart together. Each meal indicates the number of servings from each G-List group. The numbers you see in parentheses are calories. I include them to help you learn how many calories your body needs and to give you a backup reference to use when you're swapping foods. This way, you can be sure that you're portioning correctly and not eating too much—or too little.

THE NITTY-GRITTY OF GHRELIN

Before you know it, you'll be zipping through the Belly Fat Fix like a pro. But getting up to speed will take a little practice. Here are some guidelines to make the road less bumpy.

APPLES TO APPLES

Never trade proteins for carbs. If you trade food groups, you run the risk of throwing off your ghrelin level and feeling hungry. You can, however, switch foods *within* the same G-List food category for an equal portion of another food. Let's break this down. Say you made the Pork Chops with Cran-Apple Relish recipe on page 243. (It's delicious!) You loved the couscous, and you're longing to eat more. You may even be willing to reduce the amount of pork so that you can have more of the couscous.

That's a no-no. Trading one food group for another is not allowed on the Belly

Meal Plan Chart

Meal Plans	1,400	1,600	1,800	2,000	2,200	2,400
Breakfast	2 Carb (150) 1 Protein (75) 1 Fruit (60) **285**	2 Carb (150) 1.5 Protein (115) 1 Fruit (60) **325**	3 Carb (225) 2 Protein (150) 1 Fruit (60) **435**	3 Carb (225) 2 Protein (150) 1 Fat (50) 1 Fruit (60) **485**	3 Carb (225) 2 Protein (150) 2 Fat (100) 1.5 Fruit (90) **565**	3 Carb (225) 2 Protein (150) 2 Fat (100) 1.5 Fruit (90) **565**
Lunch	2 Carb (150) 2 Protein (150) 1 Fat (50) 2 Veggie (50) 1 Fruit (60) **460**	2 Carb (150) 3 Protein (225) 1 Fat (50) 2 Veggie (50) 1 Fruit (60) **535**	2 Carb (150) 3 Protein (225) 2 Fat (100) 2 Veggie (50) 1 Fruit (60) **585**	3 Carb (225) 3 Protein (225) 2 Fat (100) 2 Veggie (50) 1 Fruit (60) **660**	3 Carb (225) 3 Protein (225) 2 Fat (100) 3 Veggie (75) 1.5 Fruit (90) **715**	3 Carb (225) 3 Protein (225) 2 Fat (100) 3 Veggie (75) 1.5 Fruit (90) **715**
Snack	Snack List **200**	Snack List **200**	Snack List **200**	Snack List **200**	Snack List **200**	*Double snack* Snack List **400**
Dinner	1 Carb (75) 3 Protein (225) 1 Fat (50) 2 Veggie (50) 1 Fruit (60) **460**	2 Carb (150) 3 Protein (225) 1 Fat (50) 2 Veggie (50) 1 Fruit (60) **535**	2 Carb (150) 3 Protein (225) 2 Fat (100) 2 Veggie (50) 1 Fruit (60) **585**	3 Carb (225) 3 Protein (225) 2 Fat (100) 2 Veggie (50) 1 Fruit (60) **660**	3 Carb (225) 3 Protein (225) 2 Fat (100) 3 Veggie (75) 1.5 Fruit (90) **715**	3 Carb (225) 3 Protein (225) 2 Fat (100) 3 Veggie (75) 1.5 Fruit (90) **715**

Fat Fix. You could, however, switch the pork for another protein, or switch the couscous for another carbohydrate.

GET BACK ON TRACK

Remember: No matter how hard you try to follow this meal plan perfectly, there will inevitably be days when you can't. Sometimes you'll be at the mercy of the foods that other people (who may not be on the Belly Fat Fix) are providing, and your choices may not be ghrelin friendly. That just means you'll have to rebalance your ghrelin later. Ghrelin Master Nichole D. (page 199), a single mom, had to do just that at a family holiday event. I'm sure you can relate. Here's the e-mail she sent me. Sound familiar?

The Ghrelin Letters

I did not do well yesterday, and I feel really bad about it. I was up 2 pounds on the scale. Yikes! My family had two events yesterday: a breakfast Easter egg hunt and a big dinner. When I tell you there were no healthy choices whatsoever, I'm not exaggerating. I did scale down what I would normally eat, but all that fat, salt, and sugar was a bit of a shock to my system. It's crazy how my body reacted to the food. I was so tired last night, much more than usual. All the foods were casseroles, like French toast, potatoes au gratin, cinnamon pineapple something—and all were made with butter, cheese, and other gooey stuff. I know I feel this way because of what I ate. I'm trying to take a different approach this time. What should I do? I want to get back on track.

—Nichole

Circumstances like this will happen again and again. Let's be honest—most of us tend to blow our diets on holidays, parties, birthdays, and vacations. Here's what to do to recover, rebalance your ghrelin, and keep your head in the game.

1. **Relax.** One day will not affect your overall loss, and it will not stop you from losing more weight if you limit it to just 1 day. Don't allow yourself to continue to overeat just because you've already "messed up."

2. **Remember that weight *fluctuates* by the hour.** After 1 day of overeating, your weight increases because of fluid retention. I call this "inventory weight." Inventory weight always goes back down within a day or two, provided you drink your water and follow your meal plan.

3. **Plan ahead.** Next time you know you're attending a food-focused extravaganza, eat according to your meal plan all day until the event. It's bound to be a disaster if you try to "save up" your food. When you do this, the only thing you're saving yourself from is having balanced ghrelin.

4. **Follow the Fast-Track** for the 3 days after you've fallen off the diet wagon. This will reset your ghrelin levels and reboot your motivation.

This is what I told Nichole—and it was exactly what she needed to hear to keep on track.

I designed this plan with a backup system. When you follow this system right away, you avoid a ghrelin disaster. There's no reason to keep eating because you messed up on the meal plan. Just get right back on the saddle.

 ## The Ghrelin Letters

I'm taking a new outlook because in the past I'd just tell myself I messed up, and let it lead into a bigger binge, but I'm done with that. The foods I'm eating on a regular basis are filling me, and I feel good. Don't get me wrong—that Easter Sunday meal was delicious, especially the ham and cheesy potatoes. But I felt terrible afterward, and my face was literally swollen this morning. I felt like I had a food hangover. I'm going to follow the Fast-Track today, drink my water, and not beat myself up.

—Nichole

HAVE A DRINK—IN MODERATION

One or two alcoholic drinks per week should be your max—and less is even better. If you plan to have alcohol with dinner, never cut back on food to compensate. Having a few drinks without eating enough ghrelin-suppressing food could make you ravenously hungry—and ravenous hunger with a good buzz is the perfect setup for out-of-control eating. I suggest you eat two ghrelin-suppressing superfoods before having that drink to ensure maximum ghrelin suppression and prevent alcohol-induced hunger cravings.

While we're on the subject of alcohol and appetite, let's talk about why it makes you so hungry. One theory is that alcohol lowers inhibitions and makes it easier for most people to let loose and eat something less healthy. If you've ever eaten a slice or two of greasy pizza at 2:00 a.m. after having a few drinks, you can relate. Chances are you never would have eaten it if you hadn't been drinking. Another theory is that alcohol breaks down in the body into simple sugars that circulate in your blood. The sugar causes a spike in insulin, which causes your blood sugar to drop quickly. This drop in blood sugar triggers hunger and ghrelin secretion. A third theory, developed by a team of researchers from the University of Sussex in the United Kingdom, is that alcohol directly affects the hypothalamus, interfering with the appetite control center. The study found that men who drank alcohol before a buffet meal ate significantly more than men who didn't drink. It also showed that those participants who drank found the food more appealing. The study cast new light on alcohol's ability to affect appetite and trigger the food reward pathway—which, by the way, is right next to the pathway that gets stimulated by alcohol and drugs.

EAT EVERYTHING ON YOUR MEAL PLAN

You'll probably be surprised by how much food you can eat on the Belly Fat Fix. That's because losing weight isn't about eating less; ironically, weight loss happens when you eat *more* of the right foods. Ghrelin-suppressing foods are rich in high-quality protein (specifically lean animal proteins), fiber, vitamins and minerals, and water. When you combine multiple G-List ghrelin-suppressing foods, you get to eat much more. The best G-List foods have a lot of volume for fewer calories, and as I explained in Chapter 3, that creates thermogenesis (heat production), which raises your metabolic rate.

JOIN THE CLEAN-PLATE CLUB

Provided you've chosen the right amount of food, be sure to clean your plate, even if you feel full before you're done. It's important to complete your meals so that you fully suppress ghrelin until your next meal. If you need to lose weight, chances are you don't remember what it feels like to be healthfully full. Most people have grown so accustomed to "starved" or "stuffed" that it all feels normal. But when you eat (and complete) your ghrelin meals, you're setting a new healthy "normal" with your sense of hunger and fullness. By completing your full meals within one sitting of about 30 to 60 minutes, your ghrelin levels will come into balance and you'll experience healthy ghrelin hunger and fullness.

LET THE CALORIES TAKE CARE OF THEMSELVES

The meal plans are based on G-List portions. If you measure your food accurately, the calories will balance out. You're not required to count calories on the Belly Fat Fix. But if you've ever counted calories in the past and just can't stop yourself from counting them now—or if you're paying close attention to the calories in your meal plan—you may notice they don't always add up perfectly. This is why I've included the calories of your G-List foods; the calories are a backup reference to help you double-check your food portions. I did this because the calories in food, even within the same food category, vary a bit. If you notice a difference of, say, 10 to 15 calories, it's no big deal. This will not affect your weight loss. But if you notice

COACHING TIP

HOLD THE FRUIT! Feeling overfull at the end of a meal? Save some of it for later. You can wait about 20 to 30 minutes to have your fruit.

BREAD BASICS When buying bread, search for varieties that contain 70 to 80 calories per slice. This way you can just enjoy the bread—without having to worry about how much of that slice you can or can't eat.

that the calories in food are *way* different from the G-List food, you should adjust the food to match. For instance, let's say you have whole wheat bread that's 110 calories per slice. On the G-List, a serving of bread is 75 calories. That means you have to have a smaller portion of that bread—about two-thirds of a slice. That's why I included the calories on your meal plan chart. Sometimes you'll have to portion out less than what your meal plan is calling for, and sometimes you'll get to portion out more. Different food manufacturers make foods in various sizes. If you scour your grocery store's bread aisle, you'll notice some major differences between different brands. Part of the obesity epidemic in this country stems from the fact that portions made by manufacturers differ so much from true serving sizes. (Review Portion Control—The Next Piece of the Puzzle on page 104 in Chapter 4.)

Don't get anxious about this. I've already devised a plan so that you don't have to eat, say, two-thirds a slice of bread. To make this easy, I researched exactly which foods and brands fit with the true portion sizes on the Belly Fat Fix plan. You'll see in your prebuilt meal plan and grocery list that certain foods are listed as particular brand items. If you buy them, you won't have to worry about having to eat only two-thirds of a slice of whole wheat bread. In my opinion, that's really annoying. If I had to do this, I'd hate it. That's why I'd never ask you to, either. Just buy exactly what I tell you to buy, enjoy the food, and lose the weight.

There are some foods that naturally vary in calories and have nothing to do with food manufacturing. Take protein, for example: 95 percent lean beef versus chicken breast versus white fish. A 2-ounce portion of beef is 90 calories; a 2-ounce portion of chicken breast is 75 calories; a 3-ounce portion of white fish is 75 calories. That's because different types of animal protein vary in fluid content and fat. As long as you're varying your protein, and portioning according to your meal plan, calorie fluctuations like this won't affect your overall weight loss.

JoAnn B.

AGE: 55

POUNDS LOST:

FAST-TRACK: 5

TOTAL: 23 in 90 days

OVERALL INCHES LOST: 19.5

Need proof that the Belly Fat Fix works? Look no further than JoAnn B.'s closet, where all her clothes are a couple of sizes smaller than they were before. "I'm down from a size 12 to almost an 8, and I plan to keep going," says JoAnn.

Exciting results—and simple, too. "I had a great experience on this plan," says JoAnn, "and it was easy to follow—unlike other diets I've tried. The meals have been a snap to prepare, and after I eat, I feel full. In fact, at times it seemed like too much food, but I went ahead and ate it anyway, so I wouldn't get hungry later."

 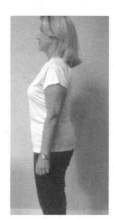

BEFORE   AFTER

Before the plan, JoAnn rarely ate on a regular schedule, and she hardly ever ate breakfast. "Like so many people my age, I was always under the impression you have to cut calories to almost nil to even lose a pound," she explains. "So I was delighted when Marjorie insisted that I could lose weight on *more* calories."

JoAnn's biggest challenge? Getting into the routine of eating at the right times for her body. She also had to pull herself out of the rut of fast-food lunches—and that meant preparing lunch ahead of time, which at first seemed like a major chore. But within a week, she was in the groove. "I kept at it religiously, and it got easier," she says.

JoAnn dropped a very encouraging 5 pounds during her 3-Day Fast-Track. Then she went straight on to the Belly Fat Fix plan, and the pounds melted at a steady pace. Much of the time, she used the food tracker to record what she ate and how she felt.

She jumped right into the exercise plan, too, adding—and loving—Zumba dance classes. Though a knee injury and a long recovery derailed her exercise program, she continued to lose weight, thanks to the healthy, pound-peeling Belly Fat Fix.

When it comes to the Belly Fat Fix, JoAnn's a true believer, and she's got some good advice for anyone who'd like to give it a try. "It may seem over-whelming, but it really isn't," she says. "At least give it a month—but I bet it won't take that long until you decide to stick with it. Once you're on it for a week, you'll be happy with the results."

GET BACK ON TRACK

The perception that you can somehow "make up" today for all the food you overate yesterday is diet blasphemy. Your body simply doesn't work this way. There's no "making up" for your overeating. That's because ghrelin works on an hourly schedule. Your hormonal system doesn't have a memory of yesterday; it's functioning to keep you alive today. You can, however, balance your ghrelin today by following your full meal plan—or better yet, following the Fast-Track if you need to rebalance it.

EAT YOUR VEGGIES

The Belly Fat Fix is easily adaptable for ovo-lacto vegetarians. Vegetarian proteins fall into the ghrelin-neutral list and should be paired with G-List ghrelin-suppressing carbs and fats for maximum ghrelin suppression. You'll find vegetarian recipes in Chapter 7. You can easily modify a recipe to make it vegetarian by using your G-List to swap a meat protein for a G-List vegetarian protein.

THE GHRELIN PREBUILT 7-DAY MEAL PLANS

Now it's time to get down to business. If you've read carefully, you know exactly which meal plan to follow; you know that every meal is interchangeable; you know how to switch foods that you a) don't like or b) don't have on hand. This prebuilt meal plan is your guide. If you're ever unsure of what to eat, or how much, simply refer to the following pages. Enjoy delicious, healthy foods while you watch the pounds disappear.

Note: The Ghrelin menus are based on cooked portions unless otherwise stated.

COACHING TIP

COLOR CUES Put a colored paper clip on day 1 on the next page, so you can quickly and easily flip open the book to see your prebuilt meal plan anytime.

The Ghrelin Prebuilt 7-Day Meal Plans

DAY 1	1,400	1,600	1,800
BREAKFAST			
Arnold Healthfull 10 Grain Bread	2 slices toast	2 slices toast	3 slices toast
Fat-free plain Greek yogurt	⅔ cup yogurt	1 cup yogurt	1⅓ cups yogurt
Strawberries	1 cup strawberries	1 cup strawberries	1 cup strawberries
Sunflower seeds			
LUNCH			
Frozen corn	⅔ cup corn	⅔ cup corn	⅔ cup corn
5-ounce can tuna in water, drained	½ can tuna	1 can tuna	1 can tuna
Low-fat shredded cheese	1½ ounces cheese	1½ ounces cheese	1 ½ ounces cheese
Mixed salad greens	1 teaspoon olive oil	1 teaspoon olive oil	2 teaspoons olive oil
Tomato	1 tablespoon balsamic vinegar	1 tablespoon balsamic vinegar	1 tablespoon balsamic vinegar
Olive oil	1 cup salad greens	1 cup salad greens	1 cup salad greens
Balsamic vinegar	1 tomato	1 tomato	1 tomato
Dried cranberries	2 tablespoons dried cranberries	2 tablespoons dried cranberries	2 tablespoons dried cranberries
SNACK			
Fat-free deli meat	1 ounce deli meat	1 ounce deli meat	1 ounce deli meat
Laughing Cow Light cheese wedges	1 cheese wedge	1 cheese wedge	1 cheese wedge
Wasa Sourdough Crispbread	2 Wasa crackers	2 Wasa crackers	2 Wasa crackers
Small apple	Small apple	Small apple	Small apple
DINNER			
Brown rice	⅓ cup brown rice	⅔ cup brown rice	⅔ cup brown rice
Shrimp, frozen	9 ounces shrimp	9 ounces shrimp	9 ounces shrimp
Pine nuts	1 tablespoon pine nuts	1 tablespoon pine nuts	2 tablespoons pine nuts
Broccoli	1 cup cooked broccoli	1 cup cooked broccoli	1 cup cooked broccoli
Grapefruit	1 small grapefruit	1 small grapefruit	1 small grapefruit

2,000	2,200/2,400	Preparation

3 slices toast
1⅓ cups yogurt
1 cup strawberries
1 tablespoon
  sunflower seeds
	3 slices toast
	1⅓ cups yogurt
	1½ cups strawberries
	1 tablespoon
	  sunflower seeds
		Slice the strawberries into a small bowl. Add the yogurt and sunflower seeds, if appropriate, and mix. Spread on the toast or use strips of the toast to dip.

1 cup corn
1 can tuna
1 ½ ounces cheese
2 teaspoons olive oil
1 tablespoon
  balsamic vinegar
1 cup salad greens
1 tomato
2 tablespoons
  dried cranberries
	1 cup corn
	1 can tuna
	1½ ounces cheese
	2 teaspoons olive oil
	1 tablespoon
	  balsamic vinegar
	2 cups salad greens
	1 tomato
	3 tablespoons
	  dried cranberries
		Mix together the corn, tuna, cheese, greens, tomato, oil, vinegar, and cranberries. Add additional seasonings, if desired.

1 ounce deli meat 1 cheese wedge 2 Wasa crackers Small apple	1 ounce deli meat 1 cheese wedge 2 Wasa crackers Small apple 2,400 *Double Snack*	Slice the apple. Spread the cheese on the slices or on the crackers. Top with chunks of deli meat.

1 cup brown rice
9 ounces shrimp
2 tablespoons pine
  nuts
2 cups cooked
  broccoli
1 small grapefruit
	1 cup brown rice
	9 ounces shrimp
	2 tablespoons pine
	  nuts
	2 cups cooked
	  broccoli
	1 large grapefruit
		Cook the rice according to the package directions, but without adding fat. Steam the broccoli separately. In a nonstick pan sprayed with cooking oil, cook the shrimp and pine nuts. Season with salt, pepper, and paprika.
		
		When shrimp is cooked, toss it together with the rice and broccoli. Serve hot. Serve the grapefruit on the side.

The Ghrelin Prebuilt 7-Day Meal Plans—cont.

DAY 2	1,400	1,600	1,800
BREAKFAST			
Cheerios cereal Fat-free milk Walnuts Blueberries	1⅓ cups Cheerios ⅔ cup milk 1 cup blueberries	1⅓ cups Cheerios 1 cup milk 1 cup blueberries	2 cups Cheerios 1⅓ cups milk 1 cup blueberries
LUNCH			
Red pepper hummus Chicken breast Avocado Shredded carrots Cucumber Romaine lettuce leaves Cantaloupe cubes	¼ cup hummus 4 ounces chicken breast 2 tablespoons avocado ¼ cup shredded carrots 1 small cucumber 3 romaine leaves 1 cup cantaloupe	¼ cup hummus 6 ounces chicken breast 2 tablespoons avocado ¼ cup shredded carrots 1 small cucumber 3 romaine leaves 1 cup cantaloupe	¼ cup hummus 6 ounces chicken breast 4 tablespoons avocado ¼ cup shredded carrots 1 small cucumber 3 romaine leaves 1 cup cantaloupe
SNACK			
Low-fat cheese stick La Tortilla Low Carb Original Tortilla Granny Smith apple	1 cheese stick 1 tortilla Small apple	1 cheese stick 1 tortilla Small apple	1 cheese stick 1 tortilla Small apple
DINNER			
Baked potato Ground turkey Sour cream Onion and pepper mix, chopped Orange	3 ounces baked potato 6 ounces turkey 2 tablespoons sour cream 1 cup onion and pepper mix Orange	6 ounces baked potato 6 ounces turkey 2 tablespoons sour cream 1 cup onion and pepper mix Orange	6 ounces baked potato 6 ounces turkey 4 tablespoons sour cream 1 cup onion and pepper mix Orange

2,000	2,200/2,400	Preparation
2 cups Cheerios 1⅓ cups milk 4 walnut halves 1 cup blueberries	2 cups Cheerios 1⅓ cups milk 8 walnut halves 1½ cups blueberries	Top the cereal with the milk, blueberries, and walnut halves, if using.
⅓ cup hummus 6 ounces chicken breast 4 tablespoons avocado ¼ cup shredded carrots 1 small cucumber 3 romaine leaves 1 cup cantaloupe	⅓ cup hummus 6 ounces chicken breast 4 tablespoons avocado ¼ cup shredded carrots 1 small cucumber 3 romaine leaves 1½ cups cantaloupe	Chop the chicken into small pieces. Mix it with the hummus, avocado, and carrots. Wrap the mixture in romaine lettuce leaves. Slice the cucumber. Serve the cucumber and cantaloupe on the side.
1 cheese stick 1 tortilla Small apple	1 cheese stick 1 tortilla Small apple 2,400 *Double Snack*	Wrap the cheese stick with the tortilla. Serve the apple on the side.
9 ounces baked potato 6 ounces turkey 4 tablespoons sour cream 1 cup onion and pepper mix Orange	9 ounces baked potato 6 ounces turkey 4 tablespoons sour cream 2 cups onion and pepper mix Large orange	Brown the turkey with the chopped onions and peppers. Add salt, pepper, oregano, and garlic to taste. Warm the potato, then open it from end to end and fill with the turkey mixture and sour cream. Serve the fruit on the side.

The Ghrelin Prebuilt 7-Day Meal Plans—cont.

DAY 3	1,400	1,600	1,800
BREAKFAST			
Thomas' 100% whole grain English muffin Laughing Cow Light cheese wedges Whole almonds Granny Smith apple	1 English muffin 2 cheese wedges Small apple	1 English muffin 3 cheese wedges Small apple	1½ English muffins 4 cheese wedges Small apple
LUNCH			
Whole wheat pasta Tofu chucks Edamame, frozen and shelled Steamer bag veggie mix Olive oil Mixed fruit salad	1 cup pasta 2 ounces tofu ⅓ cup edamame 1 teaspoon olive oil 1 cup steamed veggies 4 ounces fruit salad	1 cup pasta 4 ounces tofu ⅓ cup edamame 1 teaspoon olive oil 1 cup steamed veggies 4 ounces fruit salad	1 cup pasta 4 ounces tofu ⅓ cup edamame 2 teaspoons olive oil 1 cup steamed veggies 4 ounces fruit salad
SNACK			
Fat-free cottage cheese Fiber One cereal Slivered almonds	½ cup cottage cheese ½ cup Fiber One 1 tablespoon almonds	½ cup cottage cheese ½ cup Fiber One 1 tablespoon almonds	½ cup cottage cheese ½ cup Fiber One 1 tablespoon almonds
DINNER			
Black beans, rinsed and drained Eggs and egg whites Raw spinach and chopped tomato mixed Avocado Kiwifruit	⅓ cup black beans 2 eggs 4 egg whites 1 cup spinach and tomato mix 2 tablespoons avocado 2 small kiwifruit	⅔ cup black beans 2 eggs 4 egg whites 1 cup spinach and tomato mix 2 tablespoons avocado 2 small kiwifruit	⅔ cup black beans 2 eggs 4 egg whites 1 cup spinach and tomato mix 4 tablespoons avocado 2 small kiwifruit

2,000	2,200/2,400	Preparation
1½ English muffins 4 cheese wedges 10 whole almonds Small apple	1½ English muffins 4 cheese wedges 10 whole almonds Large apple	Seed and thinly slice the apple. Toast the English muffin, spread with the cheese, and top with the apple slices. Serve the almonds on the side, if appropriate.
1½ cups pasta 4 ounces tofu ⅓ cup edamame 2 teaspoons olive oil 1 cup steamed veggies 4 ounces fruit salad	1½ cups pasta 4 ounces tofu ⅓ cup edamame 2 teaspoons olive oil 1½ cups steamed veggies 6 ounces fruit salad	Cook the pasta and the veggie steamer bag separately, as directed. While hot, combine the pasta, edamame, tofu, and oil. Add salt and pepper to taste. Serve hot. Serve the fruit salad on the side.
½ cup cottage cheese ½ cup Fiber One 1 tablespoon almonds	½ cup cottage cheese ½ cup Fiber One 1 tablespoon almonds 2,400 *Double Snack*	Mix the cottage cheese, cereal, and almonds. Add vanilla extract or cinnamon, if desired.
1 cup black beans 2 eggs 4 egg whites 1 cup spinach and tomato mix 4 tablespoons avocado 2 small kiwifruit	1 cup black beans 2 eggs 4 egg whites 2 cups spinach and tomato mix 4 tablespoons avocado 3 small kiwifruit	Beat the eggs and egg whites with salt and pepper. Heat a nonstick skillet coated with cooking spray over medium heat. Combine the eggs, beans, spinach, and chopped tomato and add to the skillet. When cooked, top with the avocado. Serve the kiwifruit on the side.

The Ghrelin Prebuilt 7-Day Meal Plans—cont.

DAY 4	1,400	1,600	1,800
BREAKFAST			
Thomas' plain Mini Bagels Applegate turkey sausage links Butter Melon	1 mini bagel 2 turkey sausage links 1 cup cut melon	1 mini bagel 3 turkey sausage links 1 cup cut melon	1 mini bagel 4 turkey sausage links 1 cup cut melon
LUNCH			
Arnold Real Jewish Marble Rye Bread Amy's California Veggie Burgers Mayonnaise Lettuce/tomato/onion Sliced cucumber Grapes	2 slices rye bread 1 veggie burger 1 tablespoon mayonnaise 2 lettuce leaves 2 slices tomato 2 slices onion 1 cup sliced cucumber 4 ounces grapes	2 slices rye bread 1½ veggie burgers 1 tablespoon mayonnaise 2 lettuce leaves 2 slices tomato 2 slices onion 1 cup sliced cucumber 4 ounces grapes	2 slices rye bread 1½ veggie burgers 2 tablespoons mayonnaise 2 lettuce leaves 2 slices tomato 2 slices onion 1 cup sliced cucumber 4 ounces grapes
SNACK			
Fat-free cottage cheese Pineapple chunks, drained Ground flaxseed	½ cup cottage cheese 4 ounces pineapple 2 tablespoons flaxseed	½ cup cottage cheese 4 ounces pineapple 2 tablespoons flaxseed	½ cup cottage cheese 4 ounces pineapple 2 tablespoons flaxseed
DINNER			
Quinoa Pork loin Olive oil Kale Baby carrots Raisins	⅓ cup quinoa 6 ounces pork loin 1 teaspoon olive oil ½ cup steamed kale ½ cup baby carrots 2 tablespoons raisins	⅔ cup quinoa 6 ounces pork loin 1 teaspoon olive oil ½ cup steamed kale ½ cup baby carrots 2 tablespoons raisins	⅔ cup quinoa 6 ounces pork loin 2 teaspoons olive oil ½ cup steamed kale ½ cup baby carrots 2 tablespoons raisins

2,000	2,200/2,400	Preparation
1½ mini bagels 4 turkey sausage links 1 teaspoon butter 1 cup cut melon	1½ mini bagels 4 turkey sausage links 1 teaspoon butter 1½ cups cut melon	Toast the mini bagel and spread with butter, if appropriate. Heat the turkey sausage in the microwave. Assemble and serve hot. Serve the melon on the side.
2 slices rye bread 1½ veggie burgers 2 tablespoons mayonnaise 2 lettuce leaves 2 slices tomato 2 slices onion 1 cup sliced cucumber 6 ounces grapes	2 slices rye bread 1½ veggie burgers 2 tablespoons mayonnaise 2 lettuce leaves 2 slices tomato 2 slices onion 2 cups sliced cucumber 6 ounces grapes	Heat the veggie burger in the microwave or in a dry skillet. Assemble the sandwich. Serve the grapes on the side.
½ cup cottage cheese 4 ounces pineapple 2 tablespoons flaxseed	½ cup cottage cheese 4 ounces pineapple 2 tablespoons flaxseed 2,400 *Double Snack*	Mix the cottage cheese, pineapple, and flaxseed.
1 cup quinoa 6 ounces pork loin 2 teaspoons olive oil ½ cup steamed kale ½ cup baby carrots 2 tablespoons raisins	1 cup quinoa 6 ounces pork loin 2 teaspoons olive oil 1 cup steamed kale ½ cup baby carrots 3 tablespoons raisins	Preheat oven to 325°F. Rub the pork with half the oil and season with salt, pepper, and rosemary. Mix baby carrots with remaining oil. Place pork and carrots in a baking pan and cover with foil. Bake for 60 minutes, or until a thermometer inserted in center of pork registers 155°F. Meanwhile, prepare quinoa according to package directions. When done, fluff with a fork and mix in raisins. Serve pork and carrots over quinoa and kale.

The Ghrelin Prebuilt 7-Day Meal Plans—cont.

DAY 5	1,400	1,600	1,800
BREAKFAST			
Steel-cut oats	¼ cup uncooked oats	¼ cup uncooked oats	⅓ cup uncooked oats
Fat-free milk	⅔ cup milk	1 cup milk	1⅓ cups milk
Peanut butter	4 ounces banana	4 ounces banana	4 ounces banana
Banana	(½ medium)	(½ medium)	(½ medium)
LUNCH			
Thomas' Sahara Pita Pockets 100% whole wheat	½ pita	½ pita	½ pita
Corn kernels	⅓ cup corn	⅓ cup corn	⅓ cup corn
Hard-cooked eggs	1 hard-cooked egg	2 hard-cooked eggs	2 hard-cooked eggs
Hard-cooked egg whites	4 egg whites	4 egg whites	4 egg whites
Avocado	2 tablespoons avocado	2 tablespoons avocado	4 tablespoons avocado
Dijon mustard	1 teaspoon Dijon mustard	1 teaspoon Dijon mustard	1 teaspoon Dijon mustard
Cilantro, chopped	2 tablespoons cilantro	2 tablespoons cilantro	2 tablespoons cilantro
Tomato, sliced	1 tomato	1 tomato	1 tomato
Baby spinach	5 baby spinach leaves	5 baby spinach leaves	5 baby spinach leaves
Grapefruit	1 small grapefruit	1 small grapefruit	1 small grapefruit
SNACK			
Low-fat cheese stick	1 cheese stick	1 cheese stick	1 cheese stick
Hummus	2 tablespoons hummus	2 tablespoons hummus	2 tablespoons hummus
Celery sticks	3 celery sticks	3 celery sticks	3 celery sticks
DINNER			
Buckwheat pasta	½ cup pasta	1 cup pasta	1 cup pasta
95% lean ground beef	6 ounces lean beef	6 ounces lean beef	6 ounces lean beef
Parmesan cheese	1 tablespoon Parmesan	1 tablespoon Parmesan	1 tablespoon Parmesan
DeLallo Marinara fat-free Sauce	¼ cup marinara sauce	¼ cup marinara sauce	¼ cup marinara sauce
Mixed salad	1½ cups salad	1½ cups salad	1 ½ cups salad
Low-fat dressing	1 tablespoon dressing	1 tablespoon dressing	2 tablespoons dressing
Peach, sliced	1 small peach	1 small peach	1 small peach

2,000	2,200/2,400	Preparation
⅓ cup uncooked oats 1⅓ cups milk 1½ teaspoons peanut butter 4 ounces banana (½ medium)	⅓ cup uncooked oats 1⅓ cups milk 1 tablespoon peanut butter 6 ounces banana (⅔ medium)	Prepare the oatmeal as directed using milk. Add the peanut butter, if appropriate, and top with banana, sliced.
1 pita ⅓ cup corn 2 hard-cooked eggs 4 egg whites 4 tablespoons avocado 1 teaspoon Dijon mustard 2 tablespoons cilantro 1 tomato 5 baby spinach leaves 1 small grapefruit	1 pita ⅓ cup corn 2 hard-cooked eggs 4 egg whites 4 tablespoons avocado 1 teaspoon Dijon mustard 2 tablespoons cilantro 2 tomatoes 5 baby spinach leaves 1 large grapefruit	Combine the eggs, avocado, corn, mustard, and cilantro. Season with salt and pepper, if desired. Fill the pita with the egg mixture, tomatoes, and spinach. Serve the grapefruit on the side.
1 cheese stick 2 tablespoons hummus 3 celery sticks	1 cheese stick 2 tablespoons hummus 3 celery sticks 2,400 *Double Snack*	Tear the cheese stick lengthwise into 3 to 5 strips, place the strips into the celery sticks, and top with the hummus.
1½ cups pasta 6 ounces lean beef 1 tablespoon Parmesan ¼ cup marinara sauce 1½ cups salad 2 tablespoons dressing 1 small peach	1½ cups pasta 6 ounces lean beef 1 tablespoon Parmesan ½ cup marinara sauce 2 cups salad 2 tablespoons dressing 1 large peach	Cook the pasta according to the package directions. Meanwhile, brown the beef in a skillet, then drain the excess fat. Add the marinara sauce and heat through. Toss in the cooked pasta. Serve hot topped with the cheese. Mix the salad with your favorite low-fat dressing. Serve peach on the side.

The Ghrelin Prebuilt 7-Day Meal Plans—cont.

DAY 6	1,400	1,600	1,800
BREAKFAST Fiber One cereal Silk Original almond milk Almonds, chopped Strawberries, sliced	⅔ cup Fiber One ⅔ cup almond milk 1 cup strawberries	1⅓ cups Fiber One 1 cup almond milk 1 cup strawberries	1⅓ cups Fiber One 1⅓ cups almond milk 1 cup strawberries
LUNCH Chickpeas Baked chicken breast Low-fat Caesar dressing Salad greens Red onion, chopped Granny Smith apple	⅔ cup chickpeas 4 ounces chicken breast 1 tablespoon Caesar dressing 2 cups salad greens ¼ cup onion 1 small apple	⅔ cup chickpeas 6 ounces chicken breast 1 tablespoon Caesar dressing 2 cups salad greens ¼ cup onion 1 small apple	⅔ cup chickpeas 6 ounces chicken breast 2 tablespoons Caesar dressing 2 cups salad greens ¼ cup onion 1 small apple
SNACK Edamame Whole wheat couscous Pine nuts	⅓ cup edamame ⅓ cup couscous 1 tablespoon pine nuts	⅓ cup edamame ⅓ cup couscous 1 tablespoon pine nuts	⅓ cup edamame ⅓ cup couscous 1 tablespoon pine nuts
DINNER Sweet potato, baked Top sirloin steak Low-fat Italian dressing Sour cream Broccoli, steamed Mango chunks	3 ounces sweet potato 6 ounces steak 1 tablespoon sour cream 1 cup steamed broccoli 4 ounces mango chunks	6 ounces sweet potato 6 ounces steak 1 tablespoon sour cream 1 cup steamed broccoli 4 ounces mango chunks	6 ounces sweet potato 6 ounces steak 2 tablespoons sour cream 1 cup steamed broccoli 4 ounces mango chunks

2,000	2,200/2,400	Preparation
1⅓ cups Fiber One 1⅓ cups almond milk 1 tablespoon almonds 1 cup strawberries	1⅓ cups Fiber One 1⅓ cups almond milk 1 tablespoon almonds 1½ cups strawberries	Combine the cereal and milk. Top with the almonds, if appropriate, and the sliced strawberries.
1 cup chickpeas 6 ounces chicken breast 2 tablespoons Caesar dressing 2 cups salad greens ¼ cup onion 1 small apple	1 cup chickpeas 6 ounces chicken breast 2 tablespoons Caesar dressing 3 cups salad greens ¼ cup onion 1 small apple	Slice the cooked chicken and set aside. Dice the apple and mix with the chickpeas, dressing, salad greens, and onion. Top with the sliced chicken.
⅓ cup edamame ⅓ cup couscous 1 tablespoon pine nuts	⅔ cup edamame ⅔ cup couscous 2 tablespoons pine nuts 2,400 *Double Snack*	Mix the edamame, couscous, and pine nuts together with salt and pepper to taste.
9 ounces sweet potato 6 ounces steak 2 tablespoons sour cream 1 cup steamed broccoli 4 ounces mango chunks	9 ounces sweet potato 6 ounces steak 2 tablespoons sour cream 2 cups steamed broccoli 6 ounces mango chunks	Marinate the steak in the dressing overnight. Preheat the oven to 425°F. Puncture the potato in several places with a fork and wrap in foil. Place the potato in the oven alongside the steak. Bake the steak for 25 minutes, or until cooked to the desired temperature. Let stand for 5 minutes before serving. Bake the potato for 20 to 30 minutes. Top with the sour cream and a side of steamed broccoli. Serve the mango on the side.

The Ghrelin Prebuilt 7-Day Meal Plans—cont.

DAY 7	1,400	1,600	1,800
BREAKFAST			
Thomas' Sahara 100% Whole Wheat Wraps	1 wrap	1 wrap	1½ wraps
Hard-cooked egg whites	2 hard-cooked egg whites	4 hard-cooked egg whites	6 hard-cooked egg whites
Laughing Cow Light cheese wedges	1 cheese wedge	1 cheese wedge	1 cheese wedge
Large black olives	1 small pear	1 small pear	1 small pear
Pear			
LUNCH			
Quinoa	⅔ cup quinoa	⅔ cup quinoa	⅔ cup quinoa
Canned salmon, water-packed	4 ounces canned salmon	6 ounces canned salmon	6 ounces canned salmon
Olive oil	1 teaspoon olive oil	1 teaspoon olive oil	2 teaspoons olive oil
Spinach leaves	1 cup spinach leaves	1 cup spinach leaves	1 cup spinach leaves
Onion, chopped	¼ cup onion	¼ cup onion	¼ cup onion
Tomato, chopped	½ tomato	½ tomato	½ tomato
Mixed fruit cup	4 ounces mixed fruit cup	4 ounces mixed fruit cup	4 ounces mixed fruit cup
SNACK			
Fat-free deli ham	2 ounces deli ham	2 ounces deli ham	2 ounces deli ham
Athenos Baked Pita Chips	7 baked pita chips	7 baked pita chips	7 baked pita chips
Pineapple salsa	2 tablespoons pineapple salsa	2 tablespoons pineapple salsa	2 tablespoons pineapple salsa
DINNER			
Cooked brown rice and corn, in equal amounts	⅓ cup brown rice and corn	⅔ cup brown rice and corn	⅔ cup brown rice and corn
Tilapia	9 ounces tilapia	9 ounces tilapia	9 ounces tilapia
Canola oil	1 teaspoon canola oil	1 teaspoon canola oil	2 teaspoons canola oil
Red and yellow bell peppers, thinly sliced	1 cup peppers	1 cup peppers	1 cup peppers
Frozen blueberries	1 cup blueberries	1 cup blueberries	1 cup blueberries

2,000	2,200/2,400	Preparation
1½ wraps 6 hard-cooked egg whites 1 cheese wedge 5 large black olives 1 small pear	1½ wraps 6 hard-cooked egg whites 1 cheese wedge 5 large black olives 1 medium pear	Chop the eggs and the olives, if appropriate. Warm with the cheese in a microwave oven for 10 seconds. Wrap up. Serve the pear on the side.
1 cup quinoa 6 ounces canned salmon 2 teaspoons olive oil 1 cup spinach leaves ¼ cup onion ½ tomato 4 ounces mixed fruit cup	1 cup quinoa 6 ounces canned salmon 2 teaspoons olive oil 2 cups spinach leaves ¼ cup onion ½ tomato 6 ounces mixed fruit cup	Cook the quinoa with water, according to the package directions. Drain the salmon. Mix the quinoa, salmon, and oil together. Serve over the spinach, tomato, and onion. Serve the fruit cup on the side.
2 ounces deli ham 7 baked pita chips 2 tablespoons pineapple salsa	2 ounces deli ham 7 baked pita chips 2 tablespoons pineapple salsa 2,400 *Double Snack*	Dice the ham into small pieces and mix with the salsa. Dip with the pita chips.
1 cup brown rice and corn 9 ounces tilapia 2 teaspoons canola oil 2 cups peppers 1 cup blueberries	1 cup brown rice and corn 9 ounces tilapia 2 teaspoons canola oil 2 cups peppers 1½ cups blueberries	Warm a skillet on medium heat and coat with half the oil. Rub the remaining oil on the tilapia and season with salt and lemon pepper. Sauté the tilapia with the sliced peppers for 4 or 5 minutes on each side, flipping twice. Warm the rice and corn. Serve the blueberries on the side.

Ghrelin-Friendly Snacks

In addition to the prebuilt meal plan, I've included an extra 30 ghrelin-friendly snacks for you to choose from. All the snacks are about 200 calories. This is important because your snack needs to be substantial enough to suppress your ghrelin all the way to dinner. Remember from Chapter 2 how ghrelin rises slightly between the hours of 1:00 and 3:00 p.m.? For a refresher, go back and reread the "Snack Time!" sidebar on page 47.

I created this snack list for two purposes: 1) to suppress your ghrelin long enough to reach dinnertime and 2) to keep your taste buds excited and satisfied. If you think some of these snacks look too good to be true and that they can't possibly fit into your diet, trust me—they do. I meticulously calculated every single one of them. The calories are even listed for you. There are 10 savory and crunchy, 10 sweet and creamy, and 10 quick and easy snacks. You can have one snack per day. The ideal time to eat your snack is between lunch and dinner. But if your schedule is unpredictable, have your snack in between the two meals that are spaced farthest apart.

30 Quick and Delicious Ghrelin Snacks

SAVORY AND CRUNCHY

1 Yogurt-Dill Veggie Dip *(210 calories total)*

⅔ cup fat-free plain Greek yogurt (80)

1 teaspoon olive oil (45)

½ teaspoon garlic powder

1 tablespoon chopped dill

1 cup sliced cucumber (25)

5 whole wheat saltines (60)

Mix the yogurt, oil, garlic powder, and dill together. Use the cucumber and crackers for dipping.

2 Meaty Potato Snack *(190 calories)*

3-ounce baked potato (75)

2 ounces cooked lean ground turkey (80)

½ ounce low-fat Cheddar cheese (25)

2 tablespoons salsa (10)

Top the potato with the turkey and cheese; heat in a microwave oven for 1 minute. Serve with the salsa on top.

3 Mini Smoked Salmon Sandwich *(200 calories)*

Thomas' whole grain English muffin (120)

1 tablespoon low-fat cream cheese (35)

1 ounce smoked salmon (35)

1 tablespoon capers (5)

1 slice tomato (3)

1 slice onion (2)

Toast the muffin and spread with the cream cheese. Top with the salmon, capers, tomato, and onion. Serve as a sandwich.

4 Honey Ham and Spinach Spread *(208 calories)*

2 ounces fat-free honey ham, chopped (70)

⅓ cup fat-free Greek yogurt (40)

¼ cup frozen chopped spinach, thawed (7)

¼ teaspoon each of salt, pepper, garlic powder, onion powder

1½ Wasa sesame crackers (90)

Mix it with the yogurt, spinach, and seasonings. Use as a spread on the crackers.

5 Egg White and Chickpea Salad *(193 calories)*

4 cooked egg whites, chopped (75)

¼ cup fat-free salsa (20)

⅓ cup chickpeas (73)

2 tablespoon low-fat shredded Cheddar cheese (25)

Mix the eggs, salsa, chickpeas, and cheese.

6 Garlic and Spice Popcorn *(187 calories)*

3 cups air-popped popcorn (92)

1 teaspoon olive oil (45)

2 tablespoons grated Parmesan cheese (50)

¼ teaspoon garlic powder

Mix the popcorn with the oil. Top with the cheese and garlic powder.

7 Open-Faced Creamy Bean Sandwich *(195 calories)*

½ Thomas' whole grain English muffin (70)

2 tablespoons Trader Joe spicy black bean dip (30)

1 Laughing Cow Light cheese wedge (35)

4-ounce Granny Smith apple, sliced (60)

Toast the muffin. Spread on the bean dip and the cheese. Top with the apple slices—or enjoy the apple on the side.

8 Chipotle Cottage Cheese Spread *(195 calories)*

¼ cup fat-free cottage cheese (40)

¼ cup chipotle salsa (30)

2 tablespoons avocado (45)

1 slice Arnold Real Jewish Marble Rye bread (80)

Mix the cheese, salsa, and avocado. Top it on the toasted bread.

9 Veggie Burger, Avocado, and Rice *(207 calories)*

1 MorningStar Farms veggie burger (110)

⅓ cup cooked brown rice (75)

1 tablespoon avocado (22)

Cut the veggie burger into small pieces. Heat the burger and rice. Mix with the avocado and serve.

10 Open-Faced Pesto Chicken Sandwich *(188 calories)*

2 teaspoons pesto (38)

1 ounce sliced Italian bread (80)

2 ounces grilled boneless, skinless chicken breast (70)

Spread 1 teaspoon of the pesto on the bread. Spread the remaining pesto on the chicken. Place the chicken on the bread and warm in a microwave oven for 7 seconds.

I'm Still Hungry!

So now you understand how your hunger hormone works. But one thing science can't always answer is, *Why am I still hungry?* In Chapter 1, you learned about the different types of hunger. If you've been practicing mindfulness, you're starting to distinguish between them. But what happens when you've ruled out other hungers and you know you're truly ghrelin hungry, even though you've already eaten everything on your meal plan?

Here's what to do: Eat a ghrelin-friendly snack. Some days, you'll just be hungrier than others. Try one of the savory, animal-based protein snacks, because they have the highest ghrelin-suppressing effect. You're better off having a second snack for the day than dealing with elevated ghrelin.

SWEET AND CREAMY

1 Tropical Cottage Cheese *(201 calories)*

½ cup fat-free cottage cheese (80)

½ cup water-packed pineapple chunks, drained (45)

2 tablespoons unsweetened shredded coconut (76)

Mix the cottage cheese, pineapple, and coconut together. Serve chilled.

2 Fruity Cinnamon Raisin Toast *(195 calories)*

1 slice whole wheat cinnamon raisin bread (80)

2 tablespoons low-fat strawberry cream cheese (70)

½ cup mashed blueberries (45)

Toast the bread, spread with the cream cheese, and top with the mashed berries.

3 Kiwifruit Yogurt Parfait *(211 calories)*

⅔ cup fat-free plain Greek yogurt (80)

1 kiwifruit, chopped (50)

½ cup Fiber One cereal (60)

1 teaspoon honey (21)

Layer the yogurt, kiwifruit, and cereal. Top with the honey.

4 Frozen Berry Bliss *(209 calories)*

3 honey-wheat pretzel twists (33)

½ cup strawberries (25)

½ cup blueberries (40)

1 cup Blue Diamond unsweetened almond milk (40)

2 tablespoons fat-free vanilla Greek yogurt (21)

1 teaspoon vanilla extract

1 tablespoon chopped walnuts (50)

Chop the pretzels into small pieces and set aside. Blend the strawberries, blueberries, milk, yogurt, and vanilla in a blender on low speed. Once blended, mix in the pretzels and nuts by hand. Freeze for 1 or more hours. Serve frozen.

5 Sweet Potato and Honey Pecan Mash *(191 calories)*

3-ounce sweet potato, baked and cooled (77)

⅓ cup fat-free plain Greek yogurt (40)

1 tablespoon chopped pecans (53)

1 teaspoon honey (21)

¼ teaspoon ground cinnamon

Mash the sweet potato and mix in the yogurt and nuts. Top with the honey and cinnamon.

6 Chocolate, Peach, and Coconut Milk *(207 calories)*

1 cup unsweetened So Delicious coconut milk (50)

½ cup frozen peaches (30)

½ tablespoon cocoa powder (6)

½ tablespoon peanut butter (46)

1 Kashi whole grain frozen waffle (75)

Blend the milk, peaches, and cocoa powder in a blender on low speed. Chill for 1 hour. Toast the waffle, top with the peanut butter, and serve on the side with the coconut beverage.

7 Chocolate Mousse and Oats *(196 calories)*

⅔ cup fat-free plain Greek yogurt (80)

½ tablespoon cocoa powder (6)

¼ cup rolled oats (75)

½ teaspoon vanilla extract

1 tablespoon mini dark chocolate chips (35)

Mix the yogurt, cocoa, oats, and vanilla. Melt the chocolate chips in a microwave oven for 6 seconds and blend into the yogurt mixture. Serve chilled or frozen.

8 Peanut Buttery Popcorn *(214 calories)*

1½ teaspoons creamy all-natural peanut butter (72)

2 tablespoons raisins (50)

3 cups air-popped popcorn (92)

¼ teaspoon ground cinnamon (optional)

Warm the peanut butter with the raisins for 6 to 8 seconds in a microwave oven. Drizzle the mixture over the popcorn and sprinkle with the cinnamon, if desired.

9 Mango-Sweetened Cottage Cheese and Sunflower Seeds *(195 calories)*

½ cup fat-free cottage cheese (80)

1 tablespoon light whipped cream cheese (30)

½ cup frozen mango chunks, thawed (40)

1 tablespoon sunflower seeds (45)

Mix the cottage cheese, cream cheese, and mango. Top with the seeds.

10 Almond Butter and Chocolate Cake Frozen Yogurt *(215 calories)*

1 tablespoon almond butter (85)

½ deep chocolate Vitatop muffin, crumbled (50)

¼ teaspoon vanilla extract

⅔ cup fat-free plain Greek yogurt (80)

Mix the almond butter, crumbled muffin, and vanilla into the yogurt. Freeze for 1 hour or longer before serving.

QUICK AND EASY

1   1 low-fat cheese stick (80) wrapped in 1 small high-fiber wrap (75) with a side of 1 tablespoon pine nuts (45)
Total = 200 calories

2   7 whole wheat saltines (67) topped with 2 ounces Starkist Tuna Creations Sweet & Spicy tuna packet (75), with 4-ounce apple (60)
Total = 202 calories

3   2 Laughing Cow Light cheese wedges (70) spread on a 6-ounce pear (80) with 1 cup baby carrots (50)
Total = 200 calories

4   1 tablespoon avocado (25) spread on 1 MorningStar Farms Garden Veggie Patty (110) on top of 1 slice whole wheat bread (80)
Total = 215 calories

5   ⅔ cup low-sodium tomato soup (74) with 1 low-fat cheese stick (80) and 5 large olives (45)
Total = 199 calories

6   1 Baby Bell white Cheddar cheese (75) wrapped in 2 ounces fat-free turkey (65) with 1 cup cantaloupe (60)
Total = 200 calories

7   1 tablespoon sunflower seeds (45) and 1 mandarin orange snack pack in water (80) mixed in 1 snack pack 1% cottage cheese (90)
Total = 215 calories

8   2 teaspoons peanut butter (60) spread on 2 rice cakes (80) and topped with ¼ cup mashed banana (50)
Total = 190 calories

9 ⅓ cup edamame (75) mixed with ½ cup cherry tomatoes (25), ¼ cup salsa (25), and ¼ cup shredded three-cheese blend (80)
Total = 205 calories

10 1 chopped hard-cooked egg (80) mixed with 1 teaspoon honey-Dijon mustard (10), wrapped in 1 high-fiber wrap (100)
Total = 190 calories

There you are. Now you have a month's worth of snacks to enjoy and absolutely no excuse to miss that afternoon snack. You'll avoid that slump that drives up your ghrelin levels and causes you to be ravenous at dinner.

Let's hope these whet your appetite for more ghrelin-friendly recipes. You'll find delicious dishes in Chapter 7.

Nichole D.

AGE: 34

POUNDS LOST:

FAST-TRACK: 3.7

TOTAL: 13 in 35 days

OVERALL INCHES LOST: 7.25

Ask any new mom. One of the biggest challenges after that bouncing baby arrives—apart from the inevitable sleep deprivation—is dropping the pregnancy weight and fitting back into the pre-baby wardrobe. That's how it was for Nichole, who put on 50 pounds when she was expecting her son. "The last 12 were the hardest to take off," she recalls. "Nothing fit, and I was practically at my breaking point when I heard about the Belly Fat Fix. I knew that if I didn't work at this right after the pregnancy, I'd have a much harder time getting those

pounds off later. So I was more than ready to commit." Fortunately, the Belly Fat Fix did the trick.

At first, Nichole recalls, the food preparation was tough. "I couldn't just pop into the neighborhood mini-mart and get what I needed," she said. "And getting to the store when you have a new baby isn't the easiest." But she managed. Quinoa and couscous became staples for her because they cook so quickly and they're easy to make. She also began eating more meat than she ever had before, because she learned to appreciate the way it filled her up and kept her full. At lunch, she often had a salad mixed with canned tuna.

Nichole's other big challenge? Withdrawing from fats and sugars. "I definitely had a difficult time with this, but I stuck with it. You have to get creative about seasoning your food," she says. Eating fruit helped appease her sweet tooth. So did adding sweet potatoes, which she ate just about every day.

In the past, Nichole didn't eat on a regular schedule—and motherhood didn't help. But, she says, the plan forced her to eat at regular times. Another strategy that worked for her was the food tracker.

These days, it's tough for Nichole to fit in the exercise plan, but instead she walks her newborn in the stroller every day and hopes to get back on a fitness routine soon. When she does, she's confident she'll be able to lose—within 6 months—another dozen or so pounds, putting her back into those pre-baby clothes and setting the stage for a healthy new life as a mom.

BEFORE

AFTER

CHAPTER 7

Simple, Delicious, Ghrelin-Friendly Recipes

It's easier to stick with a diet if you really like what you're eating and don't feel you have to give up *all* the foods you crave. I want you to succeed on the Belly Fat Fix, so I searched high and low to find the most delicious, simple-to-prepare recipes for you. I've even included some of my personal favorites that I've developed over the years as part of my weight-loss experience.

I figured that if you are going to succeed, having an arsenal of recipes is crucial. I kept the recipes simple because I know that few people have hours to spend in the kitchen preparing daily meals. The one exception: the dessert recipes. Some are a bit more complicated to prepare, but the delicious taste makes it well worth the effort. Later in this chapter, you'll find scrumptious recipes for desserts with names like Coconut Custard Trifle (page 263) and Warm Chocolate Caramel Banana (page 264).

These are special occasion treats—not for everyday meals. Having dessert every day is irresponsible dieting that will keep you from reaching your weight-loss goals. But that doesn't mean you can't enjoy dessert once in a while. This way, you don't feel deprived. And if you don't feel deprived, you'll have one less reason to cheat.

With that in mind, I've included nine delicious desserts that fit in to the Belly Fat Fix. Each is labeled with its G-List serving information. The Gluten-Free Black Bean Brownies (page 260), for instance, count for 1 carbohydrate serving and 1 fat serving. They're my favorite. The brownies are delicious, easy to prepare, and ghrelin suppressing. (As you may recall from Chapter 3, beans contribute protein, which also makes them filling. What a bonus!)

In this chapter, you'll find recipes for every meal of the day. Vegetarians, there are options for you, too. I've tested each recipe and tweaked them all to get the nutrition just right. I can assure you that they'll provide some memorable dining experiences.

I hope the pleasure of adding these 60 new recipes to your repertoire—along with the 7 days of prebuilt meal plans and the 30 snack recipes in Chapter 6—will energize you and make it a pleasure to eat the ghrelin way for the rest of your life. I want to ensure that you have more than enough choices and that you experience for yourself how enjoyable it can be to eat what your body needs to stay slim and healthy.

What makes these recipes unique? They incorporate the up-to-the-minute food science behind the Belly Fat Fix foods that taste good and are simple to make. You won't find this winning combination anywhere else.

To make this easier for you, I made sure that each recipe tells you:

- The protein, carbohydrate, fat, vegetable, and fruit G-List food servings so you know how many servings you're getting relative to your meal plan
- The variations to make to create a super-ghrelin-suppressing meal
- The number of calories and the grams of protein, fat, saturated fat, fiber, and so on

With these recipes, you'll never have to struggle to figure out what to eat. Plus, I've added a "portion tip" to most recipes, so you can adjust the amount to fit your meal plan perfectly and make the plan effortless to follow.

To incorporate these recipes into your prebuilt meal plans and know what *else* you can eat at that meal, refer to the Meal Plan Chart on page 168. Let's say you're on the 1,600-calorie meal plan and having the Grilled Steak Salad (page 218) for lunch. You'll see it provides 2 servings of protein, 2 servings of fat, and 2 servings of vegetables. So you should add 2 servings of carbs, 1 serving of fruit and follow the portion tip to complete your full Belly Fat Fix meal. You'll also see a suggested "Super Ghrelin Meal" pairing of a 6-ounce potato. I took a lot of time to create the Super Ghrelin Meal suggestions. If you follow them, your meal will be not only tasty but also super ghrelin suppressing.

Always refer to the Meal Plan Chart when using these recipes to make sure you're not missing an important component of your meal—or eating too much. If you don't keep an eye on the chart, you run the risk of throwing your ghrelin off.

So here are the recipes. Enjoy!

Recipes Index

Southwestern Omelet

MAKES 1 SERVING   PREP TIME: 10 MINUTES ▪ TOTAL TIME: 15 MINUTES

G-LIST SERVINGS = 2 PROTEINS, 2 FATS

6 large egg whites

2 tablespoons fat-free milk

1 teaspoon olive oil

1 scallion, sliced

1 small red bell pepper, finely chopped

¼ cup shredded reduced-fat Colby Jack cheese

1 tablespoon cilantro, optional

MAKE IT A
Super Ghrelin Meal:
Have 2 slices of high-fiber toast and a small Granny Smith apple.

Portion tip:
If you only need 1 Protein, omit the Cheddar cheese from this recipe and use only 4 egg whites.

1. In a medium bowl, whisk together the egg whites and milk.

2. Heat the oil in a small nonstick skillet over medium-high heat. Add the egg mixture and tilt the pan to spread the mixture across the bottom surface.

3. Cook, pushing in the edges with a spatula to let the uncooked egg flow underneath, for 3 minutes, or until just set.

4. Top half of the omelet with the scallion, pepper, and cheese. Fold the other half over the top. Cover and let stand for 2 minutes to heat the filling and melt the cheese. Slide the omelet carefully onto a plate. Top with chopped cilantro, if desired.

PER SERVING: 254 calories, 31 g protein, 10 g carbohydrates, 10 g total fat, 4 g saturated fat, 2 g fiber, 580 mg sodium

French Toast with Fruity Topping

MAKES 1 SERVING   PREP TIME: 5 MINUTES ■ TOTAL TIME: 15 MINUTES

G-LIST SERVINGS = 1 PROTEIN, 2 CARBOHYDRATES, 1 FRUIT

3 egg whites, beaten

¼ cup fat-free milk

½ teaspoon vanilla or almond extract

½ teaspoon ground cinnamon

⅛ teaspoon ground nutmeg

2 slices whole wheat bread

¼ cup 0% plain Greek yogurt

1 cup sliced strawberries

MAKE IT A
Super Ghrelin Meal:
Have a chopped Granny Smith apple for your fruity topping instead. This could be a seasonal replacement.

Portion tip:
If you need 2 Proteins, have ⅔ cup of 0% plain Greek yogurt on the side.

1. In a large bowl, whisk together the egg whites, milk, vanilla or almond extract, cinnamon, and nutmeg. Dip the bread slices in the mixture, turning to coat completely.

2. Coat a large nonstick skillet with cooking spray and place over medium heat. Add the bread slices and cook, turning once, for 6 to 8 minutes, or until browned.

3. Place the toast on a plate and top with the yogurt and strawberries.

PER SERVING: 299 calories, 26 g protein, 43 g carbohydrates, 3 g total fat, 0.5 g saturated fat, 8 g fiber, 478 mg sodium

Blueberry Cardamom Flaxseed Muffins

MAKES 6 SERVINGS   PREP TIME: 15 MINUTES ■ TOTAL TIME: 35 MINUTES

G-LIST SERVINGS = 2 CARBOHYDRATES, 1 FAT

¾ cup almond meal or almond flour

⅓ cup ground flaxseed

½ teaspoon ground cardamom or
   1 teaspoon cinnamon

1 teaspoon baking powder

2 eggs

¼ cup Spoonable Stevia One to One

¼ cup fat-free milk

1 tablespoon olive oil

1 tablespoon vanilla extract

½ cup fresh blueberries

MAKE IT A
Super Ghrelin Meal:
Pair this recipe with ⅔ cup of 0% plain Greek yogurt mixed with a chopped Granny Smith apple.

Portion tip:
If you need 3 Carbohydrates, have 1½ muffins.

1. Preheat the oven to 350°F. Coat a nonstick 6-cup muffin pan with cooking spray or line with paper or foil liners.

2. In a medium bowl, whisk together the almond meal/flour, flaxseed, cardamom or cinnamon, and baking powder.

3. In a separate medium bowl, whisk together the eggs, stevia, milk, oil, and vanilla. Stir in the blueberries and the flour mixture.

4. Divide the batter among the muffin cups.

5. Bake for 18 minutes, or until a wooden pick inserted into the center of a muffin comes out clean.

PER SERVING: 221 calories, 7 g protein, 16 g carbohydrates, 14 g total fat, 2 g saturated fat, 4 g fiber, 128 mg sodium

Vanilla Fruit and Yogurt Dip with Pita Crisps

MAKES 1 SERVING   PREP TIME: 5 MINUTES ■ TOTAL TIME: 15 MINUTES

G-LIST SERVINGS = 1 PROTEIN, 1 CARBOHYDRATE, 1 FAT, 1 FRUIT

½ cup 0% vanilla Greek yogurt

3 dried apricots or dried apple rings, finely chopped

¼ teaspoon ground cinnamon

1 small (4") whole wheat pita

1½ teaspoons butter, melted

THIS IS A
Super Ghrelin Meal.
Portion tip:
Omit the butter if your meal plan does not include Fat at breakfast.

1. In a small bowl, stir the yogurt, dried fruit, and cinnamon.

2. Toast the pita, brush on the butter, and cut into wedges. Dip the pita crisps into the yogurt mixture.

PER SERVING: 254 calories, 14 g protein, 37 g carbohydrates, 7 g total fat, 4 g saturated fat, 4 g fiber, 250 mg sodium

Turkey-Apple Sliders

MAKES 1 SERVING   PREP TIME: 10 MINUTES ■ TOTAL TIME: 10 MINUTES

G-LIST SERVINGS = 2 PROTEINS, 2 CARBOHYDRATES, 1 FAT, 1 VEGETABLE, 1 FRUIT

- 1 teaspoon deli mustard
- 2 soft mini slider buns
- 2 ounces thinly sliced low-sodium deli turkey breast
- ½ small Granny Smith apple, cored and thinly sliced
- 1 ounce (2 thin slices) reduced-fat provolone cheese (optional)
- ½ cup shredded lettuce
- 1 thin slice red onion, halved

MAKE IT A
Super Ghrelin Meal:
Have 1 cup of raw baby carrots on the side.

Portion tip:
If you need 3 Proteins, increase the amount of turkey breast to 6 ounces.

1. Spread the mustard on the bottom of each bun.

2. Divide the turkey, apple, cheese (if desired), lettuce, and onion between the buns. Cover with the tops of the buns.

PER SERVING: 353 calories, 30 g protein, 52 g carbohydrates, 12 g total fat, 3 g saturated fat, 6 g fiber, 753 mg sodium

Tex-Mex Chicken Wrap

MAKES 2 SERVINGS   PREP TIME: 10 MINUTES ■ TOTAL TIME: 15 MINUTES

G-LIST SERVINGS = 2 PROTEINS, 2 CARBOHYDRATES, 1 FAT, 1 VEGETABLE

1 large boneless, skinless chicken breast (6 ounces), cut into thin strips

1 small onion, sliced

1 small bell pepper, sliced

1 cup water

2 teaspoons taco seasoning

¼ teaspoon garlic powder

¼ teaspoon salt

2 small (7") whole wheat low-carbohydrate tortillas

1 cup rinsed and drained canned no-salt-added pinto beans

½ cup shredded reduced-fat Cheddar cheese

Salsa (optional)

MAKE IT A
Super Ghrelin Meal:
Have a super fruit on the side.

Portion tip:
If you need 3 Proteins, have 5 ounces of cooked chicken per serving.

1. Coat a medium nonstick skillet with cooking spray and place over medium heat. Cook the chicken, onion, and pepper for 5 to 7 minutes, or until the chicken is no longer pink and the vegetables are tender.

2. Add the water, taco seasoning, garlic powder, and salt. Cook, stirring, for 5 minutes, or until the liquid has evaporated and the chicken is cooked through.

3. Meanwhile, place the tortillas between 2 sheets of paper towel. Microwave on high power for 30 seconds, or until softened. Place them on serving plates.

4. Divide the chicken mixture, beans, and cheese between the tortillas. Serve with salsa, if desired.

PER SERVING: 348 calories, 38 g protein, 36 g carbohydrates, 9 g total fat, 4 g saturated fat, 14 g fiber, 766 mg sodium

Tuna Melt

MAKES 1 SERVING   PREP TIME: 5 MINUTES ■ TOTAL TIME: 5 MINUTES

G-LIST SERVINGS = 3 PROTEINS, 2 CARBOHYDRATES, 1 FAT, 1 VEGETABLE

1 small (7") whole wheat tortilla or wrap

1 can (5 ounces) low-sodium water-packed albacore tuna, drained

1 ounce low-sodium Swiss cheese, thinly sliced

1½ teaspoons light sour cream

½ teaspoon Dijon mustard

1 cup shredded Romaine lettuce

MAKE IT A
Super Ghrelin Meal:
Have a super fruit on the side.

Portion tip:
If you need 2 Proteins, make with a half can of tuna.

1. On a microwaveable plate, lay the tortilla flat. Spread the tuna evenly on top of the wrap. Top with the cheese.

2. In a small bowl, mix the sour cream and mustard.

3. Microwave the wrap on high power for 30 seconds, or until the cheese is almost melted.

4. Drizzle the sour cream mixture over the cheese. Top with the lettuce and fold one side over.

PER SERVING: 411 calories, 48 g protein, 25 g carbohydrates, 12 g total fat, 5 g saturated fat, 3 g fiber, 353 mg sodium

Hearty Vegetable Soup

MAKES 8 SERVINGS   PREP TIME: 30 MINUTES ■ TOTAL TIME: 1 HOUR 5 MINUTES

G-LIST SERVINGS = 1 CARBOHYDRATE, 1 VEGETABLE

- 1 tablespoon olive oil
- 2 ribs celery, chopped
- 1 carrot, thinly sliced
- 1 onion, chopped
- 1 large green bell pepper, chopped
- 2 ounces sliced mushrooms (about 1 cup)
- 8 cups low-sodium vegetable or chicken broth
- 1 can (14.5 ounces) no-salt-added diced tomatoes
- 1 cup fresh or frozen and thawed corn kernels
- 3 to 4 small red potatoes (10 ounces), cubed
- 1 teaspoon salt
- 1 zucchini, sliced
- 1 cup frozen peas
- ½ head green cabbage, shredded (6 cups) (optional)

MAKE IT A
Super Ghrelin Meal:
Pair with Balsamic Chicken with Arugula (page 230). Have a super fruit on the side.

Portion tip:
If you need 2 Carbohydrates, double the red potatoes in the recipe.

1. Heat the oil in a large Dutch oven over medium-high heat. Cook the celery, carrot, onion, pepper, and mushrooms for 5 minutes, or until lightly browned.

2. Add the broth, tomatoes, corn, and potatoes. Bring to a boil over high heat. Reduce the heat to low, cover, and simmer for 20 minutes. Add the salt, zucchini, peas, and cabbage (if desired). Cover and simmer for 10 minutes or until the vegetables are tender.

PER SERVING: 110 calories, 3 g protein, 20 g carbohydrates, 2 g total fat, 0.5 g saturated fat, 4 g fiber, 472 mg sodium

Yellow Lentil Soup with Cilantro and Yogurt

MAKES 4 SERVINGS   PREP TIME: 5 MINUTES ■ TOTAL TIME: 30 MINUTES

G-LIST SERVINGS = 2 CARBOHYDRATES, 1 FAT, 1 VEGETABLE

- 2 tablespoons butter
- 1 onion, chopped
- 1 rib celery, chopped
- 1 carrot, chopped
- 5 cups low-sodium vegetable broth
- ¾ cup dry yellow lentils or yellow split peas
- ½ teaspoon salt
- ¼ cup 0% plain Greek yogurt
- 2 tablespoons chopped fresh cilantro

MAKE IT A
Super Ghrelin Meal:
Pair with 4 ounces of grilled white fish and have a super fruit on the side.

Portion tip:
If you need 2 Fats, mix 2 tablespoons of cubed avocado into the soup.

1. In a large saucepan over medium-high heat, melt the butter. Cook the onion, celery, and carrot for 5 minutes, or until softened.

2. Add the broth and bring to a boil over high heat. Reduce the heat to medium-low. Stir in the lentils and salt. Cook for 10 to 15 minutes, or until the vegetables are very tender.

3. Divide the soup among 4 bowls. Top each with 1 tablespoon of the yogurt and a sprinkle of the cilantro.

PER SERVING: 223 calories, 12 g protein, 30 g carbohydrates, 7 g total fat, 4 g saturated fat, 8 g fiber, 536 mg sodium

Curried Autumn Vegetable Soup

MAKES 4 SERVINGS   PREP TIME: 5 MINUTES ▪ TOTAL TIME: 25 MINUTES

G-LIST SERVINGS = 1 PROTEIN, 2 CARBOHYDRATES

- 2 teaspoons canola oil
- 1 pound sweet potatoes, peeled and chopped into small pieces
- 2 large carrots, chopped
- 1 pound butternut squash, seeds removed, peeled and cubed (about 3 cups)
- 1 teaspoon curry powder
- ¼ teaspoon ground cinnamon
- ½ teaspoon salt
- 2 cups fat-free milk
- ½ cup 0% plain Greek yogurt

MAKE IT A
Super Ghrelin Meal:
Pair with Italian-Style Chicken Meat Loaf (page 225). Have a super fruit on the side.

Portion tip:
If you need 1 Fat, top the soup with 2 tablespoons of sour cream.

1. Heat the oil in a large nonstick saucepan over medium heat. Stir in the sweet potatoes, carrots, squash, curry powder, cinnamon, and salt. Cover and cook, stirring occasionally, for 15 minutes, or until the sweet potatoes are tender.

2. Add the milk. Reduce the heat to low and cook for 5 minutes, or until heated through.

3. Transfer the soup to a blender or food processor. Blend until smooth. Divide soup into 4 bowls. Stir 2 tablespoons of the yogurt into each serving.

PER SERVING: 219 calories, 10 g protein, 42 g carbohydrates, 3 g total fat, 0.5 g saturated fat, 6 g fiber, 432 mg sodium

Beef and Lentil Chili

MAKES 8 SERVINGS   PREP TIME: 5 MINUTES ■ TOTAL TIME: 8 HOURS 15 MINUTES

G-LIST SERVINGS = 2 PROTEINS, 2 CARBOHYDRATES, 2 FATS, 1 VEGETABLE

2 tablespoons canola oil

2 pounds 95% extra-lean ground beef

1 onion, chopped

1 green bell pepper, chopped

1 red bell pepper, chopped

1 package (1.25 ounces) chili seasoning mix

2 cans (14.5 ounces) no-salt-added diced tomatoes

1 pound (2 cups) brown lentils

1½ cups water

MAKE IT A
Super Ghrelin Meal:
Have a super fruit on the side.

Portion tip:
If you need 3 Proteins, make the recipe with 2½ pounds extra-lean beef.

1. Heat the oil in a large saucepan over medium-high heat. Add the beef, onion, and bell peppers and cook, stirring, for 8 minutes, or until the beef is no longer pink. Add the seasoning mix, stirring to combine.

2. Place the mixture in a 4- to 6-quart slow cooker. Add the tomatoes, lentils, and water. Stir until blended. Cook on high for 2½ to 4 hours or on low for 6 to 8 hours, depending on desired thickness.

PER SERVING: 436 calories, 40 g protein, 44 g carbohydrates, 10 g total fat, 3 g saturated fat, 18 g fiber, 250 mg sodium

Roasted Chicken and Spinach Salad

MAKES 2 SERVINGS · PREP TIME: 10 MINUTES ■ TOTAL TIME: 10 MINUTES

G-LIST SERVINGS = 2 PROTEINS, 2 FATS, 2 VEGETABLES, 1 FRUIT

2 tablespoons red wine vinegar

2 teaspoons extra-virgin olive oil

1 teaspoon Dijon mustard

¼ teaspoon salt

⅛ teaspoon ground black pepper

1 bag (6 ounces) baby spinach

1 boneless, skinless chicken breast (about 6 ounces), roasted or grilled and thinly sliced

2 pears, peeled, cored, and thinly sliced

½ red onion, thinly sliced

¼ cup shaved Parmesan cheese

MAKE IT A
Super Ghrelin Meal:
Pair with a baked sweet potato.

Portion tip:
If you need 3 Proteins, make the recipe with 10 ounces of chicken breast.

1. In a large serving bowl, whisk together the vinegar, oil, mustard, salt, and pepper.

2. Add the spinach, chicken, pears, and onion. Toss to coat well.

3. Top each salad with the cheese.

PER SERVING: 390 calories, 34 g protein, 40 g carbohydrates, 12 g total fat, 4 g saturated fat, 10 g fiber, 781 mg sodium

Shrimp and Red Grapefruit Salad

MAKES 1 SERVING   PREP TIME: 10 MINUTES ■ TOTAL TIME: 10 MINUTES

G-LIST SERVINGS = 2 PROTEINS, 1 CARBOHYDRATE, 2 FATS, 1 VEGETABLE, 1 FRUIT

2 cups mixed baby greens

¼ pound large shrimp, cooked, peeled, and deveined

1 small red grapefruit, separated into segments

½ small red onion, sliced

1 tablespoon lime juice

1 tablespoon olive oil

¼ avocado, chopped

1 whole wheat pita, toasted (optional)

THIS IS A
Super Ghrelin Meal.
Portion tip:
If you need 3 Proteins and 1 Fat, make the recipe with 6 ounces of shrimp, top with 2 tablespoons of low-fat feta cheese, and use 1 tablespoon of oil.

1. Place the greens on a plate. Top with the shrimp, grapefruit, and onion.

2. In a small bowl, whisk together the lime juice and oil. Drizzle over the salad. Top with the avocado. Serve with the pita, if desired.

PER SERVING: 395 calories, 28 g protein, 27 g carbohydrates, 21 g total fat, 3 g saturated fat, 8 g fiber, 286 mg sodium

Grilled Steak Salad

MAKES 2 SERVINGS   PREP TIME: 15 MINUTES ■ TOTAL TIME: 25 MINUTES

G-LIST SERVINGS = 2 PROTEINS, 2 FATS, 2 VEGETABLES

½ pound lean flank steak, trimmed

¼ teaspoon salt

¼ teaspoon ground black pepper

1 small romaine lettuce heart, chopped (about 4 cups)

2 plum tomatoes, seeded and chopped

1 cucumber, peeled and chopped

½ cup small red onion, thinly sliced

1 tablespoon chopped fresh basil

2 tablespoons red wine vinegar

1 tablespoon olive oil

MAKE IT A
Super Ghrelin Meal:
Pair with a steamed red potato, cubed, tossed in the salad. Have a super fruit on the side.

Portion tip:
If you need 3 Proteins, top the salad with 2 ounces of shredded low-fat Cheddar cheese.

1. Coat a grill or broiler-pan rack with cooking spray. Preheat the grill or the broiler.

2. Sprinkle the flank steak with the salt and pepper. Grill or broil the steak, turning once, for 10 minutes, or until a thermometer inserted in the center registers 145°F for medium-rare. Transfer the steak to a cutting board and let stand for 10 minutes. Thinly slice the steak.

3. Meanwhile, in a large bowl, toss the lettuce, tomatoes, cucumber, and onion. In a small bowl, whisk together the vinegar, basil, and oil. Add to the salad mixture and toss to coat well.

4. Divide the salad between 2 bowls and top with the sliced steak.

PER SERVING: 277 calories, 27 g protein, 11 g carbohydrates, 14 g total fat, 3 g saturated fat, 3 g fiber, 366 mg sodium

Quinoa Salad with Grapes and Toasted Walnuts

MAKES 4 SERVINGS   PREP TIME: 10 MINUTES ■ TOTAL TIME: 30 MINUTES

G-LIST SERVINGS = 2 CARBOHYDRATES, 2 FATS, 1 FRUIT

1 cup quinoa, rinsed

¼ teaspoon salt

2 tablespoons white wine vinegar

1 tablespoon olive oil

1 rib celery, chopped

2 cups red seedless grapes, halved

½ cup dried cranberries

¼ cup walnut pieces, lightly toasted

MAKE IT A
Super Ghrelin Meal:
Pair the salad with lean beef and steamed kale. Have a fruit on the side.

Portion tip:
If you need only 1 Fat, omit the walnuts.

1. Prepare the quinoa according to package directions. Remove from the heat, add the salt, and let stand for 5 minutes.

2. Meanwhile, in a large bowl, whisk together the vinegar and oil. Add the quinoa, celery, grapes, and cranberries. Toss to coat well. Sprinkle with the walnuts. Serve warm or at room temperature.

PER SERVING: 314 calories, 8 g protein, 49 g carbohydrates, 11 g total fat, 1 g saturated fat, 5 g fiber, 163 mg sodium

Roasted Sweet Potato and Red Onion Salad

MAKES 4 SERVINGS   PREP TIME: 5 MINUTES ■ TOTAL TIME: 30 MINUTES

G-LIST SERVINGS = 2 CARBOHYDRATES, 2 FATS, 1 VEGETABLE

¾ pound sweet potatoes, peeled and cut into ½" cubes (about 2 cups)

1 red onion, cut into eighths

2 tablespoons apple cider vinegar

¼ teaspoon salt

2 tablespoons olive oil, divided

8 ounces baby spinach (about 8 cups)

2 tablespoons lemon juice

½ cup semi-soft goat cheese

MAKE IT A
Super Ghrelin Meal:
Pair with cooked chicken breast. Have a super fruit on the side.

Portion tip:
If you need 1 Fat, make the salad with 1 tablespoon of olive oil.

1. Preheat the oven to 425°F.

2. In a medium bowl, toss the potatoes and onion with the vinegar, salt, and 1 tablespoon of the oil. Spread the mixture on a baking sheet. Roast for 10 to 15 minutes, or until just tender. Set aside to cool for 10 minutes.

3. Meanwhile, in the same bowl, combine the spinach, lemon juice, and the remaining 1 tablespoon oil. Toss well.

4. Divide the spinach among 4 plates. Top with the potatoes and onion. Sprinkle evenly with the cheese.

PER SERVING: 241 calories, 8 g protein, 23 g carbohydrates, 14 g total fat, 6 g saturated fat, 5 g fiber, 384 mg sodium

Beefy Barley Salad

MAKES 4 SERVINGS   PREP TIME: 15 MINUTES ▓ TOTAL TIME: 30 MINUTES

G-LIST SERVINGS = 2 PROTEINS, 1 CARBOHYDRATE, 1 FAT, 2 VEGETABLES

⅔ cup quick-cooking barley

3 tablespoons lemon juice

2 tablespoons olive oil

½ teaspoon garlic powder

1 pound lean deli roast beef, cut into bite-size pieces

1 cup fresh asparagus pieces, lightly steamed (about 6 thin spears, trimmed)

1 tomato, chopped

3 scallions, sliced

2 tablespoons finely chopped parsley

MAKE IT A
Super Ghrelin Meal:
Have a super fruit on the side.

Portion tip:
If you need 3 Proteins and 2 Carbohydrates, make the recipe with 1½ pounds of roast beef, and add 1⅓ cups of corn kernels to step 3.

1. Cook the barley according to package directions. Drain and rinse under cold water.

2. Meanwhile, in a large bowl, combine the lemon juice, oil, and garlic powder.

3. Add the beef, asparagus, tomato, scallions, parsley, and cooked barley. Toss to coat well. Serve immediately or refrigerate to serve chilled.

PER SERVING: 319 calories, 28 g protein, 23 g carbohydrates, 13 g total fat, 3 g saturated fat, 4 g fiber, 403 mg sodium

Greek Tuna Salad

MAKES 2 SERVINGS   PREP TIME: 15 MINUTES ■ TOTAL TIME: 15 MINUTES

G-LIST SERVINGS = 2 PROTEINS, 1 CARBOHYDRATE, 2 FATS, 2 VEGETABLES

- 2 tablespoons red wine vinegar
- 1 tablespoon olive oil
- ¼ teaspoon dried oregano
- ½ head romaine lettuce, chopped
- 1 small seedless cucumber, sliced
- 1 plum tomato, seeded and chopped
- ¼ red onion, chopped
- ⅔ cup canned no-salt-added chickpeas, drained and rinsed
- 2 cans (5 ounces each) low-sodium water-packed albacore tuna, drained
- 2 tablespoons reduced-fat feta cheese
- 4 kalamata olives, pitted and sliced

MAKE IT A
Super Ghrelin Meal:
Top the salad with a chopped Granny Smith apple.

Portion tip:
If you need 3 Proteins and 2 Carbohydrates, make the recipe with 3 cans of tuna and 1 can of chickpeas.

1. In a large bowl, whisk together the vinegar, oil, and oregano. Add the lettuce, cucumber, tomato, onion, chickpeas, and tuna. Toss to coat well.

2. Divide the mixture between 2 plates and top with the cheese and olives.

PER SERVING: 405 calories, 41 g protein, 31 g carbohydrates, 13 g fat, 2 g saturated fat, 8 g fiber, 349 mg sodium

Chicken Salad with Asian Dressing

MAKES 4 SERVINGS   PREP TIME: 25 MINUTES ▪ TOTAL TIME: 40 MINUTES

G-LIST SERVINGS = 2 PROTEINS, 1 FAT, 3 VEGETABLES

2 tablespoons light soy sauce

2 tablespoons lemon juice

1 tablespoon toasted sesame oil

1 clove garlic, finely chopped

½ teaspoon crushed red-pepper flakes

1 pound cooked chicken breast, shredded

1 pound Napa cabbage, sliced (5 cups)

1 small cucumber, sliced

½ carrot, shredded

¼ cup finely chopped cilantro

2 tablespoons sliced almonds

MAKE IT A
Super Ghrelin Meal:
Pair the salad with cooked lentils. Have a super fruit on the side.

Portion tip:
If you need 3 Proteins, make the recipe with 1½ pounds of shredded chicken.

1. In a large bowl, whisk together the soy sauce, lemon juice, oil, garlic, and red-pepper flakes.

2. Add the chicken, cabbage, cucumber, and carrots. Toss to coat well.

3. Divide the salad among 4 plates and sprinkle evenly with the cilantro and almonds.

PER SERVING: 276 calories, 38 g protein, 8 g carbohydrates, 9 g total fat, 2 g saturated fat, 3 g fiber, 379 mg sodium

Grilled Apple-Turkey Burgers

MAKES 4 SERVINGS · · · · · PREP TIME: 10 MINUTES ▪ TOTAL TIME: 25 MINUTES

G-LIST SERVINGS = 2 PROTEINS, 2 CARBOHYDRATES, ½ FAT, ½ FRUIT

1 pound extra-lean ground turkey

2 Granny Smith apples, finely chopped

2 tablespoons ground flaxseed

½ red onion, finely chopped

½ cup shredded Cheddar cheese

½ teaspoon dried sage

¼ teaspoon salt

¼ teaspoon ground black pepper

4 whole wheat hamburger rolls

Lettuce (optional)

Tomato slices (optional)

MAKE IT A
Super Ghrelin Meal:
Top the burger with 1 slice of avocado and ½ of a thinly sliced Granny Smith apple. Have baby carrots on the side.

Portion tip:
If you need 3 Proteins, make the recipe with 1½ pounds of extra-lean ground turkey.

1. Coat a grill or broiler-pan rack with cooking spray. Preheat the grill or the broiler.

2. In a large bowl, combine the turkey, apples, flaxseed, onion, cheese, sage, salt, and pepper. Shape into 4 patties.

3. Grill or broil, turning once, for 10 to 15 minutes, or until a thermometer inserted in the center registers 165°F and the meat is no longer pink.

4. Serve on rolls with lettuce and tomato, if desired.

PER SERVING: 352 calories, 36 g protein, 35 g carbohydrates, 10 g total fat, 3 g saturated fat, 6 g fiber, 653 mg sodium

Italian-Style Chicken Meat Loaf

MAKES 4 SERVINGS   PREP TIME: 15 MINUTES ▪ TOTAL TIME: 1 HOUR 25 MINUTES

G-LIST SERVINGS = 2 PROTEINS, ½ CARBOHYDRATE

1 pound extra-lean ground chicken breast

2 egg whites, beaten

2 cloves garlic, finely chopped

3 tablespoons Lipton Onion Soup mix

¼ cup grated Parmesan cheese

¼ cup chopped parsley

⅓ cup rolled oats

1 cup no-salt-added tomato sauce, divided

Dash of ground black pepper (optional)

1 teaspoon Italian seasoning

MAKE IT A
Super Ghrelin Meal:
Pair with a baked sweet potato, topped with sour cream, and a side of steamed carrots. Have a super fruit on the side.

Portion tip:
If you need 3 Proteins, divide the recipe into 3 servings to equal 3 Proteins and 1 Carbohydrate per serving.

1. Preheat the oven to 350°F.

2. In a large bowl, combine the chicken, egg whites, garlic, soup mix, cheese, parsley, oats, ½ cup of the tomato sauce, and the pepper, if desired. Stir until well mixed.

3. Form the mixture into a loaf shape and place in a 13" x 9" baking dish, or pack the mixture into a 9" x 5" loaf pan or 2 mini loaf pans.

4. In a small bowl, combine the Italian seasoning and the remaining ½ cup tomato sauce. Brush over the meat loaf.

5. Bake for 50 to 60 minutes, or until a thermometer inserted in the center registers 165°F and the meat is no longer pink. Let stand for 10 minutes before slicing and serving.

PER SERVING: 201 calories, 31 g protein, 14 g carbohydrates, 3 g total fat, 1 g saturated fat, 2 g fiber, 672 mg sodium

Slow-Cooker Turkey and Lentil Sloppy Joes

MAKES 6 SERVINGS   PREP TIME: 20 MINUTES ■ TOTAL TIME: 4 HOURS 30 MINUTES

G-LIST SERVINGS = 2 PROTEINS, 2 CARBOHYDRATES, 1 VEGETABLE

1½ pounds extra-lean ground turkey breast

1 onion, finely chopped

2 cups no-salt-added tomato sauce

2 tablespoons tomato paste

⅓ cup dried lentils

1 tablespoon Worcestershire sauce

¼ teaspoon salt

¼ teaspoon ground black pepper

¼ teaspoon crushed red-pepper flakes

6 whole wheat hamburger buns

MAKE IT A
Super Ghrelin Meal:
Have a green side salad with low-fat dressing and fruit on the side.

Portion tip:
If you need 3 Proteins, make the recipe with 2¼ pounds turkey breast.

1. In a medium nonstick skillet, cook the turkey and onion over medium-high heat, stirring often, for 6 to 8 minutes, or until browned.

2. Use a slotted spoon to transfer the mixture to a 4- to 6-quart slow cooker. Stir in the tomato sauce, tomato paste, lentils, Worcestershire sauce, salt, black pepper, and red-pepper flakes. Cover and cook on low for 2½ to 4 hours.

3. Place the rolls, split side up, on 6 serving plates. Top with the turkey mixture.

PER SERVING: 326 calories, 35 g protein, 41 g carbohydrates, 4 g total fat, 0.5 g saturated fat, 7 g fiber, 450 mg sodium

Pesto-Parmesan Chicken

MAKES 2 SERVINGS   PREP TIME: 5 MINUTES ■ TOTAL TIME: 30 MINUTES

G-LIST SERVINGS = 3 PROTEINS, 2 FATS

2 tablespoons light mayonnaise

2 tablespoons basil pesto

2 tablespoons grated Parmesan cheese

¾ teaspoon Italian seasoning

2 boneless, skinless chicken breast halves (5 to 6 ounces each)

MAKE IT A
Super Ghrelin Meal:
Pair with White Bean and Parmesan Mashed Potatoes (page 249) and have a super fruit on the side.

Portion tip:
If you need 2 Proteins, make the recipe with 2 small chicken breasts.

1. Preheat the oven to 375°F. Coat a 9" x 13" baking pan with cooking spray.

2. In a small bowl, combine the mayonnaise, pesto, cheese, and Italian seasoning.

3. Place the chicken in the pan. Spread the mayonnaise mixture evenly over the chicken.

4. Bake for 20 to 22 minutes, or until a thermometer inserted in the thickest portion registers 165°F and the juices run clear.

PER SERVING: 309 calories, 35 g protein, 2 g carbohydrates, 17 g total fat, 4 g saturated fat, 0.5 g fiber, 461 mg sodium

Mushroom Cheeseburgers

MAKES 4 SERVINGS   PREP TIME: 20 MINUTES ■ TOTAL TIME: 35 MINUTES

G-LIST SERVINGS = 3 PROTEINS, 1 CARBOHYDRATE

1 pound extra-lean ground turkey breast

1 cup (4 ounces) shredded Swiss cheese

5 ounces button mushrooms, finely chopped

1 small onion, finely chopped

3 cloves garlic, finely chopped

¼ teaspoon salt

2 whole wheat pitas

Lettuce (optional)

Tomatoes slices (optional)

MAKE IT A
Super Ghrelin Meal:
Have with a side of kale, sauteed in olive oil, and a super fruit on the side.

Portion tip:
If you need 2 Carbohydrates, have one whole wheat pita.

1. In a large bowl, combine the turkey, cheese, mushrooms, onion, garlic, and salt. Shape into 4 equal patties.

2. Coat a large nonstick skillet with cooking spray and place over medium-low heat. Cook the burgers, turning once, for 15 minutes or until a thermometer inserted in the center registers 165°F and the meat is no longer pink.

3. Cut the pitas in half crosswise to make 4 open pockets. Serve the burgers in the pitas with lettuce and tomato, if desired.

PER SERVING: 291 calories, 40 g protein, 17 g carbohydrates, 10 g total fat, 3 g saturated fat, 5 g fiber, 395 mg sodium

Cheesy Chicken Pasta Casserole

MAKES 6 SERVINGS   PREP TIME: 10 MINUTES ■ TOTAL TIME: 1 HOUR 5 MINUTES

G-LIST SERVINGS = 2 PROTEINS, 1 CARBOHYDRATE

4 ounces high-fiber elbow macaroni (1 cup)

1 tablespoon olive oil

1 pound extra-lean ground chicken breast

1 small onion, chopped

1 can (14.5 ounces) Italian-style diced tomatoes

1 can (8 ounces) tomato sauce

½ cup 0% plain Greek yogurt

¼ teaspoon salt

¼ teaspoon ground black pepper

2 teaspoons Italian seasoning

¾ cup shredded part-skim mozzarella cheese

MAKE IT A
Super Ghrelin Meal:
Have with a mixed green salad, topped with olive oil, and a super fruit on the side.

Portion tip:
If you need 3 Proteins and 2 Carbohydrates, make the recipe with 1½ pounds of chicken and 2 cups of (uncooked) high-fiber macaroni.

1. Preheat the oven to 350°F. Coat a 3-quart baking dish with cooking spray.

2. Prepare the macaroni according to package directions. Drain and place in the baking dish.

3. Meanwhile, heat the oil in a medium nonstick skillet over medium heat. Add the chicken and onion and cook for 5 minutes, or until the chicken is no longer pink.

4. Remove the skillet from the heat. Stir in the tomatoes, tomato sauce, yogurt, salt, pepper, and Italian seasoning. Add to the pasta in the baking dish and toss to coat.

5. Bake for 35 minutes, or until bubbling. Sprinkle with the cheese. Bake for 5 to 10 minutes, or until the cheese melts.

PER SERVING: 235 calories, 26 g protein, 20 g carbohydrates, 6 g total fat, 1 g saturated fat, 3 g fiber, 574 mg sodium

Balsamic Chicken with Arugula

MAKES 4 SERVINGS   PREP TIME: 5 MINUTES ▪ TOTAL TIME: 25 MINUTES

G-LIST SERVINGS = 2 PROTEINS, 2 FATS, 1 VEGETABLE

3 cloves garlic, finely chopped

3 tablespoons fresh rosemary leaves, stripped from stems, or 2 tablespoons dried

2 tablespoons extra-virgin olive oil

3 tablespoons balsamic vinegar

¼ teaspoon salt

4 boneless, skinless chicken breasts (about 6 ounces each)

1 tablespoon lemon juice

1 6-ounce bag arugula (or other tender salad greens) (about 6 cups)

MAKE IT A
Super Ghrelin Meal:
Pair with Mediterranean Quinoa (page 248). Have a fruit on the side.

Portion tip:
If you need 3 Proteins, have 6 ounces of cooked chicken.

1. Preheat the oven to 450°F.

2. In a 13" x 9" baking dish, combine the garlic, rosemary, oil, vinegar, and salt. Add the chicken and turn to coat well.

3. Bake for 20 minutes, or until a thermometer inserted in the thickest portion registers 165°F and the juices run clear. Remove the chicken to a plate. Stir the lemon juice into the pan juices.

4. Divide the arugula among 4 serving plates. Top with the chicken, drizzle with the pan juices, and serve.

PER SERVING: 277 calories, 37 g protein, 4 g carbohydrates, 12 g total fat, 2 g saturated fat, 1 g fiber, 353 mg sodium

Roast Chicken and Kale

MAKES 4 SERVINGS   PREP TIME: 15 MINUTES ■ TOTAL TIME: 40 MINUTES

G-LIST SERVINGS = 2 PROTEINS, 1 CARBOHYDRATE, 2 FATS, 1 VEGETABLE

4 boneless, skinless chicken breast halves (about 5 ounces each)

2 small sweet potatoes, peeled and quartered

2 tablespoons olive oil, divided

2 cloves garlic, finely chopped

1 teaspoon dried thyme

¾ teaspoon salt, divided

½ onion, coarsely chopped

½ pound fresh kale leaves, chopped (4 cups)

1 to 2 tablespoons cider vinegar

MAKE IT A
Super Ghrelin Meal:
Have a steamed vegetable and a super fruit on the side.

Portion tip:
If you need 3 Proteins and 2 Carbohydrates, make the recipe with large chicken breasts and 4 sweet potatoes.

1. Preheat the oven to 375°F. Coat a large roasting pan with cooking spray.

2. Arrange the chicken and sweet potatoes in the pan. Drizzle with 1 tablespoon of the oil, the garlic, the thyme, and ½ teaspoon of the salt.

3. Bake for 20 minutes, or until a thermometer inserted in the thickest portion registers 165°F and the juices run clear. Keep warm.

4. Meanwhile, in a large nonstick skillet, heat the remaining 1 tablespoon oil over medium heat. Add the onion and cook for 2 to 3 minutes, or until lightly browned. Add the kale and cook until it is wilted. Remove from the heat and drizzle with the vinegar and sprinkle with the remaining ¼ teaspoon salt. Add to the roasting pan with the chicken and bake for 5 minutes.

5. Divide the chicken, potatoes, and kale among 4 plates and serve.

PER SERVING: 352 calories, 35 g protein, 29 g carbohydrates, 11 g total fat, 2 g saturated fat, 5 g fiber, 676 mg sodium

Lemon Tilapia with Curried Cauliflower

MAKES 2 SERVINGS   PREP TIME: 20 MINUTES ■ TOTAL TIME: 35 MINUTES

G-LIST SERVINGS = 3 PROTEINS, 1 FAT, 2 VEGETABLES

½ small head cauliflower, cut into florets (about 3 cups)

4 teaspoons olive oil, divided

½ teaspoon salt, divided

2 teaspoons curry powder

¼ teaspoon garlic powder

¼ teaspoon ground ginger

1 pound tilapia (or roughy, flounder, or red snapper fillet), cut in 2 equal pieces

2 tablespoons lemon juice

MAKE IT A
Super Ghrelin Meal:
Pair with brown rice and have a super fruit on the side.

Portion tip:
If you need 2 Fats, make the recipe with an additional 2 teaspoons of olive oil.

1. Preheat the oven to 450°F.

2. Arrange the cauliflower on a baking sheet. Drizzle with 2 teaspoons of the oil and stir to coat. Sprinkle with ¼ teaspoon of the salt.

3. In a small bowl, combine the curry powder, garlic powder, and ginger. Toss with the cauliflower. Bake, stirring once, for 10 to 15 minutes, or until golden brown. Remove from the oven.

4. Meanwhile, brush both sides of the tilapia with the lemon juice. Sprinkle with the remaining ¼ teaspoon salt.

5. Heat the remaining 2 teaspoons oil in a large nonstick skillet over medium-high heat. Cook the tilapia, turning once, for 4 to 6 minutes, or until just opaque in the center. Serve with the cauliflower.

PER SERVING: 323 calories, 47 g protein, 6 g carbohydrates, 14 g total fat, 3 g saturated fat, 2 g fiber, 720 mg sodium

Five-Spice Seared Salmon

MAKES 1 SERVING   PREP TIME: 5 MINUTES ■ TOTAL TIME: 15 MINUTES

G-LIST SERVINGS = 3 PROTEINS, 2 FATS

½ teaspoon Chinese 5-spice powder

½ teaspoon ground black pepper

¼ teaspoon sea salt

6 ounces skinless salmon fillet

2 teaspoons olive oil

1. In a small bowl, combine the spice powder, pepper, and salt. Sprinkle over both sides of the salmon.

2. Coat a medium nonstick skillet with cooking spray, add the oil, and place over medium heat. Cook the salmon, turning once, for 8 minutes, or until just opaque in the center.

MAKE IT A
Super Ghrelin Meal:
Pair with White Bean and Parmesan Mashed Potatoes (page 249). Have a super fruit on the side.

Portion tip:
If you need 2 Proteins, have 4 ounces of cooked salmon.

PER SERVING: 329 calories, 34 g protein, 2 g carbohydrates, 20 g total fat, 3 g saturated fat, 1 g fiber, 468 mg sodium

No-Fuss "Crab" Cakes

MAKES 2 SERVINGS   PREP TIME: 10 MINUTES ■ TOTAL TIME: 25 MINUTES

G-LIST SERVINGS = 2 PROTEINS, 1 FAT

2 egg whites

2 tablespoons light mayonnaise

2 tablespoons lemon juice

1 teaspoon Worcestershire sauce

2 scallions, finely chopped

½ small red bell pepper, chopped

6 ounces imitation crabmeat, shredded

2 tablespoons dry whole wheat panko crumbs

¼ cup finely shredded low-fat Cheddar cheese (optional)

MAKE IT A
Super Ghrelin Meal:
Pair with Creole Baked Sweet Potato Wedges (page 250) and a steamed veggie. Have a super fruit on the side.

Portion tip:
If you need 3 Proteins, have 3 "crab" cakes.

1. Preheat the broiler. Coat a baking sheet with cooking spray.

2. In a large bowl, whisk together the egg whites, mayonnaise, lemon juice, and Worcestershire sauce. Add the scallions, bell pepper, and crabmeat and stir with a fork to break up. Stir in the bread crumbs. Use a ⅓-cup measure to divide the mixture and shape into 4 patties. Place the patties on the baking sheet.

3. Broil 4" from the heat for 10 minutes, turning once, or until lightly browned. Sprinkle 1 tablespoon of the cheese on top of each patty, if desired, and broil for 1 minute, or until the cheese melts.

PER SERVING: 175 calories, 11 g protein, 20 g carbohydrates, 6 g total fat, 1 g saturated fat, 1 g fiber, 962 mg sodium

Almond-Crusted Cod Fillets with Mustard-Dill Sauce

MAKES 4 SERVINGS　　　　PREP TIME: 15 MINUTES ▪ TOTAL TIME: 25 MINUTES

G-LIST SERVINGS = 2 PROTEINS, 1½ FATS

Sauce

3 tablespoons 0% plain Greek yogurt

1 tablespoon light mayonnaise

2 teaspoons lemon juice

1 teaspoon Dijon mustard

1 teaspoon chopped fresh dill

¼ teaspoon salt

Cod

¼ cup dry whole wheat bread crumbs

¼ cup sliced almonds

¼ teaspoon salt

4 cod or halibut fillets (6 ounces each)

1 teaspoon extra-virgin olive oil

MAKE IT A
Super Ghrelin Meal:
Pair with Mediterranean Quinoa (page 248) and a steamed veggie. Have a super fruit on the side.

Portion tip:
If you need 3 Proteins, have 9 ounces of cooked halibut.

1. **To make the sauce:** In a small bowl, whisk together the yogurt, mayonnaise, lemon juice, mustard, dill, and salt. Refrigerate until ready to use.

2. **To make the cod:** In a blender or food processor, combine the bread crumbs, almonds, and salt. Blend or process until finely ground. Transfer to a shallow bowl. Place the cod in the bowl, turning to coat with the crumb mixture.

3. Heat the oil in a large nonstick skillet over medium heat. Cook the cod for 8 minutes, turning once, or until browned and just opaque in the center. Serve with the sauce.

PER SERVING: 226 calories, 33 g protein, 6 g carbohydrates, 7 g total fat, 1 g saturated fat, 1 g fiber, 490 mg sodium

Shrimp and Flounder "Ceviche"

MAKES 2 SERVINGS   PREP TIME: 10 MINUTES ■ TOTAL TIME: 45 MINUTES

G-LIST SERVINGS = 3 PROTEINS, 2 VEGETABLES

½ pound peeled and deveined shrimp, finely chopped

½ pound flounder, finely chopped

2 tomatoes, finely chopped

½ seedless cucumber, peeled and finely chopped

¼ red onion, finely chopped

¼ cup finely chopped dill

¼ cup freshly squeezed lemon juice

¼ teaspoon salt

MAKE IT A
Super Ghrelin Meal:
Add avocado to the ceviche. Serve with whole grain crackers and a super fruit on the side.

Portion tip:
If you need 2 Proteins, reduce the shrimp and flounder to 6 ounces each, and prepare as directed.

1. Coat a large nonstick skillet with cooking spray and place over medium heat. Cook the shrimp and flounder, stirring constantly, for 3 to 5 minutes, or until opaque. Transfer to a plate and allow to cool.

2. In a large serving bowl, combine the tomatoes, cucumber, onion, dill, lemon juice, and salt. Gently stir in the cooled fish.

3. Refrigerate for 30 minutes before serving.

PER SERVING: 265 calories, 46 g protein, 11 g carbohydrates, 4 g total fat, 1 g saturated fat, 2 g fiber, 561 mg sodium

Barbecue-Style Pork and Beans

MAKES 6 SERVINGS PREP TIME: 10 MINUTES ■ TOTAL TIME: 35 MINUTES

G-LIST SERVINGS = 2 PROTEINS, 2 CARBOHYDRATES, 1 FAT

1 onion, finely chopped

¾ pound lower-sodium bacon, cut into ½" pieces

2 cans (14–19 ounces each) no-salt-added navy beans, rinsed and drained

½ teaspoon chili powder

½ cup water

¼ cup ketchup

2 tablespoons maple syrup

1 tablespoon apple cider vinegar

1 teaspoon Dijon mustard

½ teaspoon salt

MAKE IT A
Super Ghrelin Meal:
Pair with steamed kale. Have a super fruit on the side.

Portion tip:
If you need 3 Proteins, add 2 ounces of cooked lean shredded beef to your portion.

1. Coat a large nonstick skillet with cooking spray and place over medium-high heat. Cook the onion, stirring, for 5 minutes, or until lightly browned. Add the bacon and cook, stirring, for 5 minutes.

2. Add the beans, chili powder, water, ketchup, maple syrup, vinegar, mustard, and salt. Bring to a boil. Reduce the heat to medium and simmer, stirring occasionally, for 15 minutes.

PER SERVING: 368 calories, 27 g protein, 24 g carbohydrates, 18 g total fat, 9 g saturated fat, 6 g fiber, 145 mg sodium

Pan-Grilled Steak with Creamy Buttermilk Dressing

MAKES 1 SERVING   PREP TIME: 5 MINUTES ▓ TOTAL TIME: 20 MINUTES

G-LIST SERVINGS = 2 PROTEINS, 2 CARBOHYDRATES, 3 FATS

¼ cup quinoa

4 ounces top round steak

⅛ teaspoon salt

⅛ teaspoon ground black pepper

1 tablespoon olive oil, divided

2 tablespoons buttermilk

½ teaspoon Dijon mustard

¼ teaspoon dried basil

MAKE IT A
Super Ghrelin Meal:
Pair with a steamed veggie. Have a super fruit on the side.

Portion tip:
If you need 3 Proteins and 2 Fats, make the recipe with 6 ounces of steak and ½ tablespoon of olive oil.

1. Prepare the quinoa according to package directions. Set aside.

2. Meanwhile, sprinkle both sides of the steak with the salt and pepper. Coat a nonstick grill pan with 1 teaspoon of the oil and heat over medium-high heat. Cook the steak, turning once, for 2 to 4 minutes per side or until desired doneness.

3. Place the steak on a cutting board and let it stand for 5 minutes before slicing.

4. Meanwhile, in a small bowl, whisk together the buttermilk, mustard, basil, and remaining 2 teaspoons oil.

5. Serve the steak with the quinoa. Drizzle with the buttermilk dressing.

PER SERVING: 451 calories, 33 g protein, 30 g carbohydrates, 22 g total fat, 4 g saturated fat, 3 g fiber, 450 mg sodium

Loin of Pork
with Smoky Paprika Rub

MAKES 6 SERVINGS   PREP TIME: 10 MINUTES ■ TOTAL TIME: 50 MINUTES

G-LIST SERVINGS = 3 PROTEINS

1 red onion, thickly sliced

1½ pounds boneless center-cut pork loin, trimmed

1 cup low-sodium chicken broth

1 teaspoon minced garlic

½ teaspoon smoked paprika

½ teaspoon salt

MAKE IT A
Super Ghrelin Meal:
Pair with Chard and Cannellini Beans (page 254). Have a super fruit on the side.

Portion tip:
If you only need 2 Proteins, have a 4-ounce serving of the pork.

1. Preheat the oven to 350°F. Coat a roasting pan with cooking spray.

2. Arrange the onion slices in a single layer in the pan. Top with the pork loin. Pour the broth over the top. Rub the loin with the garlic, paprika, and salt.

3. Roast for 30 minutes, or until a thermometer inserted in the center reaches 145°F and the juices run clear. Let stand for 10 minutes before slicing.

PER SERVING: 208 calories, 37 g protein, 4 g carbohydrates, 4 g total fat, 1.5 g saturated fat, 0 g fiber, 400 mg sodium

Busy-Day Beef Stew

MAKES 4 SERVINGS   PREP TIME: 20 MINUTES ■ TOTAL TIME: 8 HOURS 20 MINUTES

G-LIST SERVINGS = 2 PROTEINS, 2 CARBOHYDRATES, 1 FAT, 1 VEGETABLE

1 teaspoon canola oil

1 pound lean cubed beef stew meat

1 clove garlic, finely chopped

2 onions, chopped

1 teaspoon dried oregano

1 bay leaf

1 can (14.5 ounces) reduced-sodium beef broth

2 tablespoons tomato paste

1 can (14.5 ounces) diced tomatoes

2 carrots, sliced

1 cup frozen corn

3 red potatoes, cubed

MAKE IT A
Super Ghrelin Meal:
Top the stew with cubed avocado or sour cream. Have a fruit on the side.

Portion tip:
If you need 3 Proteins, make the recipe with 1½ pounds of lean beef.

1. Heat the oil in a medium skillet on medium-high heat. Sear the beef cubes with the garlic until browned.

2. In a slow cooker, combine the beef, onions, oregano, bay leaf, broth, tomato paste, tomatoes, carrots, corn, and potatoes.

3. Cover and cook on low for 6 to 8 hours, or on high for 4 to 6 hours.

PER SERVING: 380 calories, 29 g protein, 37 g carbohydrates, 13 g total fat, 4 g saturated fat, 5 g fiber, 317 mg sodium

Beef and Broccoli Stir-Fry

MAKES 4 SERVINGS   PREP TIME: 15 MINUTES ▪ TOTAL TIME: 30 MINUTES

G-LIST SERVINGS = 2 PROTEINS, 2 CARBOHYDRATES, 1 FAT, 2 VEGETABLES

⅔ cup quick-cooking brown rice

2 tablespoons cornstarch

2 tablespoons light soy sauce

1 teaspoon toasted sesame oil

1 cup low-sodium beef broth

¼ teaspoon crushed red-pepper flakes

1 tablespoon canola oil

1 pound boneless sirloin steak, diagonally sliced

2 cloves garlic, finely chopped

4 cups broccoli florets

1 onion, thinly sliced

MAKE IT A
Super Ghrelin Meal:
Have a super fruit on the side.

Portion tip:
If you need 3 Proteins, make the recipe with 1½ pounds boneless sirloin steak.

1. Prepare the rice according to the package directions.

2. Meanwhile, in a small bowl, whisk together the cornstarch, soy sauce, and sesame oil. Whisk in the broth and pepper flakes until smooth. Set aside.

3. Heat the oil in a large skillet or wok over medium-high heat. Cook the steak with the garlic, stirring constantly, for 5 minutes, or until beef is browned. Transfer to a bowl and set aside.

4. Add the broccoli and onion to the skillet. Cook, stirring constantly, for 5 minutes or until the vegetables are tender-crisp.

5. Add the reserved broth mixture to the skillet. Bring to a boil, stirring constantly. Reduce heat to medium, add the reserved beef, and simmer for 1 to 2 minutes, or until the liquid thickens. Serve over the rice.

PER SERVING: 402 calories, 28 g protein, 23 g carbohydrates, 22 g total fat, 7 g saturated fat, 3 g fiber, 367 mg sodium

Stuffed Red Peppers

MAKES 2 SERVINGS   PREP TIME: 10 MINUTES ▦ TOTAL TIME: 1 HOUR

G-LIST SERVINGS = 3 PROTEINS, 2 CARBOHYDRATES, 1 FAT, 2 VEGETABLES

½ cup quick-cooking brown rice

2 red bell peppers, tops cut off and seeds scooped out

1 tablespoon olive oil, divided

½ pound ground sirloin

¼ teaspoon salt

¼ cup shredded carrot

¼ cup marinara sauce

¼ cup shredded part-skim mozzarella cheese

MAKE IT A
Super Ghrelin Meal:
Use quinoa in the recipe instead of rice. Have a super fruit on the side.

Portion tip:
If you need 1 Carbohydrate, make the recipe with ¼ cup (uncooked) rice.

1. Prepare the rice according to the package directions. Preheat the oven to 350°F.

2. Fill a medium saucepan halfway with water and bring it to a boil. Add the peppers and boil for 2 to 3 minutes. Drain and run under cold water. Pat the peppers dry with a paper towel, then rub the outsides of the peppers with ½ teaspoon of the oil.

3. Heat the remaining 2½ teaspoons oil in a large nonstick skillet over medium heat. Cook the ground sirloin and salt for 3 to 5 minutes or until browned. Stir in the cooked rice, carrot, and marinara sauce and heat for 1 minute.

4. Fill the peppers with the beef-and-rice mixture. Top each evenly with the cheese. Place the filled peppers in a baking dish and bake for 20 minutes, or until they are heated through and the cheese is melted.

PER SERVING: 490 calories, 33 g protein, 48 g carbohydrates, 17 g total fat, 5 g saturated fat, 5 g fiber, 567 mg sodium

Pork Chops with Cran-Apple Relish

MAKES 4 SERVINGS — PREP TIME: 15 MINUTES ■ TOTAL TIME: 40 MINUTES

G-LIST SERVINGS = 2 PROTEINS, 2 CARBOHYDRATES, 1 FAT, 2 VEGETABLES, 1 FRUIT

2 tablespoons olive oil, divided

2 Granny Smith apples, chopped

½ cup chopped cranberries

1 onion, finely chopped

1 teaspoon chopped fresh rosemary

¾ teaspoon salt, divided

1 clove garlic, finely chopped

1 pound kale, tough stems removed and leaves chopped

2 tablespoons apple cider or apple cider vinegar

¼ teaspoon crushed red-pepper flakes

⅔ cup whole wheat couscous

4 boneless lean center-cut pork chops (4 ounces each)

THIS IS A
Super Ghrelin Meal.
Portion tip:
If you need 3 Proteins, make the recipe with 6-ounce pork chops.

1. Heat half the oil in a large skillet over medium heat. Add the apples, cranberries, onion, rosemary, ¼ teaspoon salt, and 2 tablespoons water. Cook, stirring often, for 10 minutes, or until softened. Transfer to a bowl, cover, and set aside.

2. Meanwhile, coat a large saucepan with cooking spray and place over medium-high heat. Cook the garlic and kale, stirring often, for 5 minutes.

3. Add the cider, pepper, and 2 cups water to saucepan. Bring to a boil. Stir in couscous and ¼ teaspoon salt. Remove pan from heat, cover, and let stand for 10 minutes, or until water is absorbed. Fluff couscous with a fork.

4. Rub the pork chops with ¼ teaspoon salt. In the same skillet, heat 1 tablespoon oil over medium heat. Cover and cook pork chops, turning once, for 10 minutes, or until lightly browned and a thermometer inserted in the center registers 160°F and juices run clear.

5. Divide the kale mixture among 4 plates. Top each with a pork chop and the reserved apple mixture.

PER SERVING: 459 calories, 29 g protein, 40 g carbohydrates, 22 g total fat, 6 g saturated fat, 7 g fiber, 538 mg sodium

Creamy Mac and Cheese

MAKES 4 SERVINGS · PREP TIME: 15 MINUTES ■ TOTAL TIME: 1 HOUR

G-LIST SERVINGS = 2 PROTEINS, 2 CARBOHYDRATES, 2 VEGETABLES

6 ounces whole grain elbow macaroni (1½ cups)

1 cup 1% cottage cheese

½ cup 0% plain Greek yogurt

2 egg whites

1 cup shredded reduced-fat Cheddar cheese

7 ounces firm silken tofu, drained and mashed

¼ teaspoon salt

2 cups broccoli florets, lightly steamed

2 Roma tomatoes, seeded and chopped

4 large scallions, finely chopped

MAKE IT A
Super Ghrelin Meal:
Have a small green salad drizzled with olive oil and balsamic vinegar. Have a super fruit on the side.

Portion tip:
If you need 3 Proteins, make the recipe with 1½ cups of low-fat cottage cheese and 1 cup of reduced-fat Cheddar cheese.

1. Preheat the oven to 350°F. Coat a 3-quart baking dish with cooking spray.

2. Prepare the macaroni according to package directions.

3. In a blender or food processor, combine the cottage cheese, yogurt, egg whites, Cheddar, tofu, and salt. Blend or process until well mixed. Pour into a large bowl. Stir in the broccoli, tomatoes, scallions, and cooked macaroni. Pour into the baking dish.

4. Bake for 35 minutes, or until heated through.

PER SERVING: 350 calories, 29 g protein, 38 g carbohydrates, 10 g total fat, 5 g saturated fat, 5 g fiber, 634 mg sodium

Spinach-Stuffed Shells

MAKES 4 SERVINGS   PREP TIME: 15 MINUTES ▓ TOTAL TIME: 55 MINUTES

G-LIST SERVINGS = 1 PROTEIN, 2 CARBOHYDRATES, 1 VEGETABLE

12 jumbo pasta shells

 1 bag (6 ounces) baby spinach, steamed until wilted

⅔ cup 0% plain Greek yogurt

½ cup shredded part-skim mozzarella cheese

¼ cup Parmesan cheese

 1 egg white

 2 cups marinara sauce

MAKE IT A
Super Ghrelin Meal:
Top the recipe with pesto sauce and have a super fruit on the side.

Portion tip:
If you need 3 Proteins, serve with 4 ounces of grilled chicken breast.

1. Preheat the oven to 375°F. Coat an 8" x 8" baking dish with cooking spray.

2. Prepare the shells according to the package directions.

3. In a large bowl, stir together the spinach, yogurt, mozzarella, Parmesan, and egg white. Fill each cooked shell with 2 tablespoons of the spinach mixture.

4. Place the shells in the baking dish. Spoon the marinara sauce over the shells. Cover and bake for 30 to 40 minutes, or until heated through.

PER SERVING: 261 calories, 17 g protein, 37 g carbohydrates, 5 g total fat, 2 g saturated fat, 5 g fiber, 739 mg sodium

Roasted Vegetable Lasagna

MAKES 4 SERVINGS   PREP TIME: 35 MINUTES ■ TOTAL TIME: 1 HOUR, 55 MINUTES

G-LIST SERVINGS = 1 PROTEIN, 2 CARBOHYDRATES, 1 VEGETABLE

1 cup reduced-fat ricotta cheese

2 tablespoons chopped fresh basil

2 tablespoons chopped flat-leaf parsley

1 clove garlic, chopped

4 ounces sliced mixed mushrooms

1 small zucchini, sliced

1 onion, chopped

1 teaspoon olive oil

 Salt

 Ground black pepper

1 cup marinara sauce

6 whole wheat no-boil (oven-ready) lasagna noodles

¼ cup Parmesan cheese

MAKE IT A
Super Ghrelin Meal:
Top the lasagna with basil pesto. Have a super fruit on the side.

Portion tip:
If you need 3 Proteins, incorporate 1 cup of mashed firm tofu into the cooked vegetables at the end of step 3.

1. Preheat the oven to 400°F.

2. In a food processor or blender, combine the ricotta cheese, basil, parsley, and garlic. Blend until smooth. Set aside.

3. Spread the mushrooms, zucchini, and onion on a baking sheet. Toss the vegetables with the oil and season with salt and pepper to taste. Roast for 20 minutes, tossing the vegetables once. Remove from oven.Lower the oven heat to 350 degrees.

4. To assemble the lasagna, spread ¼ cup of the marinara sauce in an 8" x8" baking dish. Top with 2 of the lasagna noodles. Layer half the vegetables over the noodles. Spread half the ricotta cheese mixture over the vegetables.

5. Repeat the layering with 2 noodles, half the remaining marinara sauce, the remaining vegetables, and the remaining ricotta cheese mixture. Top with the 2 remaining noodles and the remaining sauce. Sprinkle with the Parmesan. Cover the dish with foil.

6. Bake for 40 minutes, or until heated through. Remove the foil and bake for 5 to 10 minutes, or until the cheese is slightly browned. Let stand for 10 minutes before cutting and serving.

PER SERVING: 250 calories, 12 g protein, 34 g carbohydrates, 7 g total fat, 2.5 g saturated fat, 5 g fiber, 386 mg sodium

Meatless Monday "Meat Loaf"

MAKES 2 SERVINGS   PREP TIME: 15 MINUTES ■ TOTAL TIME: 1 HOUR 15 MINUTES

G-LIST SERVINGS = 2 PROTEINS, 1 CARBOHYDRATE, 2 FATS

1 tablespoon ketchup

1 teaspoon Dijon mustard

1 tablespoon chopped fresh or
1 teaspoon dried parsley

½ teaspoon dried oregano

¼ cup walnut halves

1 rib celery, finely chopped

½ small onion, finely chopped

1 clove garlic, finely chopped

8 ounces firm tofu, drained

2 ounces reduced-fat feta cheese

½ cup quick-cooking oats

1 tablespoon reduced-sodium Worcestershire sauce

1 teaspoon ketchup

MAKE IT A
Super Ghrelin Meal:
Pair with quinoa cooked with onions and peppers. Have a superfruit on the side.

Portion tip:
If you need 3 Proteins, make the recipe with 12 ounces of firm tofu.

1. Preheat the oven to 350°F.

2. **To make the topping:** In a small bowl, combine the ketchup, mustard, parsley, and oregano. Set aside.

3. **To make the loaf:** Using a grinder or food processor, process the walnuts to a powder and set aside.

4. Coat a medium skillet with cooking spray and place over medium heat. Cook the celery, onion, and garlic for 4 minutes, or until tender. Set aside.

5. In a large bowl, mash the tofu. Stir in the reserved walnuts, feta, oats, Worcestershire sauce, and ketchup. Stir in the reserved celery mixture.

6. Coat an 8" x 4" loaf pan or two 5" x 3" mini loaf pans with cooking spray. Pack the tofu mixture tightly into the pan(s). Brush with the reserved topping.

7. Bake for 45 to 55 minutes, until a pick comes out clean.

PER SERVING: 336 calories, 21 g protein, 27 g carbohydrates, 17 g total fat, 4 g saturated fat, 5 g fiber, 654 mg sodium

Mediterranean Quinoa

MAKES 4 SERVINGS   PREP TIME: 5 MINUTES ■ TOTAL TIME: 30 MINUTES

G-LIST SERVINGS = 1½ CARBOHYDRATES

1 cup tomato vegetable juice or low-sodium vegetable broth

⅔ cup quinoa, rinsed

1 clove garlic, finely chopped

¼ teaspoon salt

¼ teaspoon ground black pepper

2 pitted kalamata olives, finely chopped

1. In a medium saucepan, combine the vegetable juice or broth, quinoa, garlic, salt, and pepper. Bring to a boil over medium-high heat.

2. Reduce the heat to low, cover, and simmer for 25 minutes, or until the liquid is absorbed. Stir in olives.

PER SERVING: 124 calories, 4 g protein, 21 g carbohydrates, 2 g total fat, 0 g saturated fat, 3 g fiber, 220 mg sodium

White Bean
and Parmesan Mashed Potatoes

MAKES 6 SERVINGS   PREP TIME: 20 MINUTES ▓ TOTAL TIME: 50 MINUTES

G-LIST SERVINGS = 2 CARBOHYDRATES

- 3 all-purpose potatoes, peeled and chopped
- 2 cans (14–19 ounces each) no-salt-added cannellini beans, rinsed and drained
- 3 cloves garlic, finely chopped
- 1 teaspoon salt
- ¼ teaspoon ground black pepper
- ¾ cup 0% plain Greek yogurt
- ¼ cup grated Parmesan cheese

1. In a large saucepan, combine the potatoes, beans, garlic, salt, pepper, and enough water to cover. Bring to a boil over high heat. Reduce the heat to medium-low, cover, and cook for 25 to 30 minutes, or until tender.
2. Drain the potatoes and beans and return to the pot. Turn off the heat. Add the yogurt and cheese. With a potato masher or electric mixer at low speed, mash until well mixed.

PER SERVING: 176 calories, 10 g protein, 31 g carbohydrates, 2 g total fat, 1 g saturated fat, 5 g fiber, 482 mg sodium

Creole Baked Sweet Potato Wedges

MAKES 4 SERVINGS   PREP TIME: 10 MINUTES ■ TOTAL TIME: 30 MINUTES

G-LIST SERVINGS = 1 CARBOHYDRATE, 1 FAT

4 sweet potatoes, cut into ½" wedges

1 tablespoon olive oil

½ teaspoon garlic powder

¼ teaspoon ground red pepper

¼ teaspoon ground black pepper

¼ teaspoon paprika

¼ teaspoon salt

1. Preheat the oven to 400°F. Coat 2 baking sheets with cooking spray.

2. Place the sweet potatoes on the baking sheets. Drizzle with the oil. In a small bowl, combine the red pepper, black pepper, paprika, and salt. Sprinkle evenly over the sweet potatoes. Toss to coat well. Spread out into single layers.

3. Bake, turning once, for 20 minutes, or until golden brown and tender.

PER SERVING: 144 calories, 2 g protein, 27 g carbohydrates, 4 g total fat, 0.5 g saturated fat, 4 g fiber, 217 mg sodium

Mexicali Pasta and Bean Salad

MAKES 4 SERVINGS   PREP TIME: 10 MINUTES ■ TOTAL TIME: 20 MINUTES

G-LIST SERVINGS = 2 CARBOHYDRATES, 1 FAT

4 ounces whole grain penne, rotelle, or other stubby pasta shape

¼ cup lime juice

1 tablespoon olive oil

1 green bell pepper, chopped

½ red onion, chopped

1 can (14–19 ounces) no-salt-added kidney beans, rinsed and drained

½ cup fresh or frozen and thawed corn kernels

1. Cook the pasta according to the package directions. Drain and rinse with cold water.

2. Meanwhile, in a large bowl, whisk together the lime juice and oil. Add the pepper, onion, beans, corn, and drained pasta. Toss to coat well. Serve immediately or refrigerate until ready to serve.

PER SERVING: 203 calories, 8 g protein, 36 g carbohydrates, 4 g total fat, 0.5 g saturated fat, 7 g fiber, 193 mg sodium

Brown Rice
with Cauliflower and Peas

G-LIST SERVINGS = 1 CARBOHYDRATE, 1 FAT

⅔ cup quick-cooking brown rice

1 tablespoon olive oil

2 cloves garlic, finely chopped

1 small onion, finely chopped

1 cup small cauliflower florets

½ cup frozen green peas, thawed

¼ teaspoon salt

1. Prepare the rice according to the package directions.

2. Meanwhile, heat the oil in a medium saucepanover medium-high heat. Add the garlic, onion, cauliflower, peas, and salt and cook, stirring occasionally, for 3 to 5 minutes, or until the cauliflower is tender-crisp.

3. Fluff the rice with a fork. Stir in the cauliflower mixture and serve.

PER SERVING: 116 calories, 3 g protein, 17 g carbohydrates, 4 g total fat, 0.5 g saturated fat, 2 g fiber, 158 mg sodium

Couscous
with Squash and Pine Nuts

MAKES 4 SERVINGS   PREP TIME: 5 MINUTES ■ TOTAL TIME: 25 MINUTES

G-LIST SERVINGS = 1 CARBOHYDRATE, 1 FAT, ½ FRUIT

- 2 tablespoons pine nuts
- 1 teaspoon olive oil
- ½ small red onion, finely chopped
- 1 cup peeled and cubed butternut squash
- ⅔ cup low-fat, reduced-sodium chicken or vegetable broth
- ⅔ cup water
- ¼ teaspoon salt
- ⅔ cup whole wheat couscous
- ¼ cup dried cranberries

1. In a small skillet, toast the pine nuts over low heat, stirring often, for 2 minutes, or until lightly browned and fragrant. Remove the nuts from the skillet and set aside.
2. Heat the oil in a medium saucepan over medium heat. Cook the onion and squash, stirring often, for 5 minutes, or until tender. Add the broth, water, and salt. Bring to a boil.
3. Stir in the couscous and cranberries. Remove from the heat, cover, and let stand for 10 minutes or until the liquid is absorbed.
4. Fluff the couscous with a fork. Sprinkle with the reserved pine nuts.

PER SERVING: 151 calories, 4 g protein, 26 g carbohydrates, 5 g total fat, 0.5 g saturated fat, 4 g fiber, 224 mg sodium

Chard and Cannellini Beans

MAKES 2 SERVINGS   PREP TIME: 5 MINUTES ■ TOTAL TIME: 10 MINUTES

G-LIST SERVINGS = 1 CARBOHYDRATE, 1 FAT, 1 VEGETABLE

2 teaspoons olive oil

1 shallot, finely chopped

8 ounces Swiss chard leaves, chopped, thick stems removed and discarded (4 cups)

¼ teaspoon salt

⅔ cup canned no-salt-added cannellini beans, rinsed and drained

1. Heat the oil in a large skillet over medium heat. Cook the shallot for 1 minute.

2. Add the chard and salt. Cook, stirring occasionally, for 3 minutes, or until wilted.

3. Add the beans and cook until heated through.

PER SERVING: 147 calories, 7 g protein, 21 g carbohydrates, 5 g total fat, 1 g saturated fat, 4 g fiber, 471 mg sodium

Summer Vegetable Skillet

MAKES 2 SERVINGS   PREP TIME: 15 MINUTES ▦ TOTAL TIME: 20 MINUTES

G-LIST SERVINGS = 4 VEGETABLES

2 carrots, cut into matchsticks

1 cup broccoli florets

1 small red onion, thinly sliced

1 small zucchini, sliced

⅛ teaspoon salt

Coat a large skillet with cooking spray and place over medium-high heat. Addthe carrots, broccoli, onion, zucchini, and salt. Cook, stirring often, for 4 minutes, or until tender-crisp.

PER SERVING: 112 calories, 5 g protein, 26 g carbohydrates, 0.5 g total fat, 0 g saturated fat, 4 g fiber, 203 mg sodium

Pear-Apricot Dream

MAKES 2 SERVINGS   PREP TIME: 5 MINUTES ▥ TOTAL TIME: 15 MINUTES

G-LIST SERVINGS = 2 FRUITS

2 Bartlett or Bosc pears, peeled, cored, and chopped

¼ cup dried apricot halves, finely chopped

¼ cup pear or apricot nectar

1. In a medium saucepan, combine the pears, apricots, and nectar. Cook over medium heat, stirring, for 10 minutes or until tender.

2. Spoon into 2 dessert bowls and cool before serving.

PER SERVING: 140 calories, 1 g protein, 37 g carbohydrates, 0 g total fat, 0 g saturated fat, 6 g fiber, 4 mg sodium

Creamy Lemon-Blueberry Mousse

MAKES 6 SERVINGS   PREP TIME: 15 MINUTES ▇ TOTAL TIME: 2 HOURS 30 MINUTES

G-LIST SERVINGS = 1 CARBOHYDRATE, 1 FRUIT

- 1 package (3 ounces) sugar-free lemon-flavored gelatin
- 1 cup boiling water
- ½ teaspoon lemon zest
- 1 cup 0% plain Greek yogurt
- 1 cup frozen light whipped topping, thawed
- 2 cups fresh blueberries

1. In a medium bowl, whisk together the gelatin and boiling water for 1 minute, or until the gelatin dissolves. Let stand for 15 minutes, or until cooled but not set.

2. Whisk in the zest, yogurt, and dessert topping until smooth.

3. Divide the blueberries among 6 dessert cups. Pour the gelatin mixture evenly over the berries. Cover and refrigerate for at least 2 hours, or until set.

PER SERVING: 123 calories, 7 g protein, 18 g carbohydrates, 3 g total fat, 3 g saturated fat, 1 g fiber, 30 mg sodium

Baked Pumpkin Pudding

MAKES 8 SERVINGS   PREP TIME: 10 MINUTES ■ TOTAL TIME: 30 MINUTES

G-LIST SERVINGS = 2 CARBOHYDRATES

1 can (15 ounces) pumpkin

1 can (12 ounces) fat-free evaporated milk

⅓ cup packed light brown sugar

2 eggs

1 teaspoon ground cinnamon

¼ teaspoon ground nutmeg

¼ teaspoon ground ginger

1 teaspoon vanilla extract

1 cup 0% vanilla Greek yogurt

1. Preheat the oven to 350°F. Lightly coat eight 6-ounce custard cups with cooking spray.

2. In a medium bowl, whisk together the pumpkin, milk, sugar, eggs, cinnamon, nutmeg, ginger, and vanilla. Fold in the yogurt.

3. Pour the mixture into the prepared custard cups. Place the cups in a large baking dish or roasting pan. Pour 1" of water around the cups.

4. Bake for 20 minutes, or until the centers are just barely set.

PER SERVING: 127 calories, 8 g protein, 21 g carbohydrates, 1 g total fat, 0.5 g saturated fat, 2 g fiber, 87 g sodium

Gluten-Free Black Bean Brownies

MAKES 12 SERVINGS   PREP TIME: 10 MINUTES ■ TOTAL TIME: 35 MINUTES

G-LIST SERVINGS = 1 CARBOHYDRATE, 1 FAT

½ cup all-purpose gluten-free flour

½ teaspoon double-acting baking powder

1 can (14–19 ounces) no-salt-added black beans, rinsed and drained

⅓ cup packed brown sugar

¼ cup unsweetened cocoa powder

1 teaspoon instant coffee or espresso powder

2 eggs

¼ cup olive oil

¼ cup unsweetened applesauce

1 teaspoon vanilla extract

1. Preheat the oven to 350°F. Coat an 8" x 8" baking pan with cooking spray.

2. In a medium bowl, combine the flour and baking powder. Set aside.

3. In a blender or food processor, combine the beans, sugar, cocoa powder, coffee powder, eggs, oil, applesauce, and vanilla. Blend or process until very smooth. Add to the flour mixture and stir until combined. Spread into the prepared baking pan.

4. Bake for 25 minutes or until a wooden pick inserted in the center comes out clean. Cool completely before cutting into 12 squares.

PER SERVING: 117 calories, 3 g protein, 15 g carbohydrates, 6 g total fat, 1 g saturated fat, 2 g fiber, 108 mg sodium

Dark Chocolate Ice Pops

MAKES 4 SERVINGS   PREP TIME: 10 MINUTES ▦ TOTAL TIME: 8 HOURS 10 MINUTES

G-LIST SERVINGS = 1 CARBOHYDRATE, 3 FATS

- 4 ounces 85% extra-dark bittersweet chocolate, finely chopped
- 2 tablespoons light brown sugar
- ¼ teaspoon ground cinnamon
- 1 cup milk
- ½ teaspoon vanilla extract

1. In a medium glass bowl, combine the chocolate, sugar, and cinnamon.

2. In a small saucepan, bring the milk just to a simmer over medium heat. Pour over the chocolate mixture and stir until the chocolate is melted and the mixture is well blended. Add the vanilla.

3. Pour the mixture evenly into ice pop molds (or ice cube trays) and insert popsicle sticks in the center of each. Freeze for at least 8 hours, or until firm.

4. To remove the pops, run warm water over the outside of the mold for 10 seconds, or until you can gently pull the pops out by their sticks.

PER SERVING: 227 calories, 5 g protein, 20 g carbohydrates, 15 g total fat, 9 g saturated fat, 4 g fiber, 30 g sodium

Peanut Butter Bars

MAKES 10 SERVINGS   PREP TIME: 5 MINUTES ■ TOTAL TIME: 20 MINUTES

G-LIST SERVINGS = 1 CARBOHYDRATE, 3 FATS

¾ cup creamy unsalted peanut butter

¼ cup raw honey

1 tablespoon instant fat-free powdered
   milk

4 cups puffed wheat cereal

½ cup semisweet chocolate chips

1. Coat an 11½" × 8" pan with cooking spray.

2. In a large saucepan, combine the peanut butter, honey, and powdered milk. Cook over low heat, stirring often, for 2 minutes, or until smooth.

3. Stir in the cereal. Add the chocolate chips and stir to combine. Press the mixture into the prepared pan. Cool completely before cutting into 10 pieces.

PER SERVING: 219 calories, 7 g protein, 21 g carbohydrates, 14 g total fat, 4 g saturated fat, 2 g fiber, 7 mg sodium

No-Bake Blueberry or Raspberry Cheesecake

MAKES 6 SERVINGS   PREP TIME: 10 MINUTES ■ TOTAL TIME: 4 HOURS 40 MINUTES

G-LIST SERVINGS = 1 CARBOHYDRATE, 3 FATS

¼ cup finely ground walnuts

1 package (8 ounces) reduced-fat cream cheese, at room temperature

1 cup 0% vanilla Greek yogurt

½ teaspoon vanilla extract

½ teaspoon lemon zest

1 cup frozen light whipped topping, thawed

1 cup fresh blueberries or raspberries

1. Spread the finely ground walnuts in the bottom of a 9-inch springform pan.

2. In a medium bowl, with an electric mixer on medium speed, beat the cream cheese until light and fluffy. Add the yogurt, vanilla, and lemon zest. Beat until well blended. Fold in the whipped topping and berries.

3. Pour the mixture into the springform pan. Cover with plastic wrap and freeze for about 4 hours. To serve, remove the cheesecake from the freezer, unmold, and let stand at room temperature for 30 minutes before slicing.

PER SERVING: 226 calories, 8 g protein, 20 g carbohydrates, 13 g total fat, 8 g saturated fat, 1 g fiber, 177 mg sodium

Coconut Custard Trifle

MAKES 8 SERVINGS   PREP TIME: 15 MINUTES ■ TOTAL TIME: 2 HOURS 15 MINUTES

G-LIST SERVINGS = 1 CARBOHYDRATE, ½ FRUIT

2 cups fat-free milk

1 package (4-serving size) sugar-free vanilla instant pudding mix

4 ounces reduced-fat cream cheese, at room temperature

¼ teaspoon coconut extract

1 can (20 ounces) pineapple chunks, packed in juice (reserve ¼ cup juice)

1 can (11 ounces) water-packed mandarin oranges, drained

½ 10-ounce angel food cake, cut into 1" cubes (about 4 cups)

¼ cup pineapple juice (reserved from the can above), divided

¼ cup unsweetened flaked coconut (optional)

1. In a medium bowl, combine the milk and pudding mix. With an electric mixer on low speed, beat for 2 minutes. Set aside.

2. In a large bowl, beat the cream cheese and coconut extract with an electric mixer on medium-high speed for 30 seconds. Gradually add the pudding mixture, beating on low speed until well mixed.

3. Place half of the pineapple and mandarin oranges in a 1½-quart glass bowl. Top with half of the cake cubes. Drizzle the cake with 2 tablespoons of the pineapple juice and sprinkle with 2 tablespoons of the flaked coconut, if desired. Spoon half of the pudding mixture over the cake. Repeat the layers with the remaining half of the fruit, cake cubes, pineapple juice, pudding, and flaked coconut, if desired.

4. Cover and refrigerate for 2 hours.

PER SERVING: 101 calories, 4 g protein, 22 g carbohydrates, 0 g total fat, 0 g saturated fat, 1 g fiber, 209 mg sodium

Warm Chocolate Caramel Banana

MAKES 2 SERVINGS   PREP TIME: 5 MINUTES ▦ TOTAL TIME: 10 MINUTES

G-LIST SERVINGS = 1 CARBOHYDRATE, 2 FATS, 1 FRUIT

1 tablespoon butter

1 tablespoon light brown sugar

1 tablespoon rum or ¼ teaspoon rum extract

1 large firm-ripe banana, sliced ½" on the diagonal

2 tablespoons semisweet chocolate chips

1 tablespoon finely chopped pecans

¼ cup 0% vanilla Greek yogurt (optional)

1. In a small nonstick skillet over medium heat, melt the butter. Add the brown sugar and rum and cook, stirring constantly, for 1 minute, or until the sugar dissolves.

2. Stir in the banana. Cook, carefully turning over once, for 2 minutes, or until the banana is browned and caramelized. Sprinkle with chocolate chips.

3. Divide the banana between 2 dessert plates. Drizzle with the sauce from the skillet. Top with the pecans and the yogurt, if desired.

PER SERVING: 247 calories, 2 g protein, 32 g carbohydrates, 12 g total fat, 6 g saturated fat, 3 g fiber, 44 g sodium

Uma J.

AGE: 31

POUNDS LOST:

FAST-TRACK: 3.6

TOTAL: **8.2 in 30 days**

OVERALL INCHES LOST: 7.5

Uma started on the Belly Fat Fix just 2 months before her wedding. But unlike lots of other brides-to-be, she wasn't concerned about looking good on the wedding day. "What motivated me," she says, "was the desire to become healthier before I start my family."

The 31-year-old New York educational consultant admits that she and her fiancé had gotten into some bad eating habits, ordering lots of takeout and not paying much attention to calories or nutrition. In the end, their nutritional choices showed up on their waistlines.

So as Uma was attending her bridal shower, enjoying her bachelorette party, and finalizing all the details of the wedding, she started the 3-Day Fast-Track—a decision her mom wasn't too thrilled about. After all, Uma's dress already fit perfectly, and Mom was concerned that if Uma lost the weight, she'd need alterations.

Eager to begin her married life on a new, healthy footing, Uma completed just 2½ days of the Fast-Track—enough to help her break with her old ways. "The Fast-Track primed me to think about meals that were healthy. Now I keep foods like olives and edamame in the house, something I never did before. Sticking with the discipline of

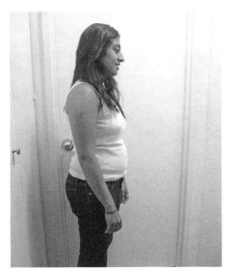

BEFORE

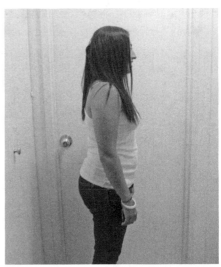

AFTER

the Fast-Track was stressful but reassuring. I knew I was doing the right thing to prepare myself to become a mother."

With the Fast-Track under her belt, she graduated to the ongoing Belly Fat Fix plan, which took a bit of getting used to. Before, Uma never planned her meals for the week. During the school day, she'd eat whatever the cafeteria was serving. And at night, if she was extra busy, she'd order takeout or run to the neighborhood grocery store to pick up the few items she needed.

All that changed on the Belly Fat Fix. Uma learned to think ahead, plan her meals for the week, and make sure she had everything she needed on hand—*that* was the key. "Having the right foods in the house was really nice on those evenings when I came home with every intention of making a meal from Marjorie's list. Then I'd be on the phone for hours with my mom, going over all the wedding details, and by the time we finished our conversation, I'd be too tired to cook. But having those ingredients on hand meant I could quickly cobble something good together. I could open my fridge at any time and realize, *Oh, there's carrots, oh, there's hummus.* I always have good foods to choose from."

The Belly Fat Fix works even when plans change at the last minute, says Uma. "Last night, our dinner with friends fell through," she explains. "In the past, I would have ordered something or had junk, but last night, there was good, healthy food in the fridge."

For Uma, there's nothing shocking about this diet—it's based on common sense and encourages good eating practices. "It's helped me become a little more aware of what's a smart choice and what's a terrible choice."

As she continued on the diet, Uma noticed two things. As she started to eat food that filled her up, suppressing her ghrelin, she realized that her stomach started "asking for less," and she began eating far less than she used to. "The other night, we went to a favorite burger place—in the past, I could eat the whole burger. This time, I ate about a third of it. I stopped when I felt full, instead of continuing to eat for the sake of eating." She also noticed that as those 6 pounds melted away, going to the gym felt a lot less daunting.

Thanks to her smarter choices—and more exercise—she's down at least one dress size and one or two pants sizes. "I just got into a dress that hasn't fit me in over a year," she says with delight. "I'm going to stay on the plan—and stay slim and healthy for good."

CHAPTER 8

The No-Sweat Exercise Program

Have you completed the 3-Day Fast-Track? If you have, you've accomplished a lot: You've reset your ghrelin in a healthy way and lost a few quick pounds to boot. You've also established a great new habit: You're using the food tracker and becoming more aware of your eating habits and your body's response to a wide variety of foods. Now it's time to move on. In this chapter, you'll learn how to harness the power of exercise to keep your ghrelin in balance, your motivation up, and your weight off.

The No-Sweat Exercise Program is designed to keep your ghrelin stable while delivering the usual benefits of exercise. It's a nonaerobic workout that uses strength training to build stronger and leaner muscles, improve your energy, increase your endurance, raise your metabolism, and keep the weight you lose from creeping back on. That's what makes the Belly Fat Fix unique. Unlike other programs, which focus on calorie-burning and weight loss, this plan incorporates a ghrelin-friendly workout that continues to support you in maintaining your ideal weight even after you've reached your goal.

I put this program together based on my own experience. When I was in college, I went to the gym about five times a week. I'd do a full hour on the elliptical at 12.0 resistance and sweat right through my shirt. It was great—I was an elliptical rock star. Problem was, even though I knew *all* about nutrition and exercise, I remained overweight. My weight bounced between 170 and 175 during my undergraduate and graduate school years. I was learning how to be a dietitian and a personal trainer, but somehow, I couldn't quite figure out what I was doing wrong.

Now I know. Truth is, I was exercising too much—and I wasn't doing any resistance training. I'd foolishly assumed that a high resistance level on the elliptical was "resistance" enough. Boy, was I wrong! It took me many years of sweating on that machine to figure it out, but once I did, it was easier to take off the weight and keep it off.

I learned firsthand that cardio exercise won't help you lose weight. In fact, it could potentially slow your weight loss or stop it entirely. Here's why: First, intense cardiovascular exercise causes ghrelin levels to spike upward, which makes you hungry. Second, that kind of exercise burns a lot of calories in a short time, sending your body into conservation mode, in which it retains fat. Sound confusing—and maybe even contradictory? You may be thinking, "If I want to lose weight, I *should* burn a lot of calories." Truth is, you shouldn't, and later on, I'll explain why.

But for now, let me share something else about myself. I wrote this book even as I was finalizing the details of my wedding—and while I managed my own nutrition and fitness coaching business in New York City. No lie. My manuscript was due 11 days before my wedding. (Crazy, I know.) Like every bride, I wanted to look my best on my big day. How to accomplish that under all that stress—seeing clients by day, writing late into the evening, getting all the wedding details just right? Here's how: I did *every single thing* I'm telling you to do. I designed the No-Sweat Exercise Program with three strategic elements so that any busy person can follow it:

1. It's a home-based program. No expensive equipment, no gym membership required. If you already belong to a gym, keep going. If you don't, no problem. Most of my clients are busy working full time and raising a family. The commute to and from a gym alone isn't always feasible. The No-Sweat Exercise Program can be easily done in your home.

2. It's quick. The No-Sweat Exercise Program can be broken up into 10-minute segments that you can do any time of the day that works for you.

3. It's adaptable for different fitness levels. Each and every exercise has an option for beginner, intermediate, and advanced fitness levels. Regardless of your exercise experience—or lack thereof—there's an option that's right for you.

THE NO-SWEAT PRINCIPLES

The No-Sweat Exercise Program has two main components:

▶ Cardio exercise for heart health rather than weight loss

▶ Resistance training for muscle building and metabolism activation

Cardio for heart heath focuses on strengthening your heart muscle to improve circulation, oxygen transport, blood pressure, and endurance. Any knowledgeable fitness trainer understands how important cardiovascular exercise is for health. But there's plenty of evidence refuting the notion that cardiovascular exercise is critical for weight loss. In fact, just one bout of intense cardiovascular exercise raises ghrelin,[1] making you hungrier and leading you into temptation. But there's a way to reap the benefits of cardiovascular exercise *without* the pitfalls of ghrelin elevation.

Resistance training for muscle building and metabolism activation focuses on muscle strengthening, toning, and flexibility. The right kind—and the right amount—of resistance training will build muscle without affecting ghrelin.[2] Muscle is more metabolically active than fat, so it burns more calories at rest than fat does. Building strong muscles over time raises your metabolic rate. The best part? You can build those muscles without ramping up your hunger—as long as you're following the No-Sweat exercise guidelines.

While the No-Sweat Exercise Program may not help you lose weight faster, here's what you *can* expect: stronger, leaner muscles; improved energy levels; more endurance; and an easier time maintaining your weight loss. That's the real purpose behind this exercise plan. Chances are, you'll see benefits from the No-Sweat program immediately. In fact, most clients who start exercising do lose weight a bit quicker, but not because of the exercise. It's because people who exercise regularly tend to stick to their diet better. Weight loss becomes a secondary benefit of the No-Sweat program.

Here's something else you can expect: an improved, improved self-confidence, and less of the stress that causes you to eat too much in the first place. Researchers at the Mayo Clinic report that just 10 minutes of physical activity stimulates various brain chemicals that leave you feeling happier and less stressed. You may also feel better about your appearance—and about yourself in general—with regular exercise, which can boost your confidence and improve your self-esteem.[3] There's a lot to be gained by doing just 10 minutes of exercise.

THE CARDIO MYTH

How exercise affects weight is one of the more vexing disputes in the weight-loss industry. Exercise burns calories—no controversy there—so in theory it should produce weight loss. This belief has propelled countless people into the gym to spend long hours jogging on a treadmill, spinning on a bike, or sweating through boot camp classes—without the results they were seeking. Studies show that intense cardio exercising does *not* yield weight loss—for both physiological and psychological reasons.[4, 5, 6]

THE PHYSIOLOGY OF CARDIO ON GHRELIN

A large body of research demonstrates that cardio exercise increases ghrelin. One study, conducted by the Department of Kinesiology at the University of Massachusetts, found that cardio burns a lot of calories quickly. Sounds good in theory—but in practice, not so much. During cardio exercise, the study found, the body's weight-regulatory system sends out a distress signal that hollers this message: *Red alert! Red alert! Body is in starvation mode. Conserve energy and fat!* In response to the crisis, the body makes more ghrelin and clamps down on the production of leptin, causing *intense hunger*—the body's way of motivating you to eat as quickly as possible to provide it with the nutrition and calories it needs. This response kicks

Ghrelin and Gender

When it comes to exercise, women are the losers—but not in a good way. After cardio exercise, women's ghrelin rises even more than for a man doing the same exercise routine.[7] This is nature's way of pre-serving fat stores for reproduction. You could say that "thunder thighs" and "muffin tops" are an unfortunate side-effect of the ability to bear children. *Lucky us.*

in several hours *after* that intense workout[8]—so if you've ever noticed that you're not hungry after working out, just wait awhile and pay attention to what happens over time. Typically, 2 to 6 hours later, your blood ghrelin levels will go sky-high.

And here's an interesting twist: This process only occurs in overweight and obese people, not in normal-weight folks.[9] So the people who need to lose weight the most are the ones who are the most negatively affected by cardio exercise.

THE PSYCHOLOGY OF CARDIO-DRIVEN EATING

Cardio exercise can *promote* reward-driven eating. If you hear yourself saying, "I can eat more because I exercised today," you're a victim of the "anticipation response" that intense exercise has been shown to create. So when you think you've burned a lot of calories exercising, your desire for food—specifically junk foods like those high in fat and sugar—rises. This phenomenon is a function of the brain's reward pathway in the hypothalamus. (See Your Brain on Ghrelin on page 9.) The real kicker here is that those people who are most likely to reward themselves with food after exercise are those with weight to lose.[10] That's self-defeating. The same study found that people who tend to look to food as a reward for exercise only need a single bout of exercise to stimulate them to seek their reward with more food. Scientists aren't quite sure what comes first with intensive cardio exercises. Does the calorie deficit spur a process in which your ghrelin levels soar? Or does the exercise itself motivate you to reward yourself with food on the way home from the gym? Either way, the end result is too much food, negating the purpose of exercise. Bottom line: Any way you look at it, cardio does *not* contribute to weight-loss success.

NO-SWEAT CARDIO EXERCISE GUIDELINES

Regardless of how much cardio raises ghrelin, it's still important for heart health. So don't abandon your workouts—just follow these guidelines. Remember that while you are actively trying to lose weight, you are highly susceptible to exercise-related ghrelin spikes. To keep your ghrelin stable, rather than driving it up and causing voracious, postworkout hunger (which spurs voracious eating), heed the following:

1. **Make your cardio workouts 30 minutes or less** for cardiovascular benefits without the calorie deficit that drives your ghrelin up.

2. **Break any sessions beyond 30 minutes of cardio into 10- to 20-minute segments over the course of a day.** You may have better luck keeping ghrelin in check by performing two 20-minute cardio sessions at different times of the day rather than 40 minutes at once.

3. **Draw a line between cardio and resistance training.** Cardio exercise should not be performed during the same workout session as your No-Sweat resistance training. Combining both types of exercise could lead to an increase in your ghrelin secretion.

4. **Do cardio should be done 1 or 2 hours after a meal,** when your ghrelin is low.

5. **Track what you've done after every session.** Studies have shown that keeping track of exercise, just like keeping track of eating, will help you stick with your routine, regardless of the type of exercise you do. A study published in the *Annals of Behavioral Medicine* found that participants who faithfully tracked their exercise were more likely to stick with their diet, make better food choices, and achieve better overall weight loss than those who didn't.[11]

FITTING THE NO-SWEAT PLAN INTO YOUR EXERCISE ROUTINE

Already have a workout routine you enjoy? Stick with it. The best form of exercise is exercise that you do regularly. But compare your current routine with the No-Sweat program. You'll probably benefit from making some minor adjustments to your current routine. With a few changes, you can be assured that you are exercising in a way that promotes muscle building and better metabolism without driving up your ghrelin. First take the quiz on page 275. Then, ask yourself these three questions to determine if your current routine is suppressing or increasing your ghrelin:

▶ **Did you pass the "Is Your Exercise Routine Ghrelin Increasing?" quiz?** If you did, great! You can stick with your current frequency of exercise each week. But that doesn't mean you should stick with your exact routine: It simply means that you're not overexercising in a way that increases ghrelin. You may still benefit from some modifications to your routine. If you didn't pass, switch to the No-Sweat program.

▶ **Is your current routine challenging all major muscles with resistance training two or three times per week?** If your current routine doesn't work all major muscle groups (upper, lower, and core) with two or more resistance-based exercises two or three times per week, you're not getting all the benefits that exercise offers. Try supplementing your current training with the No-Sweat exercises that work the body areas you've been neglecting. This way, you're still doing some (or all) of the exercises you're familiar with, while filling in the gaps with exercises that will challenge those areas of your body you've been neglecting.

▶ **Does your current routine fit into the No-Sweat cardio guidelines?** If yes, keep it up. Your cardio isn't a threat to your ghrelin levels. If not, review the No-Sweat Cardio Exercise Guidelines section (see page 273) and make adjustments ASAP. Cardio is for heart health, not weight loss. Too much cardio, especially in combination with your weight-loss efforts, will have a negative effect on your ghrelin.

Is Your Exercise Routine Ghrelin Increasing?

1. I exercise 5 or more days per week.

   ☐ True   ☐ False

2. I'm hungrier on the days I exercise.

   ☐ True   ☐ False

3. I exercise even when I feel tired or sore.

   ☐ True   ☐ False

4. I use free weights or machines less than half of my total exercise time.

   ☐ True   ☐ False

5. I generally do the same routine every time I exercise.

   ☐ True   ☐ False

6. I work out for 45 minutes or more for most exercise sessions.

   ☐ True   ☐ False

7. I no longer see results from my exercise.

   ☐ True   ☐ False

8. I often reward myself with food when I have a tough workout.

   ☐ True   ☐ False

If you answered *true* to four or more questions, your exercise routine may be hindering your weight loss. Follow the No-Sweat Exercise Program to build muscle without increasing your ghrelin.

RESISTANCE TRAINING: YOUR SECRET GHRELIN-SUPPRESSING WEAPON

My grandmother used to say, "If I had a nickel for every time I had to yell at you kids to quiet down, I'd be rich." I never understood what she meant until I became a dietitian. If I had a nickel for every time a client told me, "I have a slow metabolism," I'd be writing this book on a yacht in the Caribbean. So if you suspect you have a slow metabolism, let me set you straight. You probably don't. You're probably suffering from a lack of those healthy, strong, lean muscles that boost your metabolic rate by burning calories. When you lack healthy, strong, lean muscles, your metabolism isn't slow—in fact, it's precisely where it should be, based on your body composition (the ratio of fat to muscle).

Twenty-somethings are often told, "Things change when you turn 30." If you're over 30, as I am, you know how true this statement is. That's because after 30, women start to lose muscle mass at the rate of about a half pound per year. If you don't do something about that, your muscle-mass loss will double to 1 pound of muscle per year by the time you hit menopause. But don't freak out—you're not doomed. There's a way to stop or slow down this loss.

It's resistance training. Resistance training builds muscle, which increases your overall metabolic rate. Muscles, after all, burn about seven times more calories than fat, which adds up to between 10 and 20 calories more a day per pound. So the more muscle you have, the faster your metabolism. It doesn't matter how old or out of shape you are, you are always capable of building muscle. And when you build muscle, you increase your metabolism.

The No-Sweat Program lets you reap all the benefits of muscle building without increasing your hunger. The right kind of resistance training won't cause a spike in calorie-burning, so ghrelin will stay balanced while you build muscles. And once you build more muscles, you'll have a higher overall metabolic rate.

When you challenge muscles with resistance training, you actually injure the muscle fibers by tearing them just a little bit. Sounds terrible, but it's exactly what needs to happen for your body to build those muscles back up stronger, leaner, and more metabolically active. In fact, the *process* of muscle repair and building is also a metabolic booster. Muscle repair, after a healthy non-ghrelin-increasing dose of resistance training, is the metabolic equivalent of digestive thermogenesis. Remember how ghrelin-suppressing foods take longer to digest—and use more energy in the process? This process increases your metabolism after you've eaten. Resistance training is to your muscles what eating ghrelin-suppressing food is to your digestion. Both, over time, increase your metabolic rate.

There are a lot of other ways resistance training improves your health besides boosting metabolism and building strong, lean muscles. Among those resistance-training benefits:

- Increases stamina. As you gain strength, you won't get as tired.
- Boosts mood. Resistance training releases endorphins that keep you feeling positive.
- Improves body shape. By building firm, lean muscles, you see definition, minimize the appearance of cellulite, and, over time, experience the redistribution—in a good way—of your body weight.
- Balances sleep patterns. When you exercise regularly, you'll fall asleep and wake up more easily.
- Reduces your risk of diseases, including heart disease, diabetes, and cancers.
- Builds bone strength.
- Lowers LDL cholesterol (bad cholesterol) and raises HDL cholesterol (good cholesterol).

Do you need to feel sore afterward to know you've exercised enough to get great results? Nope. There's no evidence to support this idea. In fact, with regular resistance training, you'll get stronger even if you don't get sore. But there *may* be some rationale for the "no pain, no gain" theory.

Remember those tiny muscle-fiber tears needed to rebuild stronger muscles? Well, if you're sore after working out, it means there was damage, so muscle growth isn't far behind. The degree of soreness you feel may be a marker of the amount of muscle growth there will be.

But even if you don't exercise to the point where you feel aches and pains, you can expect to experience some discomfort, fatigue, and soreness after doing the No-Sweat exercises. Your body produces lactic acid as a normal by-product of the muscle breakdown from doing these exercises. That's what causes the fatigue and soreness. It's not pleasant, but it's a sign that you've challenged your muscles in a way that will bring results.

GETTING STARTED

The No-Sweat Exercise Program is arranged in much the same way as your prebuilt meal plan in Chapter 6. I've divided the routine into three main body regions:

upper, lower, and core (your midsection). Think of the upper body, lower body, and core sections as your breakfast, lunch, and dinner. They are the main segments of the exercise program, just as breakfast, lunch, and dinner are your main meals. They're also interchangeable, just like your prebuilt meal plans: You can mix and match the upper, lower, and core exercise sections just as you can swap breakfasts for breakfasts, lunches for lunches, and dinners for dinners. You can do whatever upper-body, lower-body, and core routine you prefer. And you can complete your exercise routine anywhere, anytime.

WARMING UP AND COOLING DOWN

It's critical that you warm up before—and cool down after—each exercise session. Warmups and cooldowns don't have to be complicated or time consuming—5 to 8 minutes of each is long enough to ensure your safety. The practice reduces your risk of injury and minimizes the aches and pains that come with exercise.

Warmups assist your circulatory system in pumping oxygen-rich blood to your working muscles. The idea is to gradually increase circulation throughout your body. A proper warmup safely prepares your body for the increased demands of exercise. Cold muscles don't absorb shock or impact as well, plus they're more susceptible to injury. As you ease into exercise, your warmup will also prepare you mentally to concentrate on the task at hand.

Afterward, the cooldown is just as important. Cooling down focuses on stretching and breathing, helping your body recover and preparing your muscles for the next workout. The cooldown is often the best part—it calms you and allows your muscles to relax. You may be tempted to skip the cooldown because you've run out of time—or steam. But taking a few minutes to stretch and breathe deeply completes your exercise routine, relaxing your muscles and circulating oxygen to the

COACHING TIP

When doing resistance training, inhale deeply through your nose during the difficult phase of the exercise, and exhale through your mouth during the easier phase. This helps ensure you're getting enough oxygen to your working muscles.

Exercise Basics

What is a set? An exercise set is a group of several exercises done in series.

What is a rep? A rep is the number of times you repeat a specific exercise as part of a set.

What is progression? That's when you progressively increase the reps, sets, and/or weight (the training stimulus) over time. Doing this increases fitness and strength, builds muscle, and helps to raise metabolic rate.

muscles you've just worked. If you skip this step, you're missing out on some important benefits.

Pre-exercise warmup: To begin your warmup, do 5 minutes of light (low intensity) physical activity such as walking, marching in place, or cycling. Pump your arms or make large, controlled, circular movements to warm up your upper body.

Postexercise cooldown: This requires stretching. The best time is right after your workout, when your muscles are still warm and most likely to respond favorably. Your cooldown lowers your risk of injury. Stretching helps to relax your muscles, restoring them to a state of rest and improving flexibility (the range of movement of your joints). Here's what to do: Stretch all the muscles you used during your exercise, stretching each muscle group for 30 seconds, twice. Starting on page 297, I'll cover the essential stretching exercises you need to do at the end of your workout to help relax your muscles.

Your No-Sweat Routine

Each section of the No-Sweat Exercise Program will take about 10 minutes and is designed to work a specific body region. You don't have to complete all three sections at once. Resistance training works just as well when you do different sections at different times, as long as you complete a full section at one time. Completing a full section is important because you must break down muscle tissue deep enough in order to build it stronger and leaner. Don't forget to allow a few extra minutes for your cooldown at the end.

EXERCISE PROGRESSION

As your muscles build strength and gain endurance, you'll need to increase your resistance. There are several ways to do this. First, make the exercise harder by referring to the descriptions and pictures for each exercise. The second way to advance is to modify the number of sets and reps. I suggest increasing them weekly. That way, you can easily keep track of your progress. Start with this progression for each body section:

- Week 1: two sets of 10 reps each
- Week 2: two sets of 12 reps each
- Week 3: three sets of 10 reps each
- Week 4: three sets of 12 reps each

NO-SWEAT RESISTANCE TRAINING

Remember, the No-Sweat program is arranged in much the same way as your pre-built meal plan in Chapter 6. The program focuses on the three main body regions: upper, lower, and core (your midsection). Each section is interchangeable, just like your prebuilt meal plans—you can mix and match exercises within the upper, lower, and core sections for your convenience. But you *must* complete a full section at a time. If you don't, you won't break down your muscles enough to stimulate rebuilding—and that's what makes them leaner and stronger.

The terms "resistance training" and "weight lifting" are often used interchangeably, but they're not the same things. Weight lifting is a form of resistance training that makes use of weights. Resistance training refers to the larger category of strength-training exercises and techniques that make use of many strategies—your own body weight, for instance, or resistance bands, pulleys, weights, and so on, to make your muscles work harder. So if you're lifting weights, then you're doing resistance training—but if you're doing resistance training, you're not necessarily lifting weights. A pushup is an example of a resistance-training exercise that doesn't use weights.

The No-Sweat Exercise Program is resistance training rather than weight lifting because it incorporates weights along with other forms of resistance, such as bands, balls, or your own body weight.

The No-Sweat Exercise Program

	Standing Routine	Sitting Routine	Lying Routine
UPPER BODY	1. Pushup 2. Back Pull 3. Front Arm Raise 4. Biceps Curl to Shoulder Push	1. Chest Squeeze 2. Shoulder Retraction 3. Curl and Press 4. Triceps Extension	1. Chest Press 2. Angel Wings 3. Triceps Extension 4. Air Punch
LOWER BODY	1. Knee Lift 2. Leg Push Back 3. Leg Side Press 4. Leg Side Pull	1. Leg Taps 2. Leg Extensions 3. Thigh Squeeze 4. Thigh Push	1. Leg Raise 2. Bottoms Up 3. Pillow Squeeze 4. Ankle Kick
CORE	1. Side Bends 2. Elbow-to-Knee Crunch	1. Abs Rotation 2. Backward Lean	1. Toe Tap 2. Tummy Hold

PUSHUP

MAIN MOVE

1. Stand at arm's length from the wall with your feet shoulder-width apart.

2. Lean forward, placing your palms against the wall at shoulder height.

3. Bend your elbows until your nose nearly touches the wall.

4. Push back to the starting position. That is 1 rep.

Make it harder: *Use one arm for half the reps and then switch to the other arm.*

Make it easier: *Stand half an arm's length from the wall; widen your stance.*

BACK PULL

MAIN MOVE

1. Stand upright. Place your feet shoulder-width apart. Grip a towel with your hands shoulder-width apart.

2. Extend the towel out in front of you. Pull back and squeeze your shoulder blades together as tight as you can. Hold for 3 seconds. That is 1 rep.

Make it harder: *Use dumbbells of 3 or more pounds instead of a towel.*

Make it easier: *Hold the rep for 1 second.*

FRONT ARM RAISE

MAIN MOVE

1. Stand upright with your feet shoulder-width apart.

2. Hold one 12-ounce water bottle in each hand, your palms facing down. Lift your arms directly in front of you to shoulder height. That is 1 rep.

Make it harder: *Use dumbbells of 3 or more pounds.*

Make it easier: *Don't use hand weights.*

BICEPS CURL TO SHOULDER PUSH

MAIN MOVE

1. Stand upright with your feet shoulder-width apart.

2. Hold one 12-ounce water bottle in each hand. Starting with your arms at your sides, lift the water bottles, with your palms facing each other, to shoulder height, then take the bottles directly over your head. That is 1 rep.

Make it harder: *Use dumbbells of 3 or more pounds.*

Make it easier: *Don't use hand weights.*

KNEE LIFT

MAIN MOVE

1. Stand upright on your right leg while supporting yourself with the back of a chair.

2. With your right knee slightly bent, raise your left knee to hip height. Hold for 3 seconds. That is 1 rep.

3. Repeat on the opposite side.

Make it harder: *Use ankle weights of 1 to 3 pounds.*

Make it easier: *Hold the rep for 1 second.*

LEG PUSH BACK

MAIN MOVE

1. Stand upright on your right leg while supporting your-self with the back of a chair.

2. With your right knee slightly bent, push your left leg back. Squeeze the gluteal muscle as tight as you can. Hold for 3 seconds. That is 1 rep.

3. Repeat on the opposite side.

Make it harder: *Use ankle weights of 1 to 3 pounds.*

Make it easier: *Hold the rep for 1 second.*

LEG SIDE PRESS

MAIN MOVE

1. Stand upright on your right leg while supporting yourself with the back of a chair.

2. With your right knee slightly bent, extend your left leg to the side as far as you can. Hold for 3 seconds. That is 1 rep.

3. Repeat on the opposite side.

Make it harder: *Use ankle weights of 1 to 3 pounds.*

Make it easier: *Hold the rep for 1 second.*

LEG SIDE PULL

MAIN MOVE

1. Stand upright on your right leg while supporting yourself with the back of a chair.

2. With your right knee slightly bent, slightly raise your left leg; pull your knee toward your middle and hold for 3 seconds. That is 1 rep.

3. Repeat on the opposite side.

Make it harder: *Use ankle weights of 1 to 3 pounds.*

Make it easier: *Hold the rep for 1 second.*

SIDE BENDS

MAIN MOVE

1. Stand upright with your feet shoulder-width apart; push your shoulders back.

2. Squeeze your sides while bending to the right; hold for 1 second. That is 1 rep.

3. Repeat on the opposite side.

Make it harder: *Hold dumbbells of 5 or more pounds in each hand.*

Make it easier: *Instead of bending from right to left, hold each side 10 seconds for 2 reps.*

ELBOW-TO-KNEE CRUNCH

MAIN MOVE

1. Stand upright on your right leg while supporting yourself with the back of a chair.

2. Squeeze your side while lifting your left knee to your left elbow. Hold for 3 seconds. Return to the starting position. That is 1 rep.

3. Repeat on the opposite side.

Make it harder: *Wear ankle weights of 3 or more pounds.*

Make it easier: *Instead of bending from right to left, hold each side 10 seconds for 2 reps.*

CHEST SQUEEZE

MAIN MOVE

1. Sit up straight on a chair, with your feet flat on the floor and shoulder-width apart.

2. Hold a lightweight ball (or pillow) at chest level; squeeze with the palms of your hands to contract chest. While continuing to squeeze, slowly push the ball in front of you at chest level until elbows are almost straight. Bend elbows and pull back to chest. That is 1 rep.

Make it harder: *Sit on a stability ball and/or use a weighted ball.*

Make it easier: *Adjust by lessening the pressure you are squeezing to your comfort level.*

SHOULDER RETRACTION

MAIN MOVE

1. Sit up straight on chair, with feet flat on floor and shoulder-width apart.

2. Make a fist, with your palms facing floor. Push arms out in front of you at chest level; do not completely straighten elbows. Bend elbows and pull them back, squeezing shoulder blades together, slightly behind your torso. Hold for 3 seconds. That is 1 rep.

Make it harder: *Sit on a stability ball and/or use dumbbells of 3 or more pounds.*

Make it easier: *Hold the rep for 1 second.*

CURL AND PRESS

MAIN MOVE

1. Sit up straight on chair, with feet flat on floor, shoulder-width apart.

2. Start with a dumbbell of 3 or more pounds in right hand at your side. Curl your arm up to a biceps curl. When you reach shoulder height, continue to push arm up and over toward your head. Slowly bring weight back down to starting position. That is 1 rep.

3. Repeat on the opposite side.

Make it harder: *Sit on a stability ball. Use heavier dumbbells and/or perform the exercise with both arms at the same time.*

Make it easier: *Don't use weights.*

TRICEPS EXTENSION

MAIN MOVE

1. Sit up straight on chair with feet flat on floor, shoulder-width apart.

2. Start with a dumbbell of 5 or more pounds; grip with both hands. Lift arms straight up over head; keep elbows slightly bent. Pause for a moment, then bend elbows, lowering weights behind head so that elbows are at 90 degrees. Straighten arm and return to starting position. That is 1 rep.

Make it harder: *Sit on a stability ball, use heavier dumbbells, or perform the exercise one arm at a time.*

Make it easier: *Don't use weights.*

SITTING ROUTINE *Lower Body*

LEG TAPS

MAIN MOVE

1. Sit up straight on a chair with feet flat on floor and shoulder-width apart. Place a ball or another object about 6 inches in front of you on floor.

2. Lift right foot and tap toes on top of the ball. Then take foot back down and tap floor. That is 1 rep. Do this as fast as you can for the set.

3. Repeat on the opposite side.

Make it harder: *Sit on a stability ball.*

Make it easier: *Slow down your reps to a comfortable level.*

LEG EXTENSIONS

MAIN MOVE

1. Sit up straight on a chair with feet flat on floor and your knees together.

2. Squeeze right quadriceps as hard as you can to straighten your leg, foot flexed. Hold for 3 seconds. Bend knee, lowering foot until you lightly touch floor. That is 1 rep.

3. Repeat on the opposite side.

Make it harder: *Sit on a stability ball and/or use ankle weights.*

Make it easier: *Hold the rep for 1 second.*

THIGH SQUEEZE

MAIN MOVE

1. Sit up straight on a chair with your feet flat on the floor and shoulder-width apart.

2. Place a ball or pillow between your knees. Squeeze the ball by contracting your inner thighs as much as you can. Hold for 3 seconds. That is 1 rep.

Make it harder: *Sit on a stability ball.*

Make it easier: *Hold the rep for 1 second.*

THIGH PUSH

MAIN MOVE

1. Sit up straight on a chair with your feet flat on the floor and shoulder-width apart.

2. Tie a resistance band around your mid-thighs. Lift your right foot slightly off the floor and step out to the right side. Tap your toe on the floor; hold for 3 seconds. Then bring your foot back to the starting position. That is 1 rep.

3. Repeat on opposite side.

Make it harder: *Sit on a stability ball and/or tie the band more tightly around your thighs.*

Make it easier: *Hold the rep for 1 second.*

SITTING ROUTINE *Core*

ABS ROTATION

MAIN MOVE

1. Sit up straight on a chair, with feet flat on floor, shoulder-width apart, while holding a 3- to 5-pound dumbbell in front of chest.

2. Contracting abs and rotating torso to the right, keep hips facing forward. Contract abs to bring yourself back to center, then rotate to left. That is 1 rep.

Make it harder: *Sit on a stability ball and lean back to engage the abs.*

Make it easier: *Don't use a weight; instead, clasp hands in front of chest.*

BACKWARD LEAN

MAIN MOVE

1. Sit up straight on a chair with feet flat on floor, shoulder-width apart.

2. Contract abs. Lean back as far as you can while still keeping feet flat on floor. Hold for 3 seconds. Return to starting position, repeat. That is 1 rep.

Make it harder: *Sit on a stability ball and/or lift one foot a few inches off the ground while leaning back.*

Make it easier: *Hold the rep for 1 second.*

LYING ROUTINE *Upper Body*

CHEST PRESS

MAIN MOVE

1. Lie faceup on the floor (or bed). Bend your knees, keeping your feet flat on the ground. Contract your abs by pushing your lower back into the floor.

2. Begin with 5- to 8-pound dumbbells in each hand. Bring your hands straight up over your chest, palms facing your feet. Bend your elbows and lower the arms until your elbows are just below the chest. Press the weights back up, without completely straightening elbows. Repeat. That is 1 rep.

Make it harder: *Use a heaver weight.*

Make it easier: *Use a lighter weight.*

ANGEL WINGS

MAIN MOVE

1. Lie facedown on the floor (or bed).

2. Lift your shoulders and chest up off the floor. Hold for 3 seconds. While you are in the holding position, sweep your arms around and hold them directly in front of you (like a reverse snow angel). Hold for 3 seconds. That is 1 rep.

Make it harder: *Lift and hold your legs up off the floor.*

Make it easier: *Hold the rep for 1 second.*

TRICEPS EXTENSION

MAIN MOVE

1. Lie faceup on the floor (or bed) with your head and shoulders on the ground. Bend your knees, keeping your feet flat on the floor.

2. Begin with 3- to 5-pound dumbbells in each hand. Bring your arms straight up over your head with palms facing forward. Bend your elbows and lower the forearms until the dumbbells are right next to your ears. Press the weights back up without completely straightening your elbows. Repeat. That is 1 rep.

Make it harder: *Use a heaver weight.*

Make it easier: *Use a lighter weight.*

AIR PUNCH

MAIN MOVE

1. Lie faceup on the floor (or bed) with your head and shoulders on the ground. Bend your knees, keeping your feet flat on the floor.

2. Punch into the air with both arms as fast as you can for 10 seconds. That is 1 rep.

Make it harder: *Hold a light dumbbell in each hand.*

Make it easier: *Start with 5-second reps, adding 1 or 2 seconds each week.*

LEG RAISE

MAIN MOVE

1. Lie faceup on the floor (or bed) with your head and shoulders on the ground. Bend your knees, keeping your feet flat on the floor.

2. Straighten your right leg and hold just above the ground. Lift the right leg up to left knee height; hold for 3 seconds. Slowly lower back to the starting position. That is 1 rep.

3. Repeat on the opposite side.

Make it harder: *Use an ankle weight.*

Make it easier: *Hold the rep for 1 second.*

BOTTOMS UP

MAIN MOVE

1. Lie faceup on the floor (or bed) with your head and shoulders on the ground. Bend your knees, keeping your feet flat on the floor.

2. Slowly lift your hips up off the floor toward the ceiling while squeezing your gluteus. Continue to squeeze and hold as high as you can for 3 seconds. Slowly drop back to the starting position. That is 1 rep.

Make it harder: *Use one leg at a time.*

Make it easier: *Hold the rep for 1 second.*

PILLOW SQUEEZE

MAIN MOVE

1. Lie faceup on the floor (or bed) with your head and shoulders on the ground. Bend your knees, keeping your feet flat on the floor.

2. Place a hard pillow (or folded pillow) between your knees. Squeeze and hold the pillow as tightly as you can for 3 seconds. That is 1 rep.

Make it harder: *Hold the rep for 5 to 8 seconds.*

Make it easier: *Hold the rep for 1 second.*

ANKLE KICK

MAIN MOVE

1. Lie facedown on the floor (or bed). Fold your arms under your head and shoulders.

2. Keeping your knees on the floor, kick your feet as fast as you can for 10 seconds while squeezing your hamstrings and gluts. That is 1 rep.

Make it harder: *Use ankle weights.*

Make it easier: *Kick for 5-second reps.*

LYING ROUTINE *Core*

TOE TAP

MAIN MOVE

1. Lie faceup on the floor (or bed) with your head and shoulders on the ground. Bend your knees, keeping your feet flat on the floor. Place both hands under the small of your back.

2. Lift both feet up off floor about 6 inches. Slowly return to the starting position and tap your feet on floor. That is 1 rep.

Make it harder: *Do the same movement with straight knees.*

Make it easier: *Use one leg at a time.*

TUMMY HOLD

MAIN MOVE

1. Lie faceup on the floor (or bed) with your head and shoulders on the ground. Bend your knees, keeping your feet flat on the floor.

2. Cross your arms over your chest. Lift your head and shoulders off the ground, squeezing your abs. Hold for 3 seconds. Return to the starting position. That is 1 rep.

Make it harder: *Hold a dumbbell across the chest for added resistance.*

Make it easier: *Hold the rep for 1 second.*

COOLDOWN STRETCHING ESSENTIALS

Be sure to finish up your workout with these cooldown stretches, which will relax your muscles and lower your risk of injury. Do each stretch twice—for 30 seconds each time—for all the muscles you just used when you were exercising.

NO-SWEAT LOWER-BODY STRETCHES

QUAD/HIP STRETCH

Stand near a wall or a piece of sturdy exercise equipment for support. Grasp your right ankle with your right hand. Gently pull your heel up and back, until you feel a stretch in the front of your thigh and hip. Tuck your hips and tighten your stomach muscles to prevent back injury. Hold for about 30 seconds. Switch legs and repeat twice.

HAMSTRING/GLUTE STRETCH:

Lie on your back on a firm surface with legs extended and the backs of your heels flat on the floor. With both hands grasping your right knee, gently pull your knee to your chest until you feel a stretch in your glute and hamstring. Hold the knee as close to your chest as comfortably possible. Keep the opposite leg relaxed in a comfortable position, either with your knee bent or with your leg extended. Hold for 30 seconds. Switch legs and repeat twice.

NO-SWEAT LOWER-BODY STRETCHES (cont.)

CALF STRETCH

Stand at arm's length from a wall. Place your right foot behind your left foot. Slowly bend your left leg forward, keeping your right knee straight and your right heel on the floor. Hold your back straight and your hips forward. Don't rotate your feet inward or outward. Hold for 30 seconds. Switch legs and repeat twice.

NO-SWEAT UPPER-BODY STRETCHES

CHEST/SHOULDER STRETCH

Stand inside a doorway facing the doorjamb. Extend your right arm straight in front of you so that your arm is parallel to the ground, then grip the outside of the doorjamb. Keep your spine tall and straight as you slowly turn your body to the left, stretching the chest, shoulder, and biceps. Hold for 30 seconds. Switch arms and repeat twice.

BACK/ARM STRETCH

Open a door and, with each hand, grasp onto a knob. Keep your feet about hip-width apart and step back, allowing your body weight to stretch your midback and arms. Your arms should be perfectly straight at this point and you should be looking down. Hold for 30 seconds and slowly release. Repeat twice.

NO-SWEAT UPPER-BODY STRETCHES (cont.)

NECK/SHOULDER STRETCH

Stand with your feet shoulder-width apart, arms at your sides. Slowly roll your head clockwise three times, and then counterclockwise three times. Then slowly roll your shoulders forward three times, and then back three times. Repeat twice.

NO-SWEAT CORE STRETCHES

ABDOMINAL STRETCH

Stand with your feet shoulder-width apart. Extend both arms and reach directly up and overhead. Lace your fingers and face your palms up toward ceiling, until you feel a stretch in your abdomen. Hold for 30 seconds. Repeat twice.

SIDE STRETCH

Stand with your feet shoulder-width apart. Extend your right arm and reach up and overhead while leaning toward your right, until you feel a stretch in your right side. Hold for 30 seconds. Switch sides and repeat twice.

POWER UP YOUR WORKOUT

The No-Sweat Exercise Program is simple, but these tips will help you get themost mileage for your efforts.

Power Up with Easy Equipment: The No-Sweat Exercise Program doesn't call for expensive equipment or workout gear. In fact, you can find appropriate substitutes for every piece of "equipment" right in your home. Here's a list of your No-Sweat equipment and the easy substitutes you can use instead.

- **Dumbbells:** Use water bottles of various sizes, and fill them with more or less water to increase or decrease resistance. Or try cans of food, like a 16-ounce can of ghrelin-suppressing black beans!
- **Weighted ball:** Use a heavy hardback book or a 2-liter bottle filled with liquid. Or buy a plastic beach ball and fill it with water instead of air.
- **Resistance bands:** Use a bungee cord.
- **Floor mat:** Use a large bath towel or beach towel.
- **Stability ball:** Stack a bunch of firm bed pillows just above knee height.

Power Up with Music: Your choice of music during exercise will have a significant impact on your motivation—and on your ability to complete your routine. A study looking at music choices on the perceived internal motivation of 34 women engaging in exercise showed that the group that could choose its favorite upbeat music while exercising experienced greater motivation and had an easier time completing the workout.[12] So listen to your favorite upbeat music while exercising. It will not only help you finish your routine, but it will make it easier to do.

COACHING TIP

Drink an extra 8 ounces of water before and after exercise. Proper hydration will help your muscles recover—and rebuild stronger than ever.

Power Up Your Feet: A pair of supportive, well-fitting sneakers is one piece of workout gear you can't do without. Good shoes will make or break your workout, so get the right pair. Follow these tips:

▶ Go to a reputable shoe store and get your feet measured. Shoe size can change over time. Working out in shoes that do not fit properly is an injury waiting to happen. When standing, you should have one thumb-width of room at the tip of your shoe.

▶ Buy a pair of cross-trainers—they're good for almost any type of exercise, including walking, jogging, and resistance training.

▶ Choose comfort and support over style.

Power Up without Bulk: For women, there's no need to avoid weight machines, free weights, and even pushups for fear of "bulking up." Gaining muscle doesn't mean you'll get bulky—in fact, I promise you won't. Here's why:

▶ Women don't have the amount of testosterone necessary to build large muscles—only men do. The average man has approximately 20 times more testosterone than the average woman. Testosterone is the reason men can build large muscles.

▶ Think of resistance training as toning. Toning is essentially bodybuilding without the testosterone. You "build" muscles by strengthening them. Strong muscles have a healthy, attractive, toned—not bulky—appearance.

▶ Bulky muscles are built from doing high-volume, heavy-weight lifting. Lower-volume resistance training, like the No-Sweat Program, is designed to build strong toned muscles—not bulky ones.

▶ "Bulking up" is dependent on calories. You need to eat more calories in order to create large bulky muscles. On the Belly Fat Fix, you're losing weight. The math simply does not add up.

Mark Q.

AGE: 57

POUNDS LOST:

FAST-TRACK: 3

TOTAL: 60 in 90 days

OVERALL INCHES LOST: 30

When you're really motivated, it's amazing what you can accomplish. Mark had been an overeater all his life, but once he committed himself to the Belly Fat Fix, he didn't waver once. That's how he achieved such spectacular results—60 pounds in 90 days, dropping from a 44-inch waist all the way down to a 34.

"I'm a having a ball buying new pants," he says. "I had 50 pair of slacks I could no longer wear, and I gave every single one of them away."

Now the 57-year-old owner of a surveillance camera company is exactly where he wants to be, and he intends to stay there. He says he's at the perfect weight to be in top form for golf, his favorite pastime—his game has improved, and those postgame backaches are a thing of the past. More important, he knows that getting down to a healthy weight again makes it more likely that he'll live longer, so he'll have more years to enjoy his grandchildren. And *that* is sure to be fun and pain free now that his knees and back feel better.

Through much of his life, Mark had maintained a healthy weight, but he started piling on the pounds over the last 10 years or so, reaching 232 pounds when he started the program. When his wife suggested he try the Belly Fat Fix,

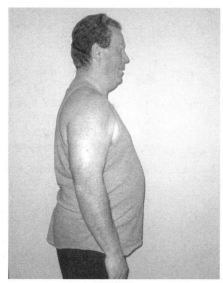

BEFORE

AFTER

he agreed to it because he knew something had to change: "My knees hurt every time I walked up a flight of stairs," he says. "I'd go to sleep at 11:00 p.m. and wake up 45 minutes later with acid reflux. I got tired of that."

Now the acid reflux is gone, and so is the snoring. Best of all, he feels *great*. His golf buddies can hardly believe how much he's changed in a single season. But Mark says he's the kind of guy who likes fast results. He doesn't have the patience for the "1 pound a month" weight loss he's observed with a family member on a commercial diet program.

Mark wasn't initially a true believer. The first time his wife gave him a bowl of Fiber One cereal, with a sliced green apple in it, he thought, *I can't eat this stuff. Now what?*

"I hated water. I just didn't like drinking it. Now I love it," he says. "And now I *want* to exercise. I have a lot more energy. I always felt young before, but now I have the energy of a younger person."

One of the changes that helped Mark the most was giving up sweets. "I was a sugar addict. I'm on the road a lot, and it was nothing for me to eat a 2-pound bag of licorice, follow it with Snickers, and then come home for dinner and have cake and a bit of ice cream for dessert—every night."

Now he brings apples or bags of sliced cucumbers on the road with him instead, and fruit provides the sweet taste he always craved. "I love those Granny Smith apples," he says. "That's my big dessert at night. I cut an apple up and throw some Cool Whip on it."

The other key for Mark? Controlling his portions. "I used to eat the whole 24-ounce steak and then feel bloated. But I've learned that a 6-ounce steak is enough for me when I combine it with the other foods."

When he started on the Belly Fat Fix, he set out to lose 40 pounds. When he reached that weight, he saw that he still had a belly, so he just kept going, eventually trimming a total of 60 pounds.

"This is not a diet; it's a new way of life for me," he insists. "It's simple and it's balanced. It's not saying *cut out carbs*. The body needs carbs, fiber, protein, fat. It's just a matter of getting the proportions and portions right."

Maintain It

CHAPTER 9

Balance Ghrelin, Regain Your Health

By now, you're getting to be an expert on ghrelin. You already know how it affects your appetite and—ultimately—your weight. In this chapter, you'll learn all about ghrelin's effects on your health. As you'll see, ghrelin impacts many body systems in a variety of ways—it could even play a role in whether or not you get cancer and how quickly that cancer spreads.

Why would a single hormone, present only in tiny quantities, be so powerful? The answer probably has something to do with the fact that ghrelin was designed with human survival in mind—and the effort you make to keep ghrelin in balance can keep you healthy and even reverse some degenerative processes that lead to disease.

Case in point: my own mother, who lost nearly 40 pounds in 4 months on the Belly Fat Fix. In that time, her borderline high LDL cholesterol dropped back into the normal range and her total cholesterol dropped from 199 to 188. Her HgbA1c—which measures long-term blood glucose concentration—dropped from a value of 5.7 (considered borderline high) into the normal range (5.3). Her blood pressure improved so much that she was able to cut in half her daily dose of blood pressure medication. Her level of thyroid-stimulating hormone (TSH)—an indication of her overall metabolism function—improved too. These positive physiological changes reduce her risk of diabetes, heart disease, and thyroid malfunction. And it all came about as a result of balancing her ghrelin on the Belly Fat Fix.

Another one of my test panelists, Mark Q., noticed dramatic changes in his health after he lost 60 pounds in 90 days. He no longer experiences the acid reflux that used to wake him up every night. He "used to eat Tums like candy, but he doesn't even have them in the house anymore," says his wife, Pat. His snoring disappeared, and his knees and back feel better all around. Another panelist, Dave H., who lost 30 pounds in 60 days, also stopped snoring. He's sleeping better and feeling well rested when he wakes up.

Such is ghrelin's power to influence your health.

Those are all good reasons to avoid becoming obese or, if you are, to make a concerted effort to lose excess weight. The more pounds you pack on, the more likely your ghrelin is off kilter—and the more deleterious the effects on your health. Researchers have found that chronic out-of-balance ghrelin plays a role in the development of obesity. This off-kilter ghrelin affects the peripheral tissues, such as adipose (or fat) tissue and the vascular tissue.

Those who are obese are likely to have lower blood levels of ghrelin than those of "normal" weight. That's problematic. In normal-weight people, the rise and fall of ghrelin before and after meals is more dramatic compared with those who are overweight and obese. *This* is ideal, since that ghrelin elevation helps people feel both normal hunger and normal satiety. Without these cues, we could eat all the time because we'd never feel quite full—or quite hungry.

Here's the good news: As we've learned, it's possible to reset ghrelin levels and nudge them back toward normal by following the 3-Day Fast-Track and then the Belly Fat Fix plan.

Losing weight the right way is crucial. Research shows that weight loss increases ghrelin concentration in those who are obese.[1] After you lose weight, ghrelin levels will drop lower after meals and rise higher before meals.[2]

No doubt about it: Getting ghrelin balanced is an important key to your all-around health. Let's look now at ghrelin's influence, body system by body system, to better understand the ghrelin-health connection.

YOUR DIGESTIVE SYSTEM

Special cells in your stomach called X/A cells supply most of the ghrelin in your body. These cells are embedded in the mucous lining of the very uppermost section of your stomach, the fundus. These highly specialized X/As account for about 20 percent of all hormone-producing stomach cells.[3] There's a larger concentration of ghrelin-producing cells in the top portion of the stomach—that's nature's way of making sure you get your hunger alerts at the right time, every time.

Remember how your empty stomach triggers ghrelin production in response to true hunger? Well, having ghrelin cells in the top part of the stomach ensures that

A Ghrelin Pill?

Stay tuned—lots of pharmaceutical companies have started to actively develop drugs that target the obesity-related functions of ghrelin and/or its receptors. A ghrelin drug isn't on the market yet, but there's a push within the industry to develop one soon.

Pharmaceutical companies are also exploring *ghrelin receptors*—blockers that would inhibit the secretion of growth hormone for the purpose of promoting weight loss, suppressing appetite, and pro-moting glucose-dependent insulin secretion.[4]

Watch the news and your favorite health magazines for updates on these drugs. But don't get too excited. Drugs that alter the negative effects of too much—or too little—ghrelin may also alter the positive and protective functions of this hormone. On the Belly Fat Fix, you'll naturally balance your ghrelin to prevent the negative effects of unbalanced ghrelin and promote the positive effects of balanced ghrelin.

ghrelin is secreted early enough, but not too early, allowing you to eat in time to keep your body's other regulatory hormones stable. By the time your last meal makes it down to the bottom of your stomach, into the small intestine, and then into your large intestine or colon, your X/A cells are already starting to produce ghrelin again.

During the hours it takes your body to digest food, fresh batches of ghrelin are secreted, pushing blood levels of ghrelin back up to the point where you feel the urge to eat again. If you act on that urge, your body will create the two kinds of ghrelin, acylated and unacylated, in the right proportions. (I explained the difference between these in the sidebar "What *Exactly* Is Ghrelin?" in Chapter 1.) If you eat when you get those first ghrelin hunger cues, you'll also save those X/A cells from having to work extra hard by pumping out more and more ghrelin until you finally pay attention and find something to nosh on. Just as significantly, by eating now, you may prevent a ghrelin imbalance that triggers your ghrelin receptors to activate the DNA in cancer cells. Yep—new research suggests that having your ghrelin out of balance may make you more vulnerable to cancer. (See Ghrelin and Cancer, page 314.)

More immediate consequences of out-of-whack ghrelin are sleep deprivation, weight gain, and obesity. In each case, your digestive system isn't capable of secreting ghrelin on a healthy schedule. Chronically high ghrelin levels—or low levels without distinct fluctuations (such as ghrelin levels in obese people)—result in fast digestion, which triggers ghrelin to be released sooner. And the sooner it's released, the sooner you want to eat again.

The X/A cells of the stomach lining secrete ghrelin directly into the bloodstream, where it circulates through your body via the cardiovascular system. Once it enters the cardiovascular system, it works its effects on the body. If ghrelin is balanced overall, it will promote health throughout the body. If it's not in balance, however, it will tip the balance toward disease and excess weight.

GHRELIN AND BOWEL DISEASES

Inflammatory bowel disease (IBD) includes a group of disorders in which the intestines become inflamed—red and swollen—as a result of the body's immune reaction against its own intestinal tissue. This affects digestion, causing weight loss and muscle weakness.

The two major types of IBD are ulcerative colitis and Crohn's disease. Ulcerative colitis is limited to the colon (large intestine). Crohn's disease can involve any part of the gastrointestinal tract from the mouth to the colon, but it most commonly affects the small intestine and/or the colon. Irritable bowel syndrome (IBS), a cluster of symptoms rather than an actual disease, is a much less serious problem in which the digestive system looks normal but doesn't work as it should.

Studies confirm that ghrelin levels are elevated in active IBD cases, suggesting a close relationship between circulating ghrelin levels and the severity of the disease.[5,6] So people with active IBD have much higher ghrelin levels than those in remission. Plus, the level of circulating ghrelin is directly linked to the severity of the disease and its symptoms, suggesting that blood ghrelin may serve as a good biomarker for IBD's onset, development, and severity.

Scientists have yet to conduct human studies on the effectiveness of ghrelin treatment for IBD sufferers, but numerous animal trials show promise. A study reported in the *International Journal of Peptides* concluded that ghrelin administration in animals produced "improvements in disease activity and systemic inflammation."[7]

Some pharmaceutical companies are developing ghrelin agonist drugs, which work by blocking ghrelin's own receptors, keeping naturally circulating ghrelin from binding with the receptor to do its job. In IBD, that means the out-of-whack ghrelin is blocked from its receptors, slowing or stopping the disease from becoming more severe. At present, these drugs are being tested on animals. Human trials are likely to begin soon.

Scientists have yet to discover the mechanism by which ghrelin suppresses IBD in animals, but they're confident they can create a drug that takes advantage of ghrelin's "ability to stimulate hunger, food intake, and digestive motility."[8] Ghrelin's ability to speed up digestion decreases the amount of time the inflamed digestive tract cells are exposed to digesting food, which may help to reduce inflammation. Meanwhile, ghrelin's ability to increase appetite and stimulate eating can offset the weight loss and muscle wasting often seen in sufferers of IBD.

YOUR CARDIOVASCULAR SYSTEM

Even your cardiovascular system has ghrelin receptors, in the heart and aortas. In one study, volunteers were injected with normal levels of ghrelin, which was shown to decrease blood pressure even as it increased the output of the heart.[9] In short, ghrelin enabled the heart to pump more oxygen-filled blood with less effort. This suggests that when ghrelin is balanced, it regulates blood pressure, which has a protective effect on the entire cardiovascular system. But unbalanced ghrelin has negative health consequences. When ghrelin is chronically low, as in people who are obese, the heart and surrounding tissues actually create more receptors. The increase in number of receptors in the heart and surrounding tissues contributes to hardening of the arteries and increased LDL (bad) cholesterol.[10]

YOUR ENDOCRINE SYSTEM

Via the cardiovascular system, ghrelin circulates and spreads through your body, quickly reaching the pancreas, an organ that functions within both the digestive and endocrine systems. In the digestive system, its job is to produce digestive enzymes and release them into the small intestine. In the endocrine system—the network of hormone-producing glands that sends messages directly into your bloodstream—the pancreas is tasked with producing and releasing insulin and other hormones that play a role in overall metabolism and blood sugar regulation.

Scientists recently discovered that there's a special kind of ghrelin produced by epsilon cells in the pancreas. This ghrelin has a different concentration—and a different purpose—than the ghrelin produced in the stomach. Instead of making the trip to the hypothalamus to stimulate hunger, this pancreatic ghrelin—which doesn't stimulate hunger at all—functions locally, attaching to receptor cells right alongside the epsilon cells.

The primary role of pancreatic ghrelin is to regulate insulin secretion and blood sugar levels to prevent life-threatening low blood sugar in times of starvation. When circulating ghrelin is chronically elevated—for instance, when you're constantly yo-yo dieting or not sleeping enough—weight gain and higher blood sugar are often the results. When you become overweight or obese, your ghrelin levels drop to a new baseline. The chronically low ghrelin then causes insulin resistance and, eventually, type 2 diabetes.[11]

GHRELIN AND DIABETES

Health experts agree we're facing a diabetes epidemic. According to the National Diabetes Fact Sheet, 25.8 million people—a little more than 8 percent of the population—have diabetes, and that percentage is expected to rise precipitously. The Centers for Disease Control and Prevention (CDC) predicts that as many as one in three adults could have diabetes by 2050 if current trends continue.[12]

Dangerous? You bet, and for a lot of reasons. Diabetes can lead to serious complications and premature death. It's the seventh-leading cause of death in the United States. Complications of diabetes include heart disease and stroke, blindness, chronic kidney disease, and even amputations.

Fortunately, type 2 diabetes can be prevented. Studies have shown that people who lose 5 to 7 percent of their body weight (about 14 pounds for a 200-pound person) and get at least 150 minutes a week of "moderate physical exercise" (like moderate-paced walking) can prevent the development of metabolic syndrome, a gateway to diabetes.

Ghrelin Treatment for Diseases

Scientists are researching ghrelin as a treatment for some autoimmune diseases such as rheumatoid arthritis and inflammatory bowel disease. Though the exact mechanism of ghrelin as a treatment isn't completely understood and a lot more research and development are required, the focus of research and development is on synthetic ghrelin agonist drugs. These are chemicals that bind to the receptor of a cell to trigger a response and mimic the action of a naturally occurring substance. Ghrelin agonist drugs work by combining with the natural ghrelin receptor, harnessing the positive functions of ghrelin to treat a disease rather than cause it.

Symptoms of metabolic syndrome include excess visceral fat—the kind that lies deep inside your body, where it blankets your heart, liver, and other nearby organs—plus high cholesterol, high blood pressure, and elevated insulin levels.

One way this plan protects against metabolic syndrome and type 2 diabetes is by giving you biological control of your appetite. If you time your meals properly so that your ghrelin levels remain stable, you'll be less likely to binge. If you don't time your meals properly or skip some meals altogether, your blood level of ghrelin will rise too high, causing you to eat more even as the foods you choose slow down your metabolism. You may recall from Chapter 1 that high ghrelin levels even make you more responsive to pictures of food and/or the actual sight of food. High ghrelin also makes you hungrier and less able to control your appetite. If you make the effort to stabilize ghrelin, you'll be satisfied with less.

Following the Belly Fat Fix conscientiously—sticking to your meal plan, focusing on ghrelin-suppressing foods, *and* exercising within your ghrelin-suppressing limits—will greatly lower your risk of succumbing to type 2 diabetes.

What If You Already Have Diabetes?

If you already have type 2 diabetes, the Belly Fat Fix can help you manage it. If you're insulin dependent, though, be sure to consult a registered dietitian or diabetes educator to make the adjustments that are right for you. Remember, this plan isn't set up to count grams of carbohydrates, something you *must* do if you are taking insulin.

If you have type 2 diabetes and you're obese, chances are excellent that your fasting ghrelin concentrations are lower than average.[13] Additionally, scientists have found that "circulating ghrelin concentrations are also reduced in healthy offspring of type 2 diabetic patients," suggesting a possible genetic component in the "regulation of ghrelin plasma levels."[14]

Some ghrelin, of course, is secreted in the pancreas, where it's thought to actively moderate insulin secretion, either assisting or obstructing the regulation of insulin release.[15] One study, undertaken with healthy young people, showed that administering extra ghrelin "impairs insulin and glucose metabolism by increasing glucose concentrations and decreasing insulin levels."[16]

This is something to strenuously work to prevent if you hope to keep diabetes at bay. So it's definitely to your benefit to get regular, non-ghrelin-increasing exercise by doing the No-Sweat Exercise Program and following your meal plan to keep your ghrelin levels in balance.

YOUR IMMUNE SYSTEM

By now, this fact will probably come as no surprise: Your immune system is *also* affected by ghrelin. This happens via the neuroendocrine pathway, a two-way communication highway between your endocrine and central nervous systems. Your immune and endocrine systems are intimately connected by this pathway, and it's here that ghrelin exerts its influence. In fact, both systems use the same ghrelin receptors. When ghrelin is balanced, it has powerful anti-inflammatory effects within your immune cells, which work to keep your immune system strong. When ghrelin is not balanced, though, inflammation ensues within the immune cells.[17] And that's a huge problem. Since every known disease is a result of inflammation, that's an important pathway by which ghrelin imbalance contributes to the development of many diseases.

GHRELIN AND CANCER

One of the most feared degenerative diseases is cancer. In 2012, an estimated 1.6 million people will be diagnosed with the disease.[18] Because it's so common, you probably know someone who has been affected by cancer. I certainly have. When I was 14, my dad died of non-Hodgkin's lymphoma, a rapidly spreading cancer of the immune system. I was struck when I learned that ghrelin plays a role in whether or not you stay cancer free. If ghrelin is functioning optimally, you may be less likely to develop cancer. When it isn't, ghrelin appears to "feed" the disease. A research group from the Institute of Health and Biomedical Innovation in Australia found that the DNA codes of cancer cells also contain codes for ghrelin, and that growing cancer cells have ghrelin receptors.[19]

Evidence suggests that an imbalance in ghrelin triggers the ghrelin receptors in a way that causes the DNA in cancer cells to be activated as well, possibly causing cancer cells to grow and spread more quickly. So a ghrelin imbalance may initiate a process that flips cancer's "on switch," allowing it to do even more damage by triggering the rapid growth, development, and spread of cancer.

Scientists still have a lot to learn here—remember, after all, that ghrelin was just discovered in 1999. It'll be years before we understand ghrelin's full role in cancer development and growth, but what we do know, according to the Australian research group, is that "ghrelin and its receptors are expressed in a number of cancers and cancer cell lines, and may play a role in processes associated with cancer progression, including cell proliferation, apoptosis, cell invasion, and migration."[20]

If that sounds kind of scary, you're getting it. It *is* scary. Even the mere suggestion that following the Belly Fat Fix can provide extra protection against cancer ought to make you more motivated to follow it.

Here's what I think is going on here. An imbalance in ghrelin causes the body to create more ghrelin receptors. We know that this happens in the cardiovascular system of obese people. Remember how the heart and aortas develop more ghrelin receptors? The body does this in an effort to make up for the lack of circulating ghrelin, which, if balanced, would have worked to regulate blood pressure.

This suggests to me that ghrelin is buried deep within our DNA. Think about it: Our body tissues don't make ghrelin receptors for no reason. The ghrelin genetic coding within human DNA tells the body to do this. That same DNA directs cancer-producing cells, too.

There's growing evidence that ghrelin plays a role in cell messaging via a system called the autocrine-paracrine signaling pathway,[21] which works by secreting hormones that bind to receptors directly on the very cell secreting the hormone. Think of the autocrine-paracrine signaling pathway as similar to the instant messaging capability of your computer. The message is sent at almost the same moment it's received, leaving a record on your computer of everything said. In much the same way, the cell containing ghrelin DNA secretes ghrelin; ghrelin instantaneously sends a message back to the same cell that secreted it. The autocrine-paracrine signaling happens within the minute space of one microscopic cell, and ghrelin's message leads to changes within that one cell.

Here's the problem: When cancer is involved, lots of cells are doing this all at once, *and* when the process is set in motion, it speeds up quickly. The cancer-causing ghrelin DNA triggers the very cells that hold that DNA—ghrelin, after all, functions "locally." So the ghrelin produced in a cell is functioning solely within that cell.

In cancer cells, the ghrelin DNA is functioning locally, triggering this signaling system and promoting cancer progression.[22] This process has been shown to happen in a bunch of cancer-producing cells throughout the body in pituitary, colon, stomach, prostate, thyroid, endocrine, pancreatic, ovarian, brain, uterine, testicular, renal, and lung cancers.[23]

In the brain, there's even a type of ghrelin-secreting cell called an astrocytoma cell, which causes brain tumors. This increases the ghrelin concentration in the brain, and the higher level causes this particular kind of brain cancer to develop and spread more quickly.[24]

There's a strong link between ghrelin and cancers of the sexual and reproductive organs, such as ovarian, prostate, uterine, endometrial, and breast cancers. Breast cancer, in particular, is strongly linked to ghrelin, say researchers in the Ghrelin Research Group at the School of Life Sciences in Brisbane, Australia.[25] A study published in *Endocrine-Related Cancer* found that normal, healthy breast tissue does not have ghrelin receptors, but that breast cancer tissue does. It also found that breast cancer will grow and spread more quickly when ghrelin and its receptors are present to flip the on switch.[26] Scientists are now using this information to look for ways to more accurately detect early-stage breast cancer or breast cancer risk.

As I suggested when I mentioned prostate cancer, men aren't immune from the dark side of ghrelin. Ghrelin and its receptors have been found in prostate cancer cell DNA and in prostate tumor cell tissue.[27] Ghrelin works the same way in prostate cancer as it does in breast cancer, flipping cancer's on switch and speeding up the growth and spread of prostate cancer cells. In prostate cancer, this process happens through a cellular signaling pathway called the MAPK pathway.[28]

This pathway functions similarly to the autocrine-paracrine signaling pathway I mentioned earlier. The MAPK pathway is a chain of proteins in a cell that sends a message from a receptor on the surface of the cell directly to the DNA in the nucleus of the same cell. Researchers who published a groundbreaking study in *Clinical Cancer Research* remarked that the "ghrelin receptor GHS-R can cross-talk with the MAPK pathway to promote cell proliferation in several cancer cell lines." (They were specifically speaking about the cancer cell lines [DNA] in liver, pancreatic, and pituitary cells.) They suggest that "activation of MAPK pathways could be involved in the increased proliferation observed in prostate cancer cells after ghrelin treatment."[29] (The "ghrelin treatment" to which they refer is the ghrelin they used in their experiments, as they explored the effect of ghrelin on prostate cancer cells.)

Ghrelin's role in cancer development and progression has led researchers to look at ghrelin as a possible diagnosis biomarker for certain cancers.[30] They're trying to figure out how ghrelin genes (DNA) in certain cells may serve as an indicator of a person's potential to develop cancer.

It would be terrific if ghrelin could be harnessed to help health professionals more quickly diagnose cancer. As you may know, many cancers are on the rise, and younger and younger people are being diagnosed. According to the World Cancer Report, global rates of cancer could go up by 50 percent over the next decade, resulting in 15 million new cases a year by 2020.

The rise of hormone-dependent cancers, such as breast and prostate cancers, is particularly virulent. These are the most common cancers in men and women in the Western world. According to research, between 1 in 6 and 1 in 10 American men is at risk of developing prostate cancer, and between 1 in 7 and 1 in 11 American women is at risk of developing breast cancer.[31]

There are many factors that determine your risk of cancer; ghrelin imbalance is only one of them. But it's a powerful one because it makes it more likely that not only will you develop cancer, but the disease will spread and become more deadly more quickly than if your ghrelin were in balance. This—combined with all the other negative effects of unbalanced ghrelin—sets you up for a perfect storm.

But before you get too worried, remember that this is within your control. Simply keep ghrelin in balance. Follow the counsel in this book and you can significantly lower your risk of cancer. Consider, too, that your risk of developing cancer and many other diseases drops dramatically when you lose excess weight.

If you've already had cancer, following the Belly Fat Fix may provide you with some protection against its recurrence. Remember—especially when you're tempted to skip meals, postpone eating longer than you should, or do without sleep—that ghrelin imbalance triggers the growth, development, and spread of cancer by activating certain cells. Then make the smart choice. If your cancer should recur, balanced ghrelin (along with your new healthy lifestyle) may prevent the cancer from growing and spreading as quickly.

GHRELIN AND ARTHRITIS

Rheumatoid arthritis (RA) is a chronic autoimmune disease leading to accelerated muscle tissue breakdown, joint damage, weakness, weight loss, and even disability. RA spurs the breakdown of cartilage, which normally protects a joint and allows the joint to move smoothly and absorb shock when pressure is placed on it as you walk. Without the normal amount of cartilage, your bones rub together, causing pain, stiffness, and swelling (inflammation), which doesn't always go away after treatment. And when it doesn't, you've got chronic arthritis.

Once again, ghrelin could be the culprit. New research shows that "variations in

Exercise Boosts Immunity

The No-Sweat Exercise Program in Chapter 8 will not only build muscle and keep your appetite at bay, it'll also work toward preventing certain degenerative diseases.

Exercise will help you maintain healthy blood sugar levels, which can prevent glycation, a process in which the level of sugar in the blood becomes so high that it's toxic to the cells. This ultimately leads to cellular degeneration, which opens the door to degenerative disease and aging. That's why exercise is a preventive strategy against diabetes.

Regular exercise helps you stick with your diet and take off those unwanted pounds. It also alters gene expression, turning "on" certain genes in the cells, rather than allowing them to remain in the "off" position. The good news: Exercise turns on the genes that create disease protective proteins, such as HSP-70, BDNF, and GRP-78, which protect brain cells and prevent cancer.

With the Belly Fat Fix— eating the right foods in the right amounts at the right time *and* doing the No-Sweat exercises— you'll not only slim down and tone up, you'll also boost your resistance to some of the most common degenerative diseases, such as diabetes and cancer, *and* delay cognitive decline.

the ghrelin gene may have an impact on rheumatoid arthritis."[32] The gene variation is not completely understood; the ghrelin gene was found to be associated with early RA onset and a faster development of chronic RA. This gene variation is now being looked at as a possible biomarker of RA development—and as a possible treatment.

A study published in the *American Journal of Physiology–Endocrinology and Metabolism* shows that a ghrelin-based drug treatment for arthritis appears to hold much promise. Researchers showed that administering a synthetic ghrelin receptor agonist reduced the symptoms of arthritis.[33] A synthetic ghrelin receptor agonist works by blocking the ghrelin receptor gene variation (this is the variation that is associated with early-onset arthritis and faster development of chronic arthritis). The ghrelin "drug" blocks natural ghrelin from triggering early RA onset and a faster development of chronic RA.

YOUR CENTRAL NERVOUS SYSTEM

Via the cardiovascular system, ghrelin eventually makes its way to your central nervous system, where it triggers the hypothalamus in your brain to stimulate eating. Ghrelin is also produced in the hypothalamus and plays lots of roles in the brain itself, where ghrelin-producing chemical messengers called neurons spread throughout the spaces between the hypothalamus and other parts of the brain. These ghrelin-producing messengers send messages through your entire body, regulating metabolism and fat storage. When circulating ghrelin levels are normal, the neurons send messages to maintain a healthy body weight. But when they're out of balance, your NPY neurons send your body a signal to store excess white fat cells in your belly. (See The Survival Effect on page 28.)

In the brain, ghrelin also influences memory formation. The hippocampus, the part of your brain in charge of memory formation and learning, has ghrelin receptors, and normally elevated ghrelin levels—for instance, just before a meal—enhance our memory. That was a boon to our ancestors, who were constantly searching for food. But research findings suggest that our memory may be negatively affected when ghrelin levels are chronically low, as they are in obesity. This may happen because ghrelin doesn't rise enough before meals. (See the Normal-Weight vs. Overweight/Obese Ghrelin Levels graph on page 45.) The ghrelin

(continued on page 322)

THE BENEFITS
OF BALANCED GHRELIN

**These are some of the benefits you will experience
when your ghrelin is balanced**

CENTRAL NERVOUS SYSTEM
Your Brain
Regulates metabolism to
maintain healthy body weight
and promotes memory
function

CARDIOVASCULAR SYSTEM
Your Heart
Protects the heart by
regulating blood pressure

DIGESTIVE SYSTEM
Your Stomach
Regulates healthy
digestion and gastric
juice secretions

ENDOCRINE SYSTEM
Your Blood Sugar
Regulation
Prevents low blood
sugar by regulating
insulin secretion

IMMUNE SYSTEM
Your Cells
Protects cells from
inflammation and
disease

Eating at the right time, getting enough sleep each night, and keeping your weight down
balance ghrelin, which contributes to the proper functioning of many systems in your body.
This keeps you healthy.

THE DANGERS OF UNBALANCED GHRELIN

These are some of the dangers you will experience when your ghrelin is not balanced

CENTRAL NERVOUS SYSTEM
Your Brain
Slows metabolism, causes weight gain, decreases memory retention

CARDIOVASCULAR SYSTEM
Your Heart
Increases blood pressure and hardening of the arteries

DIGESTIVE SYSTEM
Your Stomach
Speeds up digestion and ghrelin secretion

ENDOCRINE SYSTEM
Your Blood Sugar Regulation
Increases blood sugar and insulin resistance

IMMUNE SYSTEM
Your Cells
Causes cellular inflammation and disease progression

When ghrelin is not in balance, however, you become vulnerable to disease processes, including the ones that cause diabetes, cancer, rheumatoid arthritis, and inflammatory bowel disease.

receptors in the hippocampus may not promote memory because the receptors aren't adequately stimulated.[34]

From the brain, ghrelin sends signals throughout the entire body. One of those signals stimulates the release of ghrelin from the X/A cells in your gut. Daily, ghrelin travels through an infinite body-mind loop, affecting not only how you look but how healthy you are and how you feel—all contributing to your overall appearance. Remember, too, that ghrelin is a fast-acting hormone that can quickly turn your health for the worse when you don't keep it in balance.

See this at a glance by comparing the illustrations on pages 320 and 321.

Armed with this information, you're standing at the crossroads. Where you go from here is your choice. You can choose to set in motion a positive cascade of events that are beneficial for your overall health. Balancing your ghrelin resets your entire biological system, not only slimming you down but also promoting good overall health. If you don't do what it takes to keep your ghrelin levels in balance, however, you're setting the stage for weight gain and disease.

CHAPTER 10

Keeping It Off: Your Guide to Long-Term Success

If you've been following right along with this book, you spent 3 days on the Fast-Track, stabilized your ghrelin, and quickly dropped a few pounds. You spent another month accustoming yourself to this long-term approach to eating, and you've learned, through tracking your meals and snacks, how different foods affect you and what kinds of situations trigger your appetite. You've also begun the No-Sweat exercise routine.

Right now, you're probably feeling good about all of that—and healthier than ever.

Let's keep it that way. In this chapter, I'll tell you how to maintain your target weight instead of becoming one of the many, *many* people who lose weight and celebrate their success—then get lax and put all the weight right back on.

Your body isn't necessarily your ally here. Researchers have discovered something called a "set point," which happens when your body and your mind get used to a certain weight. When your weight drops below that amount, your body strategizes for ways to get you back to what it believes is "normal." That's probably why statistics show that 95 percent of dieters gain the weight back within just a few years. That subsequent regain has been thoroughly researched and is well documented. Maybe you've even experienced this phenomenon yourself—and maybe you fear that no diet will ever keep weight off for good.

Lose the fear. It's in your way. Focus on this bit of good news: **It is within your control to be among the 5 percent of dieters who keep the weight off.** I say that

Take a Break

Losing weight is hard, and most people can't *always* be disciplined—that's sure to lead to diet burnout, which generally happens between 3 and 6 months after starting a new diet. What to do?

My solution: Stop pressuring yourself to lose weight. If you feel that you just can't stick to your diet another day, then don't. Take a break.

But don't use your break as an excuse to gain the weight back. Plan to keep your weight stable for a while. You're better off pausing for a specific amount of time than trying to be perfect on the plan. I advise a 1- or 2-month hiatus while you maintain your current weight loss. And when you're ready to get back on board 100 percent, you can start with a clear head and no extra pounds. Keeping your weight stable will stop you from getting discouraged.

During your break, follow these three key strategies:

1. Set a 3- to 5-pound weight range to stay within.

2. Stick with your plan 75 percent of the time.

3. Continue to keep your food journal.

with full confidence. I'm doing it and so can you! In fact, I want you to stop right now and affirm that to yourself. Say right out loud, "It's within my control to keep this weight off."

Now I'll tell you how. My advice is based on the findings of the National Weight Control Registry (NWCR), an organization that has thoroughly studied people who succeed at keeping the weight off. Currently, the NWCR is following more than 10,000 people who've been successful at maintaining their weight loss. (These are people who've lost more than 30 pounds and who've kept it off for a year or more.) Although these folks have used different strategies to lose the weight, they're using a common set of strategies to *keep* it off.[1]

Here are the winning strategies that NWCR's research has identified:

- Eat a lower-fat diet, but not an unnecessarily restrictive one.
- Watch portion sizes.
- Eat breakfast every day of the week—nearly four in five successful dieters do.
- Be physically active. (Walking—rather than cardio exercise—is the most commonly enjoyed physical activity among these successful dieters.)
- Take pleasure in your healthier lifestyle. Enjoy being "set free" from the burden of dieting, watching your weight yo-yo, and then redoubling your efforts on a new diet.

Notice how well these success factors align with the key tenets of the Belly Fat Fix. That's no coincidence. I explicitly designed the Belly Fat Fix to be an eating and activity plan you can follow for the rest of your life. It's designed to take the weight off *and* keep it off.

Let me give you another bit of good news. People who successfully maintain their target weight also report that it gets easier over time. After a while, they explain, they get to know what works and what doesn't. You may have made some of these discoveries for yourself as you logged your results in your food tracker (see Chapter 11).

In time—and perhaps it's already happened for you—eating on ghrelin time, using your G-Scale, choosing and portioning foods from the G-List, and exercising within the ghrelin-suppressing limits will become second nature. Continuing to adhere to these guidelines will ensure your long-term success. So will eating three meals and one healthy snack to suppress ghrelin, using smart strategies to minimize stress, and getting plenty of sleep and exercise.

That's what will work for the physical you. But it's not just the physical you who sits down at the table—or goes "hunting" in the cabinets or fridge when you "must" have *something*. That's why I want you to continue to discern the difference between true ghrelin-induced hunger and the other hungers you've learned about—hungers that can never be fully satisfied by food. (If you're still not sure how to distinguish between these hungers, reread the sections in Chapter 1 on ghrelin and true hunger, psychological hunger, and stress; see pages 13–25.)

If you use these strategies in tandem with the package of strategies in the Belly Fat Fix, you can live the ghrelin way forever. You can reach your target weight and maintain it without a struggle. That's a promise. My clients are proving it every day. As I explained in Chapter 9, following this plan is also a great way to stay healthy and ward off the scariest degenerative diseases, like diabetes and fast-growing cancers.

RULES TO STAY SLIM BY

To keep you on your slim, healthy path, let's review the rules that will keep you that way. You can't abandon these rules if you want to maintain your figure and your health—in fact, you need to adhere to them now more than ever. There are two reasons for this: One is that if you don't continue to follow these rules, you run the risk of your ghrelin becoming out of balance, which would set you up to gain the weight back. The other is that until your body accepts this new weight as normal, it may resist and try to pack some more pounds on.

Here are the rules that will keep the weight off:

Rule 1: Use your G-Scale to determine your ghrelin level.

Rule 2: Balance your meals and snacks using the G-List.

Rule 3: Exercise within your ghrelin-suppressing limits.

Now let's look at why each rule is critical now, during weight maintenance.

Rule 1: Use your G-Scale to determine your ghrelin level. Hunger is a sensation you feel every day, several times a day, but at some point you'll experience hungers other than true hunger. When this happens—and you can bet it will—the

G-Scale is your guide. Eating outside true hunger is the gateway to weight gain and the path to obesity. Everyone eats for reasons other than true hunger sometimes, like at parties or holidays, but when it goes from an occasional splurge to a regular occurrence, watch out! Using your G-Scale daily is the best way to work with your ghrelin and avoid non–true hunger eating.

Rule 2: Balance meals and snacks using the G-List. The G-List is your guide to the foods that suppress, have little effect on, or increase ghrelin. By now, you should be familiar with the G-List; you may even have your favorite go-to foods. And if you're choosing foods mainly from the ghrelin-suppressing and ghrelin-neutral categories—great! Remember, you must balance the foods at each meal. If you're following your prebuilt meal plan, the work is done for you. You can also refer to the G-List to swap out foods within the same category.

Rule 3: Exercise within your ghrelin-suppressing limits. You know that intense cardio exercise won't help you lose weight—it'll actually increase your hunger. If you don't participate in regular exercise, now is the time to start. Remember: Only after 1 full month on the Belly Fat Fix should you start the No-Sweat Exercise Program, designed to build lean muscle and increase your metabolism over time, without affecting your hunger.

Don't abandon these rules! Think about it this way: What you do to take the weight off is the same as what you need to do to keep it off.

STRATEGIES FOR SUCCESS

To ensure your success, add these simple strategies to the basic rules. Incorporate these in your daily routine:

SET A 3- TO 5-POUND WEIGHT RANGE TO STAY WITHIN

When you reach your goal weight, it's essential that you continue to weigh yourself and keep track of the numbers. Once or twice a week is ideal. Then if your weight starts to creep up, you know right away and you can initiate corrections quickly. Make a 3- to 5-pound rule for yourself. This range represents your upper weight limit, and it's your alarm telling you to get back on track ASAP. If you weigh less than 150 pounds, I go for a 3-pound rule, and if you're over 150 pounds, make a 5-pound gain your upper limit.

Weight fluctuates daily, even hourly, so don't get all worked up if your weight is a couple of pounds higher today—unless you *know* you haven't been following your plan rules. If you've strayed and your weight is higher, the time to get back into the healthy routine is *right now.* You've worked so hard to lose weight and establish a healthier life for yourself. By monitoring your weight regularly, you're taking responsibility and holding yourself accountable. Plus, regularly seeing that number on the scale sets a new standard for you. This practice will also help you continue to understand your body better and to know exactly what you need to do to keep the weight off.

How to Trick Your Body Out of a Weight-Loss Plateau

You're following your diet, but you've hit a plateau—every dieter's fear.

First, don't freak out. (Remember that stress can trigger your appetite.)

That plateau won't last forever. Your body just needs to readjust to your new lower weight and improved eating habits. Your best option? Wait it out and follow the "Take a Break" guidelines on page 324. This gives your body time to adjust hormonally to your new weight.

Once that happens, your survival mechanism will shut off and the pounds will go. It's that simple.

But what if you absolutely have to lose that weight *now*? Here are some strategies to get your body to switch out of the plateau and back into slim-down mode. The key is to do *all* these tricks, not just one or two.

1. **Follow the meal plan above yours for 2 days.** For example, if you're on the 1,600-calorie meal plan, follow the 1,800-calorie meal plan for 2 days. Your body is sensing major nutrition and calorie withdrawal; by providing the nutrition it perceives it needs, you can flip that starvation-mechanism switch. A couple of days of

STICK WITH YOUR PLAN
75 PERCENT OF THE TIME

Obviously, if you want *to lose* weight, you have to stick with your diet. Generally speaking, you must follow your meal plan 90 percent of the time to lose weight. That leaves you a 10 percent margin for error on the Belly Fat Fix, so you can relax when you make a portioning mistake or occasionally overindulge. But for the most part, you need to be on the diet to take off the weight. When you reach your target weight and enter the weight-maintenance phase, follow your meal plan 75 percent of the time. You'll have a larger margin of error, but by no means should you stop following the plan.

eating one meal plan higher will not cause you to gain weight.

2. **Take a 20- to 30-minute walk before breakfast.** Not for the calorie-burning, but to wake your body up by changing your routine. Often weight-loss plateaus happen because your body gets used to the same routine day in and day out. A morning walk can be just enough for your body to shift gears and restart your metabolism.

3. **Switch around your No-Sweat Exercise Program routines.** Change the times you work out and the order of your exercises. *Don't exercise more.* After all, if your body's in survival mode already, burning more calories won't help, but changing your routine will. When you break down different muscles more effectively, your body works harder to repair and rebuild those muscles. Remember that muscle repair and rebuilding is a metabolic booster. So by switching up your No-Sweat program, you can increase your metabolic daily calorie-burning without actually burning a lot of calories at one time.

CONTINUE TO KEEP A FOOD TRACKER

The key to preserving your target weight is keeping up with your food tracker. The goal is to own your mistakes and indulgences and to learn the nuances of your hungers and your body's responses to food and timing. Writing in the tracker may not prevent every dieting mistake or episode of indulgence. That's not realistic—it's normal to have a bad eating day at some point. We all do. But the key is to not let a bad eating day turn into a bad eating week, month, or year. That's how keeping your tracker can help. You can keep a log on paper, in a notebook, or on your computer or smartphone. You can photocopy the trackers in Chapter 11. Whatever method you choose—just do it.

Dining Out on the Belly Fat Fix

The National Restaurant Association says the average American adult purchases a meal or a snack from a restaurant about five times per week. If you're an "average American," you probably dine out or order takeout meals often. On the Belly Fat Fix, there's no reason to write off eating out—and even if you wanted to, you probably couldn't. There's bound to be a birthday, wedding, or holiday that requires you to eat out—and you should. Dining out and celebrating are healthy parts of life—and they needn't be an excuse to binge.

Just remember that you have control over what you order and how much of it goes in your mouth. The Ghrelin-Friendly Restaurant Guide (page 332)—and these ground rules—will make it possible to stay on your plan:

1. **Order separates.** Ordering a meal with separate food items gives you the ability to figure out how much you should or should not eat. You can't use measuring cups or spoons at a restaurant, but you can use the "Easy Ghrelin Portion Guide" in Chapter 4 (page 105) to figure out the right portion. For instance, a burrito may sound like a good option, and the ingredients may be all ghrelin-suppressing or ghrelin-neutral foods, but you still have to watch how much you put on

THE END

I say "the end" in jest. Honestly, it's just the beginning. I'm excited—along with you—about what can happen when you follow the Belly Fat Fix. You'll learn to understand your eating habits better; gain biological control of your appetite and strategic control of the impulse to binge (thus preventing sliding and weight regain); bring your ghrelin into its optimal, balanced state; fill up with delicious, nutritious food; slim down; and get healthy. Very likely, this will motivate you to continue on the plan, just as the Ghrelin Masters in this book are choosing to do.

My goal in writing this book is to help you get there and be the healthier, slimmer, more energetic "you" you've always imagined. But I know for a fact that it's not easy.

---

your plate. The better choice? Skip the burrito and opt for grilled steak fajitas with fixings on the side. Steak is a ghrelin superfood, and you can make the fajitas the way you like them and then portion it according to the Belly Fat Fix. Problem solved.

2. **Swap out sides.** Many of my clients tell me, "There was nothing healthy on the menu." But I guarantee that if you swap out a side or two, many high-calorie/high-fat ghrelin-increasing meals will do just fine. Take the all-American burger with cheese, a side of fries, and coleslaw, adding up to a whopping 1,200-calorie ghrelin-increasing meal. But if you elimi-

nate the coleslaw and cheese, switch the fries for extra lettuce, tomato, and onion, and request sliced bread instead of a bun, you'll have a well-balanced ghrelin meal.

3. **Eat only from your plate.** We all love to share appetizers and trade entrées, but if you want to stick with the Belly Fat Fix, eat the food on your plate—and only your plate. Eating your kid's leftovers or trying a bite of everyone else's meal will only get you in trouble. Plus, make a mental note: The breadbasket is *not* your plate. Exception: If you choose to have dessert (which I encourage on occasion), share it and eat only half.

Ghrelin-Friendly Restaurant Guide

Cuisine	Ghrelin Increasing	Ghrelin Friendly	Common Menu Items and What Each Means
Asian	BBQ ribs, curry sauce, egg rolls, fried rice, General Tso, gow gee, gyoza, nut dishes, seitan, spring rolls, sweet-and-sour sauce, tempura	Brown rice, mirin, miso soup, ponzu, shoyu, soba noodles, steamed dumplings, summer rolls, sushi, tofu soup, wasabi *Even the healthiest options tend to be high in sodium.*	"Baked, broiled, or steamed"—prepared with little fat; ask for sauce on the side. "Build your own"—choose soba noodles or brown rice, lean protein, and double the veggies (sauce on the side). "Maki"—rolled in seaweed. "Negimaki"—grilled beef wrapped with scallions. "Sashimi"—raw fish minus the rice. "Shabu"—dipped meats/veggies in a simmering broth (not fat). "Yaki"—grilled or broiled.
Indian	Biryani, chutneys, ghee, korma, naan, pakora, poori, samosas	Cauliflower curry, chickpeas, dal, lassi	"Raita"—cool yogurt sauce made with cucumber; excellent option on the side of many dishes. "Tandoori"—clay oven for cooking meats with spices. "Tikka"—skewers of meat and veggies; be sure to order chicken.
Italian	Alfredo sauce, alla vodka sauce, carbonara sauce, eggplant Parmesan, garlic bread, lasagna, manicotti, ravioli, risotto	Baked fish, clam sauce, marinara sauce, meat sauce, minestrone soup, pasta e fagioli soup, polenta, whole wheat pasta	"Al forno"—from the oven, or baked. "Cacciatore"—made with tomato, onion, herbs, peppers, and wine. "Marsala"—reduced wine with onions, shallots, mushrooms, and herbs. "Piccata"—sautéed. *All usually appears as fish, chicken, or beef dishes. Be sure to ask for sauce on the side, and portion your pasta.*
Mediterranean	Avgolemono, bastilla, brek, falafel, lavash flatbread, potpie, shawarma	Baba ghanoush, bakoula, chermoula, couscous, grilled veggies and meats, harira soup, hummus, immouzer, legumes, tabbouleh	"Arobi"—mixed grills; avoid the higher-fat meats. "Chicken gyro"—okay minus the sauces and half of the pita. "Dolmades"—grape or cabbage leaves stuffed with herbs, rice, and meat. "Stifado"—baked stew with beef, onion, tomato, and wine.
Mexican	Burritos, chili con queso, chiles rellenos, chimichangas, enchiladas, quesadillas, refritos, sour cream, taco salad, tamales	Ceviche, escabeche, guacamole, mole sauce, pico de gallo, posole, salsa verde, vegetable salsa	"Fajitas"—grilled; you can build your own to load up on veggies and lean meat. Be sure to shake off excess oil. "Fish tacos"—ask for grilled fish and corn tortillas. "Marisco"—seafood. "Pescado"—fresh fish.

Copy this page and slip it into your wallet or your supermarket coupon organizer.

Succeeding on the Belly Fat Fix doesn't require you to be perfect, but it does demand a degree of consistency. To be consistent, you must first be committed. And first, you must commit to yourself.

I wrote this book to help you understand how ghrelin works in your body and realize that all those times you blamed yourself for being lazy or lacking willpower, much of the fault lay with your out-of-whack ghrelin. Once your ghrelin is balanced, your health is restored, your appetite is more within your control, you can move forward, and you can live a long, healthy, slender life. The motivation to lose weight may be what got you here, but it is the motivation to live a good life that will ultimately keep you here.

I see this every day with my clients. It's truly a gift to witness the metamorphosis that comes from following the plan. The biggest gift I got from this plan has been seeing the success of my mother, Lisa N. (Her story is featured on page 68.) Her weight loss not only improved her health, it also brought us closer together. I think that's because when the people you love take care of their health, it reminds you how truly precious life is—and how excess weight compromises your relationships.

I can't begin to tell you how proud I am of my mom for following the Belly Fat Fix. I bet if you take a moment to think about it, you know someone in your life who will feel the same way about you after you take your health back by balancing your ghrelin. The best part for me is that my mom walked me down the aisle on my wedding day weighing almost 40 pounds less than she did before the plan.

As I walked proudly down that aisle with my mom, I realized this: The power of weight loss is so much more than the excitement of fitting into a smaller pair of jeans. It's about your dreams coming true.

The Scoop on Supplements

More than half of all American adults take supplements, so I'm never surprised when a client asks, "Are there any supplements that will help me to lose weight?"

The answer is no. The right ones can help keep you healthy and may stop a disease process dead in its tracks, but they won't take off the pounds. I rarely tell clients they *have* to take a supplement, but there are a few that I regularly recommend. Check out the chart that follows and decide for yourself. Before you buy any supplements, follow these two suggestions to ensure you're buying a quality product and not overdosing:

1. Look for a USP label. *USP* stands for the United States Pharmacopeial Convention. The USP is a dietary supplement verification program, a voluntary testing and auditing procedure that ensures the quality of supplements. The USP-verified mark indicates that the product has been tested and meets industry standards. The USP specifically tests supplements to ensure that they:

1. Contain the ingredients listed on the label, in the declared potency and amount.

2. Don't contain harmful levels of specified contaminants.

3. Will break down and release into your body within a specific amount of time.

4. Have been made using sanitary, well-controlled procedures according to the FDA's Current Good Manufacturing Practice regulations.

2. Follow the recommended dosage. Don't spend extra money on megavitamins—or lots of different vitamins—while on the Belly Fat Fix, since the plan draws, in a balanced way, from all the food groups. When you choose a supplement, check that it supplies no more than 100 percent of the Recommended Dietary Allowance (RDA).

Supplement	Why?	How much?
Multivitamin	A multivitamin is an insurance policy. Studies are inconclusive, but it won't hurt. If you're deficient in a particular vitamin or mineral, a general multivitamin can provide what you need.	• Take one multivitamin daily or a few times per week.
Vitamin D3	Vitamin D deficiency is common. Those who don't get enough sun, especially in northern climates, are at risk. The deficiency also occurs in sunny climates, perhaps because people stay indoors more, covering up when outside, or using sunscreens consistently to reduce skin cancer risk.	• RDA for adults: 600 IU daily; upper limit: 4,000 IU per day. • For most adults, 1,000–2,000 IU per day is adequate. • Can be taken in larger doses once per week.
Calcium	Most people can easily get at least half of the calcium they need from food, so the other half may be lacking. Women are especially at risk, as calcium deficiency leads to osteoporosis.	• Women: 1,200 mg daily. Men: 1,000 mg daily. • Take in 500–600 mg doses with food for best absorption.
Omega-3 fatty acids	Omega-3 fatty acids or, polyunsaturated fatty acids (PUFAs), are lacking in the standard American diet; important for many bodily functions, including relaxation and contraction of muscles, blood clotting, digestion, fertility, cell division, growth, and movement of calcium and other substances in and out of cells.	• 600–1,000 mg daily. • Take with a meal for best absorption.

Pat Q.

AGE: 54

POUNDS LOST:

FAST-TRACK: 3

TOTAL: 14 in 60 days

OVERALL INCHES LOST: 11.5

In the cosmetics business, looking good is more than just a matter of vanity—it's a professional necessity. That's what motivated Pat, who supervises a team of beauty consultants for a well-known line of cosmetics products, to go on the Belly Fat Fix to get rid of those 14 extra pounds she was carrying around.

Her other motivation? Her husband, Mark, who needed to lose more weight than she did. (See his success story on page 302.) She convinced him to go on the plan with her—and they are delighted with the results.

 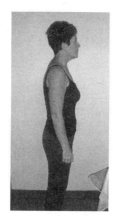

BEFORE   AFTER

Because Pat prepared food for both of them, she found cooking all the foods for the Fast-Track a bit daunting. "That was a lot of cooking—and that's not something I tend to get a lot of joy from. There were times when I wished we had a personal chef!"

But ultimately, the effort paid off. Mark and Pat each lost 3 pounds on the Fast-Track, and they went on to reach their target weights. Pat was amazed at how much food she was allowed on the Fast-Track—she couldn't finish it all.

It wasn't long before Pat figured out how to simplify meals to cut down on food prep. "We had a lot of salads" augmented with the right ghrelin-suppressing proteins and carbohydrates, she says.

"I also appreciated the variety of meal plans. Mark and I tend to eat the same things over and over, and this got us out of our rut."

Pat enjoyed the ability to be flexible within the parameters of the plan. "We stayed very true to the Fast-Track, but after that, though we stayed within the menu, we didn't necessarily copy everything."

Pat's made some minor adjustments in the way she prepares meals. For instance, now she'll use just the egg whites and not the yolks when she makes egg dishes, and instead of choosing red apples, she buys green Granny Smiths, which are higher in pectin and thus help to extend that feeling of fullness longer. (Read more about Granny Smith apples on page 90.)

Now Pat is not only slimmer, she also feels better in lots of ways. "This is a very healthy eating plan," she says. "It's certainly worked for us!"

CHAPTER 11

Write Your Way to Success: Your 30-Day Food Tracker

Once you've completed the 3-Day Fast-Track, you're ready to use this food tracker faithfully for the next 30 days. Don't blow it off; it'll really help you. Tracking is a proven weight-loss success strategy. In fact, it's one of the most important things you can do on a weight-loss program to take off pounds and keep them off or good.

Need proof? In a study published in the *American Journal of Preventive Medicine*, researchers looked at the effectiveness of various behavioral weight-loss interventions in more than 1,500 overweight and obese adults. Participants were taught lifestyle interventions that included weekly group sessions, regular exercise, following a heart-healthy diet, reducing alcohol consumption, and keeping food diaries.

After 5 months, all the participants (even those who didn't keep a food diary) lost weight—an average of almost 13 pounds, a significant amount. Those who kept a food diary more than 5 days a week, however, *lost almost twice as much weight* as those who didn't. Perhaps more impressive, they kept the weight off.[1]

That's why I urge you to use the food tracker I created. **Recording your progress daily helps you reach your goal.**

I speak from my own experience. I've been a food-tracking junkie for years, so I know what it's like to slip up and forget to write in my tracker for a day or two. I know what it's like to say, "I'll start over tomorrow. What's the point in bothering today? After all, I've already messed up." And I know what it's like to lose a whole week before I could get myself back on track again.

It was only when I fully committed to logging every single thing I ate, every single day—and noting all the circumstances going on in my life—that I managed to lose that last 10 pounds I hadn't been able to drop before. The science—and my personal experience—proves my point: You *must* log everything you eat, no matter what you eat and no matter how far you stray from your diet.

Tracking isn't always easy. But here's how it serves you: Maintaining a daily food tracker will keep you honest about how much you're eating and when. I found that writing down my mistakes didn't always prevent me from succumbing to temptation, but it did give me the mental and emotional will to keep a bad day from turning into a bad week. That's because when I write down everything, I can't pretend that I didn't slip up. Acknowledging my mistakes—without berating myself for them—gets me back on track faster.

I urge you to do the same. Be honest with yourself. Write down everything you eat on your good days *and* your bad days. If you've fallen off the wagon, look at what you've written, learn from your mistake, and love yourself anyway. Determine to do better next time.

Sure, you'll still have bad days—in fact, I pretty much guarantee it. But if you own what you ate and silence that inner critic—who will make you feel so bad that you'll want to reach for yet another piece of chocolate cake—you can stop a bad day from becoming a bad week. Or a bad month, for that matter!

Here's the other benefit you gain when you write in the food tracker every day:

You'll become more aware of the nuances of your hunger, emotions, and eating patterns. I can't tell you how important this is. The more you learn about yourself, the easier it will be for you to tell whether your hunger is coming from your body's need for nutrients (which prompts ghrelin to rise and stimulates your appetite) or from stress, anxiety, or feelings you don't want to feel. The better you get at discerning the difference, the easier it will be to head off binges at the pass. You'll begin to think: *This isn't real hunger, so let me figure out what I really need to feel satisfied.*

Recognizing your emotional connection with food is *critical* if you want to lose weight and keep it off. The few minutes you spend logging daily entries in this food tracker—and the discoveries you make about your body and mind when you do— will make it much easier to keep the weight off. And because it's not easy, you want to marshal every success strategy you can. Keeping a food tracker is definitely at the top of the list.

Here are some tips for making the most of your food tracker:

1. You're going to have "bad eating days" where you're tempted to skip writing in your tracker. Make yourself write in it anyway. Log every bit of food you put in your mouth, including the brownie mix you licked off the beaters. Be prepared for the bad days, because they will happen.

2. *Don't* allow yourself to say, "I'll skip the tracker today and start over again tomorrow. Meanwhile, since I'm taking the day off, I'll eat what I want." If you do this, it could end up taking you a week or more to get back to business. Write down everything you ate today—*today*. Acknowledge it. Own it. Then move on.

3. Don't worry about spelling or punctuation. Your food tracker is for your eyes only.

4. Write your true feelings, challenges, and thoughts—even if they don't seem to have any connection with food. This allows you to learn your own unique patterns. Once you do, you can change them.

Deal? Okay—go for it. You'll be happy you did.

FOOD TRACKER *Sample*

MEAL PLAN	MEAL CHOICE

BREAKFAST

2 + CARBS: 2 slices fiber bread	TIME: **7:30** a.m.
1 + PROTEIN: non-fat Greek yogurt	G-SCALE: (gray) • white • black
FAT:	
1 FRUIT: strawberries	CHALLENGES / THOUGHTS: Still not used to
✓ 12 oz water with lemon	eating breakfast. I just don't feel hungry in the morning.
✓ 8 oz coffee (optional)	

LUNCH

2 + CARBS: 2 tbsp hummus/wheat wrap	TIME: **1:00** p.m.
2 + PROTEIN: 4 oz. chicken breast	G-SCALE: gray • white • (black)
1 = FAT: 1.5 tsp peanut butter	
1 FRUIT: half banana	CHALLENGES / THOUGHTS: Eating in front of my
VEGETABLE: baby carrots	computer again. Work has been so stressful lately! I could
✓ 12 oz water with lemon	barely wait until my break to eat. I am definitely more hungry
	for lunch when I eat breakfast.

GHRELIN-SUPPRESSING SNACK

Wasa crackers and 2 cheese wedges	TIME: **4:20** p.m.
	G-SCALE: gray • (white) • black

DINNER

1 + CARBS: 3 oz baked potato	TIME: **7:30** p.m.
2 + PROTEIN: 4 oz. lean ground beef	G-SCALE: gray • white • (black)
1 = FAT: 1 tbsp regular sour cream	
1 FRUIT: frozen blackberries	CHALLENGES / THOUGHTS: I want to eat more,
VEGETABLE: onion/peppers/broccoli	but I know I'm not hungry! Why do I always want to eat
✓ 12 oz water with lemon	more after dinner? I think I am just bored. I need to do
	something productive.

ACTIVITY/EXERCISE

	CHALLENGES / THOUGHTS:
20 minute after dinner walk	I feel good, I don't feel like eating anymore. A walk was the
	perfect distraction!

FOOD TRACKER

Day 1

MEAL PLAN	MEAL CHOICE

BREAKFAST

CARBS:	TIME:
PROTEIN:	G-SCALE: gray • white • black
FAT:	
FRUIT:	CHALLENGES / THOUGHTS:
☐ 12 oz water with lemon	
☐ 8 oz coffee (optional)	

LUNCH

CARBS:	TIME:
PROTEIN:	G-SCALE: gray • white • black
FAT:	
FRUIT:	CHALLENGES / THOUGHTS:
VEGETABLE:	
☐ 12 oz water with lemon	

GHRELIN-SUPPRESSING SNACK

	TIME:
	G-SCALE: gray • white • black

DINNER

CARBS:	TIME:
PROTEIN:	G-SCALE: gray • white • black
FAT:	
FRUIT:	CHALLENGES / THOUGHTS:
VEGETABLE:	
☐ 12 oz water with lemon	

ACTIVITY/EXERCISE

	CHALLENGES / THOUGHTS:

FOOD TRACKER   *Day 2*

MEAL PLAN	MEAL CHOICE

BREAKFAST

CARBS: _____

PROTEIN: _____

FAT: _____

FRUIT: _____

☐ 12 oz water with lemon
☐ 8 oz coffee (optional)

TIME: _____

G-SCALE: gray • white • black

CHALLENGES / THOUGHTS:
_____
_____

LUNCH

CARBS: _____

PROTEIN: _____

FAT: _____

FRUIT: _____

VEGETABLE: _____

☐ 12 oz water with lemon

TIME: _____

G-SCALE: gray • white • black

CHALLENGES / THOUGHTS:
_____
_____

GHRELIN-SUPPRESSING SNACK

TIME: _____

G-SCALE: gray • white • black

DINNER

CARBS: _____

PROTEIN: _____

FAT: _____

FRUIT: _____

VEGETABLE: _____

☐ 12 oz water with lemon

TIME: _____

G-SCALE: gray • white • black

CHALLENGES / THOUGHTS:
_____
_____

ACTIVITY/EXERCISE

CHALLENGES / THOUGHTS:
_____

FOOD TRACKER
Day 3

MEAL PLAN	MEAL CHOICE

BREAKFAST

CARBS:

PROTEIN:

FAT:

FRUIT:

☐ 12 oz water with lemon

☐ 8 oz coffee (optional)

TIME:

G-SCALE: gray • white • black

CHALLENGES / THOUGHTS:

LUNCH

CARBS:

PROTEIN:

FAT:

FRUIT:

VEGETABLE:

☐ 12 oz water with lemon

TIME:

G-SCALE: gray • white • black

CHALLENGES / THOUGHTS:

GHRELIN-SUPPRESSING SNACK

TIME:

G-SCALE: gray • white • black

DINNER

CARBS:

PROTEIN:

FAT:

FRUIT:

VEGETABLE:

☐ 12 oz water with lemon

TIME:

G-SCALE: gray • white • black

CHALLENGES / THOUGHTS:

ACTIVITY/EXERCISE

CHALLENGES / THOUGHTS:

FOOD TRACKER

Day 4

MEAL PLAN	MEAL CHOICE

BREAKFAST

CARBS:

PROTEIN:

FAT:

FRUIT:

☐ 12 oz water with lemon

☐ 8 oz coffee (optional)

TIME:

G-SCALE: gray • white • black

CHALLENGES / THOUGHTS:

LUNCH

CARBS:

PROTEIN:

FAT:

FRUIT:

VEGETABLE:

☐ 12 oz water with lemon

TIME:

G-SCALE: gray • white • black

CHALLENGES / THOUGHTS:

GHRELIN-SUPPRESSING SNACK

TIME:

G-SCALE: gray • white • black

DINNER

CARBS:

PROTEIN:

FAT:

FRUIT:

VEGETABLE:

☐ 12 oz water with lemon

TIME:

G-SCALE: gray • white • black

CHALLENGES / THOUGHTS:

ACTIVITY/EXERCISE

CHALLENGES / THOUGHTS:

FOOD TRACKER

Day 5

MEAL PLAN	MEAL CHOICE

BREAKFAST

CARBS:	TIME:
PROTEIN:	G-SCALE: gray • white • black
FAT:	
FRUIT:	CHALLENGES / THOUGHTS:
☐ 12 oz water with lemon	
☐ 8 oz coffee (optional)	

LUNCH

CARBS:	TIME:
PROTEIN:	G-SCALE: gray • white • black
FAT:	
FRUIT:	CHALLENGES / THOUGHTS:
VEGETABLE:	
☐ 12 oz water with lemon	

GHRELIN-SUPPRESSING SNACK

	TIME:
	G-SCALE: gray • white • black

DINNER

CARBS:	TIME:
PROTEIN:	G-SCALE: gray • white • black
FAT:	
FRUIT:	CHALLENGES / THOUGHTS:
VEGETABLE:	
☐ 12 oz water with lemon	

ACTIVITY/EXERCISE

	CHALLENGES / THOUGHTS:

FOOD TRACKER

Day 6

MEAL PLAN	MEAL CHOICE

BREAKFAST

CARBS:

PROTEIN:

FAT:

FRUIT:

☐ 12 oz water with lemon
☐ 8 oz coffee (optional)

TIME:

G-SCALE: gray • white • black

CHALLENGES / THOUGHTS:

LUNCH

CARBS:

PROTEIN:

FAT:

FRUIT:

VEGETABLE:

☐ 12 oz water with lemon

TIME:

G-SCALE: gray • white • black

CHALLENGES / THOUGHTS:

GHRELIN-SUPPRESSING SNACK

TIME:

G-SCALE: gray • white • black

DINNER

CARBS:

PROTEIN:

FAT:

FRUIT:

VEGETABLE:

☐ 12 oz water with lemon

TIME:

G-SCALE: gray • white • black

CHALLENGES / THOUGHTS:

ACTIVITY/EXERCISE

CHALLENGES / THOUGHTS:

FOOD TRACKER

Day 7

MEAL PLAN	MEAL CHOICE
BREAKFAST	

CARBS: TIME:

PROTEIN: G-SCALE: gray • white • black

FAT:

FRUIT: CHALLENGES / THOUGHTS:

☐ 12 oz water with lemon
☐ 8 oz coffee (optional)

| **LUNCH** | |

CARBS: TIME:

PROTEIN: G-SCALE: gray • white • black

FAT:

FRUIT: CHALLENGES / THOUGHTS:

VEGETABLE:

☐ 12 oz water with lemon

| **GHRELIN-SUPPRESSING SNACK** | |

TIME:

G-SCALE: gray • white • black

| **DINNER** | |

CARBS: TIME:

PROTEIN: G-SCALE: gray • white • black

FAT:

FRUIT: CHALLENGES / THOUGHTS:

VEGETABLE:

☐ 12 oz water with lemon

| **ACTIVITY/EXERCISE** | |

CHALLENGES / THOUGHTS:

FOOD TRACKER
Day 8

MEAL PLAN	MEAL CHOICE

BREAKFAST

CARBS:

PROTEIN:

FAT:

FRUIT:

☐ 12 oz water with lemon
☐ 8 oz coffee (optional)

TIME:

G-SCALE: gray • white • black

CHALLENGES / THOUGHTS:

LUNCH

CARBS:

PROTEIN:

FAT:

FRUIT:

VEGETABLE:

☐ 12 oz water with lemon

TIME:

G-SCALE: gray • white • black

CHALLENGES / THOUGHTS:

GHRELIN-SUPPRESSING SNACK

TIME:

G-SCALE: gray • white • black

DINNER

CARBS:

PROTEIN:

FAT:

FRUIT:

VEGETABLE:

☐ 12 oz water with lemon

TIME:

G-SCALE: gray • white • black

CHALLENGES / THOUGHTS:

ACTIVITY/EXERCISE

CHALLENGES / THOUGHTS:

FOOD TRACKER

Day 9

MEAL PLAN	MEAL CHOICE

BREAKFAST

CARBS:	TIME:
PROTEIN:	G-SCALE: gray • white • black
FAT:	
FRUIT:	CHALLENGES / THOUGHTS:
☐ 12 oz water with lemon	
☐ 8 oz coffee (optional)	

LUNCH

CARBS:	TIME:
PROTEIN:	G-SCALE: gray • white • black
FAT:	
FRUIT:	CHALLENGES / THOUGHTS:
VEGETABLE:	
☐ 12 oz water with lemon	

GHRELIN-SUPPRESSING SNACK

	TIME:
	G-SCALE: gray • white • black

DINNER

CARBS:	TIME:
PROTEIN:	G-SCALE: gray • white • black
FAT:	
FRUIT:	CHALLENGES / THOUGHTS:
VEGETABLE:	
☐ 12 oz water with lemon	

ACTIVITY/EXERCISE

	CHALLENGES / THOUGHTS:

FOOD TRACKER

Day 10

MEAL PLAN	MEAL CHOICE
BREAKFAST	

CARBS: ___

PROTEIN: ___

FAT: ___

FRUIT: ___

☐ 12 oz water with lemon
☐ 8 oz coffee (optional)

TIME: ___

G-SCALE: gray • white • black

CHALLENGES / THOUGHTS:

___

LUNCH

CARBS: ___

PROTEIN: ___

FAT: ___

FRUIT: ___

VEGETABLE: ___

☐ 12 oz water with lemon

TIME: ___

G-SCALE: gray • white • black

CHALLENGES / THOUGHTS:

___

GHRELIN-SUPPRESSING SNACK

TIME: ___

G-SCALE: gray • white • black

DINNER

CARBS: ___

PROTEIN: ___

FAT: ___

FRUIT: ___

VEGETABLE: ___

☐ 12 oz water with lemon

TIME: ___

G-SCALE: gray • white • black

CHALLENGES / THOUGHTS:

___

ACTIVITY/EXERCISE

CHALLENGES / THOUGHTS:

FOOD TRACKER   *Day 11*

MEAL PLAN	MEAL CHOICE

BREAKFAST

CARBS:

PROTEIN:

FAT:

FRUIT:

☐ 12 oz water with lemon
☐ 8 oz coffee (optional)

TIME:

G-SCALE: gray • white • black

CHALLENGES / THOUGHTS:

LUNCH

CARBS:

PROTEIN:

FAT:

FRUIT:

VEGETABLE:

☐ 12 oz water with lemon

TIME:

G-SCALE: gray • white • black

CHALLENGES / THOUGHTS:

GHRELIN-SUPPRESSING SNACK

TIME:

G-SCALE: gray • white • black

DINNER

CARBS:

PROTEIN:

FAT:

FRUIT:

VEGETABLE:

☐ 12 oz water with lemon

TIME:

G-SCALE: gray • white • black

CHALLENGES / THOUGHTS:

ACTIVITY/EXERCISE

CHALLENGES / THOUGHTS:

FOOD TRACKER

Day 12

MEAL PLAN	MEAL CHOICE

BREAKFAST

CARBS:

PROTEIN:

FAT:

FRUIT:

☐ 12 oz water with lemon

☐ 8 oz coffee (optional)

TIME:

G-SCALE: gray • white • black

CHALLENGES / THOUGHTS:

LUNCH

CARBS:

PROTEIN:

FAT:

FRUIT:

VEGETABLE:

☐ 12 oz water with lemon

TIME:

G-SCALE: gray • white • black

CHALLENGES / THOUGHTS:

GHRELIN-SUPPRESSING SNACK

TIME:

G-SCALE: gray • white • black

DINNER

CARBS:

PROTEIN:

FAT:

FRUIT:

VEGETABLE:

☐ 12 oz water with lemon

TIME:

G-SCALE: gray • white • black

CHALLENGES / THOUGHTS:

ACTIVITY/EXERCISE

CHALLENGES / THOUGHTS:

FOOD TRACKER

Day 13

MEAL PLAN	MEAL CHOICE

BREAKFAST

CARBS:

PROTEIN:

FAT:

FRUIT:

☐ 12 oz water with lemon

☐ 8 oz coffee (optional)

TIME:

G-SCALE: gray • white • black

CHALLENGES / THOUGHTS:

LUNCH

CARBS:

PROTEIN:

FAT:

FRUIT:

VEGETABLE:

☐ 12 oz water with lemon

TIME:

G-SCALE: gray • white • black

CHALLENGES / THOUGHTS:

GHRELIN-SUPPRESSING SNACK

TIME:

G-SCALE: gray • white • black

DINNER

CARBS:

PROTEIN:

FAT:

FRUIT:

VEGETABLE:

☐ 12 oz water with lemon

TIME:

G-SCALE: gray • white • black

CHALLENGES / THOUGHTS:

ACTIVITY/EXERCISE

CHALLENGES / THOUGHTS:

FOOD TRACKER
Day 14

MEAL PLAN	MEAL CHOICE

BREAKFAST

CARBS:	TIME:
PROTEIN:	G-SCALE: gray • white • black
FAT:	
FRUIT:	CHALLENGES / THOUGHTS:

☐ 12 oz water with lemon
☐ 8 oz coffee (optional)

LUNCH

CARBS:	TIME:
PROTEIN:	G-SCALE: gray • white • black
FAT:	
FRUIT:	CHALLENGES / THOUGHTS:
VEGETABLE:	

☐ 12 oz water with lemon

GHRELIN-SUPPRESSING SNACK

	TIME:
	G-SCALE: gray • white • black

DINNER

CARBS:	TIME:
PROTEIN:	G-SCALE: gray • white • black
FAT:	
FRUIT:	CHALLENGES / THOUGHTS:
VEGETABLE:	

☐ 12 oz water with lemon

ACTIVITY/EXERCISE

CHALLENGES / THOUGHTS:

FOOD TRACKER
Day 15

MEAL PLAN	MEAL CHOICE

BREAKFAST

CARBS:

PROTEIN:

FAT:

FRUIT:

☐ 12 oz water with lemon
☐ 8 oz coffee (optional)

TIME:

G-SCALE: gray • white • black

CHALLENGES / THOUGHTS:

LUNCH

CARBS:

PROTEIN:

FAT:

FRUIT:

VEGETABLE:

☐ 12 oz water with lemon

TIME:

G-SCALE: gray • white • black

CHALLENGES / THOUGHTS:

GHRELIN-SUPPRESSING SNACK

TIME:

G-SCALE: gray • white • black

DINNER

CARBS:

PROTEIN:

FAT:

FRUIT:

VEGETABLE:

☐ 12 oz water with lemon

TIME:

G-SCALE: gray • white • black

CHALLENGES / THOUGHTS:

ACTIVITY/EXERCISE

CHALLENGES / THOUGHTS:

FOOD TRACKER

Day 16

MEAL PLAN	MEAL CHOICE

BREAKFAST

CARBS:	TIME:
PROTEIN:	G-SCALE: gray • white • black
FAT:	
FRUIT:	CHALLENGES / THOUGHTS:

☐ 12 oz water with lemon
☐ 8 oz coffee (optional)

LUNCH

CARBS:	TIME:
PROTEIN:	G-SCALE: gray • white • black
FAT:	
FRUIT:	CHALLENGES / THOUGHTS:
VEGETABLE:	

☐ 12 oz water with lemon

GHRELIN-SUPPRESSING SNACK

	TIME:
	G-SCALE: gray • white • black

DINNER

CARBS:	TIME:
PROTEIN:	G-SCALE: gray • white • black
FAT:	
FRUIT:	CHALLENGES / THOUGHTS:
VEGETABLE:	

☐ 12 oz water with lemon

ACTIVITY/EXERCISE

CHALLENGES / THOUGHTS:

FOOD TRACKER
Day 17

MEAL PLAN	MEAL CHOICE

BREAKFAST

CARBS:	TIME:
PROTEIN:	G-SCALE: gray • white • black
FAT:	
FRUIT:	CHALLENGES / THOUGHTS:

☐ 12 oz water with lemon
☐ 8 oz coffee (optional)

LUNCH

CARBS:	TIME:
PROTEIN:	G-SCALE: gray • white • black
FAT:	
FRUIT:	CHALLENGES / THOUGHTS:
VEGETABLE:	

☐ 12 oz water with lemon

GHRELIN-SUPPRESSING SNACK

	TIME:
	G-SCALE: gray • white • black

DINNER

CARBS:	TIME:
PROTEIN:	G-SCALE: gray • white • black
FAT:	
FRUIT:	CHALLENGES / THOUGHTS:
VEGETABLE:	

☐ 12 oz water with lemon

ACTIVITY/EXERCISE

CHALLENGES / THOUGHTS:

FOOD TRACKER

Day 18

MEAL PLAN	MEAL CHOICE
BREAKFAST	

BREAKFAST

CARBS:

PROTEIN:

FAT:

FRUIT:

☐ 12 oz water with lemon
☐ 8 oz coffee (optional)

TIME:

G-SCALE: gray • white • black

CHALLENGES / THOUGHTS:

LUNCH

CARBS:

PROTEIN:

FAT:

FRUIT:

VEGETABLE:

☐ 12 oz water with lemon

TIME:

G-SCALE: gray • white • black

CHALLENGES / THOUGHTS:

GHRELIN-SUPPRESSING SNACK

TIME:

G-SCALE: gray • white • black

DINNER

CARBS:

PROTEIN:

FAT:

FRUIT:

VEGETABLE:

☐ 12 oz water with lemon

TIME:

G-SCALE: gray • white • black

CHALLENGES / THOUGHTS:

ACTIVITY/EXERCISE

CHALLENGES / THOUGHTS:

FOOD TRACKER

Day 19

MEAL PLAN	MEAL CHOICE

BREAKFAST

CARBS:	TIME:
PROTEIN:	G-SCALE: gray • white • black
FAT:	
FRUIT:	CHALLENGES / THOUGHTS:
☐ 12 oz water with lemon	
☐ 8 oz coffee (optional)	

LUNCH

CARBS:	TIME:
PROTEIN:	G-SCALE: gray • white • black
FAT:	
FRUIT:	CHALLENGES / THOUGHTS:
VEGETABLE:	
☐ 12 oz water with lemon	

GHRELIN-SUPPRESSING SNACK

	TIME:
	G-SCALE: gray • white • black

DINNER

CARBS:	TIME:
PROTEIN:	G-SCALE: gray • white • black
FAT:	
FRUIT:	CHALLENGES / THOUGHTS:
VEGETABLE:	
☐ 12 oz water with lemon	

ACTIVITY/EXERCISE

	CHALLENGES / THOUGHTS:

FOOD TRACKER

Day 20

MEAL PLAN	MEAL CHOICE

BREAKFAST

CARBS:

PROTEIN:

FAT:

FRUIT:

☐ 12 oz water with lemon
☐ 8 oz coffee (optional)

TIME:

G-SCALE: gray • white • black

CHALLENGES / THOUGHTS:

LUNCH

CARBS:

PROTEIN:

FAT:

FRUIT:

VEGETABLE:

☐ 12 oz water with lemon

TIME:

G-SCALE: gray • white • black

CHALLENGES / THOUGHTS:

GHRELIN-SUPPRESSING SNACK

TIME:

G-SCALE: gray • white • black

DINNER

CARBS:

PROTEIN:

FAT:

FRUIT:

VEGETABLE:

☐ 12 oz water with lemon

TIME:

G-SCALE: gray • white • black

CHALLENGES / THOUGHTS:

ACTIVITY/EXERCISE

CHALLENGES / THOUGHTS:

FOOD TRACKER
Day 21

MEAL PLAN	MEAL CHOICE

BREAKFAST

CARBS:	TIME:
PROTEIN:	G-SCALE: gray • white • black
FAT:	
FRUIT:	CHALLENGES / THOUGHTS:
☐ 12 oz water with lemon	
☐ 8 oz coffee (optional)	

LUNCH

CARBS:	TIME:
PROTEIN:	G-SCALE: gray • white • black
FAT:	
FRUIT:	CHALLENGES / THOUGHTS:
VEGETABLE:	
☐ 12 oz water with lemon	

GHRELIN-SUPPRESSING SNACK

	TIME:
	G-SCALE: gray • white • black

DINNER

CARBS:	TIME:
PROTEIN:	G-SCALE: gray • white • black
FAT:	
FRUIT:	CHALLENGES / THOUGHTS:
VEGETABLE:	
☐ 12 oz water with lemon	

ACTIVITY/EXERCISE

	CHALLENGES / THOUGHTS:

FOOD TRACKER

Day 22

MEAL PLAN	MEAL CHOICE

BREAKFAST

CARBS:

PROTEIN:

FAT:

FRUIT:

☐ 12 oz water with lemon
☐ 8 oz coffee (optional)

TIME:

G-SCALE: gray • white • black

CHALLENGES / THOUGHTS:

LUNCH

CARBS:

PROTEIN:

FAT:

FRUIT:

VEGETABLE:

☐ 12 oz water with lemon

TIME:

G-SCALE: gray • white • black

CHALLENGES / THOUGHTS:

GHRELIN-SUPPRESSING SNACK

TIME:

G-SCALE: gray • white • black

DINNER

CARBS:

PROTEIN:

FAT:

FRUIT:

VEGETABLE:

☐ 12 oz water with lemon

TIME:

G-SCALE: gray • white • black

CHALLENGES / THOUGHTS:

ACTIVITY/EXERCISE

CHALLENGES / THOUGHTS:

FOOD TRACKER
Day 23

MEAL PLAN	MEAL CHOICE

BREAKFAST

CARBS:

PROTEIN:

FAT:

FRUIT:

☐ 12 oz water with lemon

☐ 8 oz coffee (optional)

TIME:

G-SCALE: gray • white • black

CHALLENGES / THOUGHTS:

LUNCH

CARBS:

PROTEIN:

FAT:

FRUIT:

VEGETABLE:

☐ 12 oz water with lemon

TIME:

G-SCALE: gray • white • black

CHALLENGES / THOUGHTS:

GHRELIN-SUPPRESSING SNACK

TIME:

G-SCALE: gray • white • black

DINNER

CARBS:

PROTEIN:

FAT:

FRUIT:

VEGETABLE:

☐ 12 oz water with lemon

TIME:

G-SCALE: gray • white • black

CHALLENGES / THOUGHTS:

ACTIVITY/EXERCISE

CHALLENGES / THOUGHTS:

FOOD TRACKER

Day 24

MEAL PLAN	MEAL CHOICE

BREAKFAST

CARBS:	TIME:
PROTEIN:	G-SCALE: gray • white • black
FAT:	
FRUIT:	CHALLENGES / THOUGHTS:
☐ 12 oz water with lemon	
☐ 8 oz coffee (optional)	

LUNCH

CARBS:	TIME:
PROTEIN:	G-SCALE: gray • white • black
FAT:	
FRUIT:	CHALLENGES / THOUGHTS:
VEGETABLE:	
☐ 12 oz water with lemon	

GHRELIN-SUPPRESSING SNACK

	TIME:
	G-SCALE: gray • white • black

DINNER

CARBS:	TIME:
PROTEIN:	G-SCALE: gray • white • black
FAT:	
FRUIT:	CHALLENGES / THOUGHTS:
VEGETABLE:	
☐ 12 oz water with lemon	

ACTIVITY/EXERCISE

	CHALLENGES / THOUGHTS:

FOOD TRACKER

Day 25

MEAL PLAN	MEAL CHOICE

BREAKFAST

CARBS:

PROTEIN:

FAT:

FRUIT:

☐ 12 oz water with lemon
☐ 8 oz coffee (optional)

TIME:

G-SCALE: gray • white • black

CHALLENGES / THOUGHTS:

LUNCH

CARBS:

PROTEIN:

FAT:

FRUIT:

VEGETABLE:

☐ 12 oz water with lemon

TIME:

G-SCALE: gray • white • black

CHALLENGES / THOUGHTS:

GHRELIN-SUPPRESSING SNACK

TIME:

G-SCALE: gray • white • black

DINNER

CARBS:

PROTEIN:

FAT:

FRUIT:

VEGETABLE:

☐ 12 oz water with lemon

TIME:

G-SCALE: gray • white • black

CHALLENGES / THOUGHTS:

ACTIVITY/EXERCISE

CHALLENGES / THOUGHTS:

FOOD TRACKER

Day 26

MEAL PLAN	MEAL CHOICE

BREAKFAST

CARBS:

PROTEIN:

FAT:

FRUIT:

☐ 12 oz water with lemon
☐ 8 oz coffee (optional)

TIME:

G-SCALE: gray • white • black

CHALLENGES / THOUGHTS:

LUNCH

CARBS:

PROTEIN:

FAT:

FRUIT:

VEGETABLE:

☐ 12 oz water with lemon

TIME:

G-SCALE: gray • white • black

CHALLENGES / THOUGHTS:

GHRELIN-SUPPRESSING SNACK

TIME:

G-SCALE: gray • white • black

DINNER

CARBS:

PROTEIN:

FAT:

FRUIT:

VEGETABLE:

☐ 12 oz water with lemon

TIME:

G-SCALE: gray • white • black

CHALLENGES / THOUGHTS:

ACTIVITY/EXERCISE

CHALLENGES / THOUGHTS:

FOOD TRACKER

Day 27

MEAL PLAN	MEAL CHOICE

BREAKFAST

CARBS:

PROTEIN:

FAT:

FRUIT:

☐ 12 oz water with lemon
☐ 8 oz coffee (optional)

TIME:

G-SCALE: gray • white • black

CHALLENGES / THOUGHTS:

LUNCH

CARBS:

PROTEIN:

FAT:

FRUIT:

VEGETABLE:

☐ 12 oz water with lemon

TIME:

G-SCALE: gray • white • black

CHALLENGES / THOUGHTS:

GHRELIN-SUPPRESSING SNACK

TIME:

G-SCALE: gray • white • black

DINNER

CARBS:

PROTEIN:

FAT:

FRUIT:

VEGETABLE:

☐ 12 oz water with lemon

TIME:

G-SCALE: gray • white • black

CHALLENGES / THOUGHTS:

ACTIVITY/EXERCISE

CHALLENGES / THOUGHTS:

FOOD TRACKER

Day 28

MEAL PLAN	MEAL CHOICE

BREAKFAST

CARBS:

PROTEIN:

FAT:

FRUIT:

☐ 12 oz water with lemon
☐ 8 oz coffee (optional)

TIME:

G-SCALE: gray • white • black

CHALLENGES / THOUGHTS:

LUNCH

CARBS:

PROTEIN:

FAT:

FRUIT:

VEGETABLE:

☐ 12 oz water with lemon

TIME:

G-SCALE: gray • white • black

CHALLENGES / THOUGHTS:

GHRELIN-SUPPRESSING SNACK

TIME:

G-SCALE: gray • white • black

DINNER

CARBS:

PROTEIN:

FAT:

FRUIT:

VEGETABLE:

☐ 12 oz water with lemon

TIME:

G-SCALE: gray • white • black

CHALLENGES / THOUGHTS:

ACTIVITY/EXERCISE

CHALLENGES / THOUGHTS:

FOOD TRACKER
Day 29

MEAL PLAN	MEAL CHOICE
BREAKFAST	

CARBS: _____

PROTEIN: _____

FAT: _____

FRUIT: _____

☐ 12 oz water with lemon
☐ 8 oz coffee (optional)

TIME: _____

G-SCALE: gray • white • black

CHALLENGES / THOUGHTS:

_____

_____

LUNCH

CARBS: _____

PROTEIN: _____

FAT: _____

FRUIT: _____

VEGETABLE: _____

☐ 12 oz water with lemon

TIME: _____

G-SCALE: gray • white • black

CHALLENGES / THOUGHTS:

_____

_____

GHRELIN-SUPPRESSING SNACK

TIME: _____

G-SCALE: gray • white • black

DINNER

CARBS: _____

PROTEIN: _____

FAT: _____

FRUIT: _____

VEGETABLE: _____

☐ 12 oz water with lemon

TIME: _____

G-SCALE: gray • white • black

CHALLENGES / THOUGHTS:

_____

_____

ACTIVITY/EXERCISE

CHALLENGES / THOUGHTS:

FOOD TRACKER

Day 30

MEAL PLAN	MEAL CHOICE

BREAKFAST

CARBS:	TIME:
PROTEIN:	G-SCALE: gray • white • black
FAT:	
FRUIT:	CHALLENGES / THOUGHTS:
☐ 12 oz water with lemon	
☐ 8 oz coffee (optional)	

LUNCH

CARBS:	TIME:
PROTEIN:	G-SCALE: gray • white • black
FAT:	
FRUIT:	CHALLENGES / THOUGHTS:
VEGETABLE:	
☐ 12 oz water with lemon	

GHRELIN-SUPPRESSING SNACK

	TIME:
	G-SCALE: gray • white • black

DINNER

CARBS:	TIME:
PROTEIN:	G-SCALE: gray • white • black
FAT:	
FRUIT:	CHALLENGES / THOUGHTS:
VEGETABLE:	
☐ 12 oz water with lemon	

ACTIVITY/EXERCISE

	CHALLENGES / THOUGHTS:

ENDNOTES

CHAPTER 1

1   F Broglio, C Gottero, F Prodam, C Gauna, G Muccioli, M Papotti, T Abribat, AJ van der Lely, and E Ghigo, "Non-acylated ghrelin counteracts the metabolic but not the neuroendocrine response to acylated ghrelin in humans," *Journal of Clinical Endocrinology and Metabolism*, Jun 2004; 89(6):3062–65. http://ncbi.nlm.nih.gov /pubmed/15181099

2   AJ van der Lely, "Ghrelin and new metabolic frontiers," *Hormone Research*, Jan 2009; 71 suppl 1:129–33. http://ncbi.nlm.nih.gov/pubmed/19153523

3   Ibid.

4   J Liu, CE Prudom, and R Nass, "Novel ghrelin assays provide evidence for independent regulation of ghrelin acylation and secretion in healthy young men," *Journal of Clinical Endocrinology and Metabolism,* May 2008; 93(5):1980–87.

5   https://www.youtube.com/watch?v=fKnbOJ4NAvU

6   A Dor, C Ferguson, C Langwith, and E Tan, "Research report: a heavy burden: the individual costs of being overweight and obese in the United States," Sep 21, 2010; George Washington School of Public Health and Health Services.

7   DJ Pournaras and CW leRoux "Ghrelin and metabolic surgery," *International Journal of Peptides*, 2010, Article ID 217267.

8   G Frühbeck, R Nutr, MD, PhD, A Diez-Caballero, MD, PhD, MJ Gil, PhD, I Montero, BS, J Gómez-Ambrosi, PhD, J Salvador, MD, PhD, J A Cienfuegos, MD, PhD, "The decrease in plasma ghrelin concentrations following bariatric surgery depends on the functional integrity of the fundus," *Obesity Surgery*, 2004, 606–12.

9   D J Pournaras, "Ghrelin and metabolic surgery," *International Journal of Peptides*, 2010, Article ID 217267.

10 C Holdstock, BE Engstrom, M Obrvall, L Lind, M Sundborn, FA Karlsson, "Ghrelin and adipose tissue regulatory peptides: Effect of gastric bypass surgery in obese humans." *Journal of Clinical Endocrinology and Metabolism*, 2003; 88:177–3183.

11 http://www.sciencedaily.com/releases/2011/07/110712094044.htm

12 http://gupea.ub.gu.se/bitstream/2077/4421/1/gupea_2077_4421_1.pdf

13 http://healthnews.uc.edu/news/?/12898

14 G Cizza and KI Rother, "Was Feuerback right: are we what we eat?" *Journal of Clinical Investigation*, Aug 2011; 121(8):2969–71.

15 Ibid.

16 Ibid.

17 Robert Pool, *Fat: Fighting the Obesity Epidemic* (Oxford [UK]: Oxford University Press, 2001).

18 T Wells, "Ghrelin: defender of fat," *Progress in Lipid Research,* Sep 2009; 48(5):257–74.

CHAPTER 2

1 http://jeffweintraub.blogspot.com/2005/09/jared-diamond-on-why-invention-of.html

2 Ibid.

3 http://library.thinkquest.org/5443/whistory.html

4 http://www.foodtimeline.org/foodfaq7.html

5 Ibid.

6 A Rufus, "There is no biological reason to eat three meals a day—so why do we do it?" http://www.alternet.org/food/152486/there_is_no_biological_reason_to_eat_three_meals_a_day_--_so_why_do_we_do_it

7 O Carlson, B Martin, KS Stote, E Golden, S Maudsley, SS Najjar, L Ferrucci, DK Ingram, DL Longo, WV Rumpler, DJ Baer, J Egan, and MP Mattson, "Impact of reduced meal frequency without caloric restriction on glucose regulation in healthy, normal weight middle age men and women," *Metabolism,* Dec 2007; 56(12):1729–34. http://www.ncbi.nlm.nih.gov/pmc/articles/PMC2121099

8 Wells, "Ghrelin: defender of fat."

9 G Natalucci, S Riedi, A Gleiss, T Zidek, and H Frisch, "Spontaneous 24-h ghrelin secretion pattern in fasting subjects: maintenance of a meal-related pattern," *European Journal of Endocrinology,* Jun 2005; 152(6):845–50.

10 Natalucci, "Spontanous 24-h ghrelin secretion pattern in fasting subjects."

11 M Romon, S Gomila, P Hincker, B Soudan, and J Dallongeville, "Influence of weight loss on plasma ghrelin responses to high-fat and high-carbohydrate test meals in obese women," *Journal of Clinical Endocrinology and Metabolism,* Mar 2006; 91(3):1034–41.

12 S Malik, F McGlone, D Bedrossian, and A Dagher, "Ghrelin modulates brain activity in areas that control appetitive behavior," *Cell Metabolism,* May 2008; 7(5):400–409.

13 J Daubenmier, J Kristeller, FM Hecht, N Maninger, M Kuwata, K Jhaveri, RH Lustig, M Kemeny, L Karan, and E Epel, "Mindfulness intervention for stress eating to reduce cortisol and abdominal fat among overweight and obese women: an exploratory randomized controlled study," *Journal of Obesity,* 2011; 2011:651936.

14 "Obesity and shift work in the general population." http://ijahsp.nova.edu/articles/Vol8Num3/pdf/feldman.pdf

15 Ibid.

16 Ibid.

17 JC Weikel, A Wichniak, M Ising, H Brunner, E Friess, K held, S Mathias, DA Schmid, M Uhr, and A Steiger, "Ghrelin promotes slow-wave sleep in humans," *American Journal of Physiology–Endocrinology and Metabolism*, Feb 2003; 284(2):E407–15.

CHAPTER 3

1 RE Steinert, F Frey, A Töpfer, J Drewe, and C Beglinger, "Effects of carbohydrate sugars and artificial sweeteners on appetite and the secretion of gastrointestinal satiety peptides," *British Journal of Nutrition,* May 2011; 105(9):1320–28.

2 WAM Blom, A Lluch, S Vinoy, JJ Holst, G Schaafsma, and HFJ Hendriks, "Effect of a high-protein breakfast on the postprandial ghrelin response," *American Journal of Clinical Nutrition,* Feb 2006; 83(2):211–20.

3 DK Layman, EM Evans, D Erickson, J Seyler, J Weber, D Bagshaw, A Griel, T Psota, and P Kris-Etherton, "A moderate-protein diet produces sustained weight loss and long-term

changes in body composition and blood lipids in obese adults," *Journal of Nutrition*, Mar 2009; 139(3):514–21.

4 SHA Holt, JC Brand Miller, P Petocz, and E Farmakalidis, "A satiety index of common foods," *European Journal of Clinical Nutrition,* Sep 1995; 49(9):675–90.

5 P Monteleone, R Bencivenga, N Longobardi, C Serritella, and M Maj, "Differential responses of circulating ghrelin to high-fat or high-carbohydrate meal in healthy women," *Journal of Clinical Endocrinology and Metabolism,* Nov 2003; 88(11):5510–14.

6 JA Higgins, DR Higbee, WT Donahoo, IL Brown, ML Bell, and DH Bessesen, "Resistant starch consumption promotes lipid oxidation," *Nutrition and Metabolism,* Oct 2004; 1(1):8.

7 S Hylla, A Gostner, G Dusel, H Anger, HP Bartram, SU Christl, H Kasper, and W Scheppach, "Effects of resistant starch on the colon in healthy volunteers: possible implications for cancer prevention," *American Journal of Clinical Nutrition,* Jan 1998; 67(1):136–42.

8 HJ Willis, AL Eldridge, J Beiseigel, W Thomas, and JL Slavin, "Greater satiety response with resistant starch and corn bran in human subjects," *Nutrition Research,* Feb 2009; 29(2):100–105.

9 A Rahen, A Tagliabue, NJ Christensen, J Madsen, JJ Hoist, and A Astrup, "Resistant starch: the effect on postprandial glycemia, hormonal response, and satiety," *American Journal of Clinical Nutrition,* Oct 1994; 60(4):544–51.

10 Willis, "Greater satiety response."

11 Monteleone, "Differential responses of circulating ghrelin."

12 http://fnic.nal.usda.gov/dietary-guidance/dri-reports/thiamin-riboflavin-niacin-vitamin -b6-folate-vitamin-b12-pantothenic#overlay-context=dietary-guidance/dri-reports/ research-synthesis-workshop-summary

13 AC Looker, PR Dallman, MD Carroll, EW Gunter, and CL Johnson, "Prevalence of iron deficiency in the United States," *Journal of the American Medical Association*, Mar 26, 1997; 277(12):973–76.

14 Layman, "A moderate-protein diet produces sustained weight loss."

15 MA Roussell, AM Hill, TL Gaugler, SG West, JP Heuvel, P Alaupovic, PJ Gillies, and PM Kris-Etherton, "Beef in an optimal lean diet study: effects on lipids, lipoproteins, and adoiproproteins," *American Journal of Clinical Nutrition,* Jan 2012; 95(1):9–16.

16 JA Higgins, DR Higbee, WT Donahoo, IL Brown, ML Bell, and DH Bessesen, "Resistant starch consumption promotes lipid oxidation," *Nutrition and Metabolism,* Oct 6, 2004; 1(1):8

17 C Dincer, M Karaoglan, F Erden, N Tetik, A Topuz, and F Ozdemir, "Effects of baking and boiling on the nutritional and antioxidant properties of sweet potato," *Plant Foods for Human Nutrition*, Nov 2011; 66(4):341–47.

18 WJ Pasman, J Heimerikx, CM Rubingh, R van den Berg, M O'Shea, L Gambelli, HFJ Hendriks, AWC Einerhand, C Scott, HG Keizer, and LI Mennen, "The effect of Korean pine nut oil on in vitro CCK release, on appetite sensations and on gut hormones in post-menopausal overweight women," *Lipids in Health and Disease,* Mar 20, 2008; 7:10.

19 K Fujioka, F Greenway, J Sheard, and Y Ying, "The effects of grapefruit on weight and insulin resistance: relationship to the metabolic syndrome," *Journal of Medicinal Food*, spring 2006; 9(1):49–54. doi:10.1089/jmf.2006.9.49

20 HJ Silver, MS Dietrich, and KD Niswender, "Effects of grapefruit, grapefruit juice, and water preloads on energy balance, weight loss, body composition, and cardiometabolic risk in free-living obese adults," *Nutrition and Metabolism,* Feb 2, 2011; 8(1):8.

CHAPTER 4

1   KJ Melanson, TJ Angelopoulos, V Nguyen, L Zukley, J Lowndes, and JM Rippe, "High-fructose corn syrup, energy intake, and appetite regulation," *American Journal of Clinical Nutrition*, Dec 2008; 88(6):1738S–44S.

2   G Schaller, A Schmidt, J Pleiner, W Woloszczuk, M Wolzt, and A Luger, "Plasma ghrelin concentrations are not regulated by glucose or insulin: a double-blind, placebo-controlled crossover clamp study," *Diabetes*, Jan 2003; 52(1):16–20.

3   N Saravanan, A Haseeb, NZ Ehtesham, and Ghafoorunissa, "Differential effects of dietary saturated and trans-fatty acids on expression of genes associated with insulin sensitivity in rat adipose tissue," *European Journal of Endocrinology*, Jul 2005; 153(1):159–65.

4   Q Yang, "Gain weight by 'going diet?' Artificial sweeteners and the neurobiology of sugar cravings," *Yale Journal of Biology and Medicine*, Jun 2010; 83(2):101–8.

5   Steinert, "Effects of carbohydrate sugars and artificial sweeteners on appetite and the secretion of gastrointestinal satiety peptides."

6   PJ Rogers and JE Blundell, "Umami and appetite: Effects of monosodium glutamate on hunger and food intake in human subjects," *Physiology and Behavior*, Dec 1990; 48(2):801–4.

7   DE Cummings, RS Frayo, C Marmonier, R Aubert, and D Chapelot, "Plasma ghrelin levels and hunger scores in humans initiating meals voluntarily without time- and food-related cues," *American Journal of Physiology–Endocrinology and Metabolism*, Aug 2004; 287:E297–304.

8   Ibid.

9   Centers for Disease Control and Prevention. http://www.cdc.gov/healthyyouth/obesity/facts.htm

10 WS Agras, LD Hammer, F McNicholas, HC Kraemer, "Risk factors for childhood overweight: a prospective study from birth to 9.5 years," *Journal of Pediatrics*, Jul 2004; 145(1):20–25.

11 H Patrick and TA Nicklas, "A review of family and social determinants of children's eating patterns and diet quality," *Journal of the American College of Nutrition*, Apr 2005; 24(2):83–92.

12 DB Abrams and MJ Follick, "Behavioral weight-loss intervention at the worksite: feasibility and maintenance," *Journal of Consulting and Clinical Psychology*, Apr 1983; 51(2):226–33.

CHAPTER 8

1   TA Hagobian, CG Shaeroff, and B Braun, "Effects of short-term exercise and energy surplus on hormones related to regulation of energy balance," *Metabolism–Clinical and Experimental*, Mar 2008; 57(3):393–98.

2   T Kizaki, T Maegawa, T Sakuria, and J Ogasawara, "Voluntary exercise attenuates obesity-associated inflammation through ghrelin expressed in macrophages," *Biochemical and Biophysical Research Communications*, Sep 30, 2011; 413(3):454–59.

3   "Exercise: 7 benefits of regular physical activity," MayoClinic.com. http://www.mayoclinic.com/health/exercise/HQ01676

4   HJ Leidy, JK Gardner, BR Frey, ML Snook, MK Schuchert, EL Richard, and NI Williams, "Circulating ghrelin is sensitive to changes in body weight during a diet and exercise program in normal weight young women," *Journal of Clinical Endocrinology and Metabolism*, Jun 2004; 89(6):2659–64.

5   HJ Leidy, KA Dougherty, BR Frye, KM Duke, and NI Williams, "Twenty-four-hour ghrelin is elevated after calorie restriction and exercise training in non-obese women," *Obesity*, Feb 2007; 15(2):446–55.

6 JB Li, A Asakawa, Y Li, K Cheng, and A Inui, "Effects of exercise on the levels of peptide YY and ghrelin," *Experimental and Clinical Endocrinology and Diabetes*, Mar 2011; 119(3):163–66.

7 Leidy, "Circulating ghrelin is sensitive to changes in body weight."

8 Leidy, "Twenty-four-hour ghrelin is elevated."

9 Ibid.

10 G Finlayson, E Bryant, JE Blundell, and NA King, "Acute compensatory eating following exercise is associated with implicit hedonic wanting for food," *Physiology and Behavior*, Apr 20, 2009; 97(1):62–67.

11 RA Carels, LA Darby, S Rydin, OM Douglass, HM Cacciapaglia, and WH O'Brien, "The relationship between self-monitoring, outcome expectancies, difficulties with eating and exercise, and physical activity and weight loss treatment outcomes," *Annals of Behavioral Medicine*, Dec 2005; 30(3):182–90.

12 JM Dwyer, "Effect of perceived choice of music on exercise intrinsic motivation," *Journal of Health Behavior, Education & Promotion*, Mar–Apr 1995; 19(2):18–26.

CHAPTER 9

1 Romon, "Influence of weight loss on plasma ghrelin responses."

2 Ibid.

3 M Kojima and K Kangawa, "Ghrelin: Structure and Function," *Physiological Reviews*, Apr 2005; 85(2):495–522.

4 F Ferrini, C Salio, L Lossi, and A Merighi, "Ghrelin in central neurons," *Current Neuropharmacology*, Mar 2009; 7(1):37–49.

5 Y Ate, B Degerteki, A Erdi, H Yama, and K Dagalp, "Serum ghrelin levels in inflammatory bowel disease with relation to disease activity and nutritional status," *Digestive Diseases and Sciences*, Aug 2008; 53(8):2215–21.

6 K Karmiris, IE Koutroubakis, C Xidakis, M Polychronaki, T Voudouri, and EA Kouroumalis, "Circulating levels of leptin, adiponectin, resistin, and ghrelin in inflammatory bowel disease," *Inflammatory Bowel Disease*, Feb 2006; 12(2):100–105.

7 MD Deboer, "Use of ghrelin as a treatment for inflammatory bowel disease: mechanistic considerations," *International Journal of Peptides*, 2011; 2001:189242.

8 S Charoenthongtrakul, D Giuliana, KA Longo, EK Govek, A Nolan, S Gagne, K Morgan, J Hixon, N Flynn, BJ Murphy, AS Hernández, J Li, JA Tino, DA Gordon, PS DiStefano, and BJ Geddes, "Enhanced gastrointestinal motility with orally active ghrelin receptor agonists," *Journal of Pharmacology and Experimental Therapeutics*, Jun 2009; 329(3): 1178–86.

9 N Nagaya, M Kojima, M Uematsu, M Yamagishi, H Hosoda, H Oya, Y Hayashi, and K Kangawa, "Hemodynamic and hormonal effects of human ghrelin in healthy volunteers," *American Journal of Physiology*, May 2001; 280(5):R1483–87.

10 AJ van der Lely, M Tschöp, ML Heiman, and E Ghigo, "Biological, physiological, pathophysiological and pharmacological aspects of ghrelin," *Endocrine Reviews*, Jun 2004; 25(3):426–57.

11 L Pulkkinen, O Ukola, M Kolemainen, and M Uusitupa, "Ghrelin in diabetes and metabolic syndrome," *International Journal of Peptides*, 2010; 2010:248949.

12 http://www.cdc.gov/Features/DiabetesFactSheet

13 Pulkkinen, "Ghrelin in diabetes and metabolic syndrome."

14 Ibid.

15 Ibid.

16 Ibid.

17 DD Taub, "Neuroendocrine interaction in the immune system," *Cellular Immunology,* Mar–Apr 2008; 252(1–2):1–6.

18 "Surveillance epidemiology and end results," National Cancer Institute. http://seer .cancer.gov/statfacts/html/all.html

19 AC Herington, LK Chopin, P Jeffery, L de Amorim, T Veveris-Lowe, L Bui, and JA Clements, "Hormone-dependent cancers: new approaches to identification of potential diagnostic and/or therapeutic biomarkers," *Asia-Pacific Journal of Molecular Biology and Biotechnology,* Jan 2010; 18(1):63–66.

20 Ibid.

21 L Chopin, C Walpole, I Seim, P Cunningham, R Murray, E Whiteside, P Josh, and A Herington, "Ghrelin and cancer," *Molecular and Cellular Endocrinology,* Jun 20, 2011; 340(1):65–69.

22 Ibid.

23 Ibid.

24 Ibid.

25 PL Jeffery, RE Murray, AH Yeh, JF McNamara, RP Duncan, GD Francis, AC Herington, and LK Chopin, "Expression and function of the ghrelin axis, including a novel preproghrelin isoform, in human breast cancer tissues and cell lines," *Endocrine-Related Cancer,* Dec 2005; 12(4):839–50.

26 Ibid.

27 Herington, "Hormone-dependent cancers."

28 Chopin, "Ghrelin and cancer."

29 AH Yeh, PL Jeffery, RP Duncan, AC Herington, and LK Chopin, "Ghrelin and a novel preproghrelin isoform are highly expressed in prostate cancer and ghrelin activates mitogen-activated protein kinase in prostate cancer," *Clinical Cancer Research,* Dec 1, 2005; 11(23):8295–303.

30 Herington, "Hormone-dependent cancers."

31 Ibid.

32 M Ozgen, SS Koca, EO Etem, H Yuce, S Aydin, and A Isik, "Ghrelin gene polymorphisms in rheumatoid arthritis," *Joint Bone Spine,* Jul 2011; 78(4):368–73.

33 M Granado, T Priego, AI Martin, MA Villanúa, and A López-Calderón, "Ghrelin receptor agonist GHRP-2 prevents arthritis-induced increase in E3 ubiquitin-ligating enzymes MuRF1 and MAFbx gene expression in skeletal muscle," *American Journal of Physiology–Endocrinology and Metabolism,* Dec 2005; 289(6):E1007–14.

34 F Ferrini, C Salio, L Lossi, and A Merighi, "Ghrelin in central neurons," *Current Neuropharmacology,* Mar 2009; 7(1):37–49.

CHAPTER 10

1 National Weight Control Registry. http://www.nwcr.ws/Research/default.htm

CHAPTER 11

1 MG Goldstein, EP Whitlock, and J DePue, "Multiple risk factor interventions in primary care," *American Journal of Preventive Medicine,* Aug 2004; 27(2):61–79.

INDEX

Underscored page references indicate sidebars and tables. **Boldface** references indicate photographs and illustrations.

A

Dry goods
    for Belly Fat Fix plan, 118
    for 3-Day Fast-Track, 112–13
Dumbbells, for No-Sweat Exercise Program, 300

E

Eating patterns
    changing, for weight loss, 35–36
    evolution of, 38–39
    of hunter-gatherers, 19, 33, 34, 35
Economic costs
    high ghrelin increasing, 18
    of obesity and overweight, 15
Edamame, 123, 266
Eggs
    Egg White and Chickpea Salad, 192
    Southwestern Omelet, 205
Electronic devices, for preventing stress eating, 25
Endocrine system, effect of ghrelin on, 311, **320, 321**
Energy balance, effect of leptin on, 34
Equipment, for No-Sweat Exercise Program, 300
Exercise. *See also* No-Sweat Exercise Program;
        No-Sweat Resistance Training; Resistance
        training
    cardio (*see* Cardio exercise)
    cooldown after, 278–79 (*see also* No–Sweat
        Stretches)
    delaying, after starting Belly Fat Fix plan,
        161–62, 327
    for diabetes prevention and control, 277, 312,
        314, 318
    evaluating current routine of, 274
    ghrelin-increasing quiz about, 274, 275
    of Ghrelin Master, 174
    for ghrelin suppression, 31
    hydration for, 300
    inflammation reduced by, 6–7
    for new mothers, 199
    prohibited in 3-Day Fast-Track, 128
    terms describing, 279
    tracking, 273
    warmup before, 278, 279
    for weight-loss maintenance, 325, 326, 327

F

Famine, 9, 18, 51
Fasting, ghrelin affected by, 44–45
Fat, body
    from excess calories, 27, 34
    high-protein diet for losing, 70
Fat(s), dietary
    in balanced meals, 101, 102, 102
    calories in, 64
    as essential nutrient, 75–76
    ghrelin-increasing, 81
    for Belly Fat Fix plan, 116

ghrelin-neutral, 80
ghrelin-suppressing, 79
as ghrelin-suppressing superfood, 88–89
in meats, 114
in recipes, 201
types of, 76–77
withdrawing from, 199
Fat cells
    leptin made by, 50
    obesogens increasing, 100
    white, 27, **28**, 43, 319
Fiber
    in recipes, 201
    sources of
        ghrelin-increasing foods, 81
        ghrelin-neutral foods, 80
        ghrelin-suppressing foods, 79
        lentils, 88
        quinoa, 87
        rolled oats, 85
        sweet potatoes, 86
    types of, 73–75
Fish, 204
    Almond-Crusted Cod Fillets with Mustard-Dill
        Sauce, 235
    calories in, 173
    Five-Spice Seared Salmon, 233
    for Belly Fat Fix plan, 117
    Greek Tuna Salad, 222
    Lemon Tilapia with Curried Cauliflower, 232
    mercury in, 85
    Mini Smoked Salmon Sandwich, 191
    Shrimp and Flounder "Ceviche," 236
    Tuna Melt, 211
    white, as ghrelin-suppressing superfood,
        84–85
Floor mat, for No-Sweat Exercise Program, 300
Flounder
    Shrimp and Flounder "Ceviche," 236
Food additives, ghrelin-increasing, 94–95, 98,
        100
    artifical flavors, 98, 99
    artificial sweeteners, 97, 99
    high-fructose corn syrup, 95–96, 99
    hydrogenated oils/trans fatty acids, 96, 99
    monosodium glutamate, 97–98, 99
    as obesogens, 100
Food choices
    for creating biological fullness, 30
    ghrelin and, 8, 16, 18
    impulsive, from ghrelin imbalance, 7
    as investment, 15
Food combinations, guidelines for, 93, 101–4
Food smells
    ghrelin increasing sensitivity to, 14, 16, 18–19
    sensory hunger from, 55

R

Raspberries
  No-Bake Blueberry or Raspberry Cheesecake, 262
Recipes, 6, 200–202. *See also specific foods*
  breakfast, 203, 205–8
  dessert, 200–201, 204, 256–64
  meat entrée, 204, 237–43
  poultry, 203, 224–31
  salad, 203, 216–23
  sandwich, 203, 209–11
  seafood, 204, 232–36
  side dish, 204, 248–55
  soup, 203, 212–15
  vegetarian, 204, 244–47
Rep, exercise, 279
Resistance bands, for No-Sweat Exercise Program, 300
Resistance training. *See also* No-Sweat Resistance Training
  benefits of, 276–77
  breathing during, 278
  evaluating current routine of, 274
  vs. weight lifting, 281
Resistant starch, 73, 74–75, 85, 86, 88
Restaurant dining
  ghrelin influencing, 55
  guidelines for, 330–31, 332
  portions quiz about, 107
Reward-driven eating, after cardio exercise, 272
Rheumatoid arthritis, 312, 318–19
Rice, brown
  Brown Rice with Cauliflower and Peas, 252
  Stuffed Red Peppers, 242
  Veggie Burger, Avocado, and Rice, 193

S

Saccharin, 97, 99
Salads
  balanced, 101
  Beefy Barley Salad, 221
  Chicken Salad with Asian Dressing, 223
  Egg White and Chickpea Salad, 192
  Greek Tuna Salad, 222
  Grilled Steak Salad, 202, 218
  Mexicali Pasta and Bean Salad, 251
  Quinoa Salad with Grapes and Toasted Walnuts, 219
  Roasted Chicken and Spinach Salad, 216
  Roasted Sweet Potato and Red Onion Salad, 220
  Shrimp and Red Grapefruit Salad, 217
Salmon. *See* Fish
Sandwiches, 203. *See also* Burgers
  Mini Smoked Salmon Sandwich, 191
  Open-Faced Pesto Chicken Sandwich, 193

Slow-Cooker Turkey and Lentil Sloppy Joes, 226
  Tex-Mex Chicken Wrap, 210
  Tuna Melt, 211
  Turkey-Apple Sliders, 209
Saturated fats, 76, 201
Scale, digital, for portion control, 106
Seafood. *See* Fish; Shellfish
Selenium, in white fish, 85
Serotonin, carbohydrates and, 22
Serving size, 104
Set, exercise, 279
Setbacks, handling, 169–70, 169, 173, 175
7-day prebuilt meal plans, 158, 159, 161, 162, 173, 175, 175, 176–89
Shellfish, 117, 204
Shells, pasta
  Spinach-Stuffed Shells, 245
Shift work, weight problems from, 51, 58–59
Shoes, for No-Sweat Exercise Program, 301
Shopping lists
  Belly Fat Fix plan, 114–18
  3-Day Fast-Track, 112–13, 126
Shrimp
  Shrimp and Flounder "Ceviche," 236
  Shrimp and Red Grapefruit Salad, 217
Side dishes, 204
  Brown Rice with Cauliflower and Peas, 252
  Chard and Cannellini Beans, 254
  Couscous with Squash and Pine Nuts, 253
  Creole Baked Sweet Potato Wedges, 250
  Mediterranean Quinoa, 248
  Mexicali Pasta and Bean Salad, 251
  Summer Vegetable Skillet, 255
  swapping, in restaurants, 331
  White Bean and Parmesan Mashed Potatoes, 249
Sleep
  exercise improving, 277
  ghrelin and, 7, 61
  for PMS, 60
  for shift workers, 59
  TV interfering with, 58
Sleep deprivation
  ghrelin and, 26, 51, **52**, 309, 311
  hunger from, 20, 58–59
  leptin decreased by, 51, **52**
Sloppy joes
  Slow-Cooker Turkey and Lentil Sloppy Joes, 226
Smells, food, ghrelin increasing sensitivity to, 14, 16, 18–19
Snacking, insulin control curbing, 11
Snacks, 201
  afternoon
    evolution of, 38–39
    importance of, 47

ghrelin-friendly, 190, 198
  quick and easy, 197–98
  savory and crunch, 191–93
  sweet and creamy, 194–96
  when to eat, 108, <u>193</u>
  for ideal weight, 39
  for preventing stress eating, 25
Sneakers, for No-Sweat Exercise Program, 301
Snoring, <u>11</u>, <u>303</u>, 307
Soda, as dehydrating, 92
Soups, 203. *See also* Chili
  Curried Autumn Vegetable Soup, 214
  Hearty Vegetable Soup, 212
  Yellow Lentil Soup with Cilantro and Yogurt, 213
Spices, <u>157</u>
Spinach
  Honey Ham and Spinach Spread, 192
  Roasted Chicken and Spinach Salad, 216
  Spinach-Stuffed Shells, 245
Spreads. *See also* Dips
  Chipotle Cottage Cheese Spread, 193
  Honey Ham and Spinach Spread, 192
Squash. *See* Butternut squash; Zucchini
Stability ball, for No-Sweat Exercise Program, 300
Starvation
  ghrelin for preventing, 9, 12, 13, 311
  ghrelin imbalance from, 26–27
  self-, in Hunger Trap, <u>39</u>
Starvation signal, 27, 51, 96
Steak. *See* Beef
Stew
  Busy-Day Beef Stew, 240
Stir-fry
  Beef and Broccoli Stir-Fry, 241
Stomach, ghrelin secreted by, <u>4</u>, 13, **14**, <u>16</u>, 25, 308–9
Stomach growling, <u>36</u>
Strawberries
  French Toast with Fruity Topping, 206
  Frozen Berry Bliss, 194
Stress
  cholesterol and, <u>5</u>
  ghrelin and, 12, 23–24, 26, 56
Stress eating, 18, 21, <u>22–23</u>, 24–25, 52
Stress hunger, **21**, 56–57
Stretching, in exercise cooldown, 278–79. *See also* No-Sweat Stretches
Success stories. *See* Ghrelin Masters
Sucralose, 97, <u>99</u>
Sugar
  substitutes for, <u>303</u>
  withdrawing from, <u>199</u>
Superfoods. *See* Ghrelin-suppressing superfoods
Super Ghrelin Meal suggestions, in recipes, 202

Supplements, <u>334–35</u>
Survival Effect loop, **28**, 52
Sweet potatoes
  Creole Baked Sweet Potato Wedges, 250
  Curried Autumn Vegetable Soup, 214
  as ghrelin-suppressing superfood, 86
  Roasted Sweet Potato and Red Onion Salad, 220
  for satisfying sweet tooth, <u>199</u>
  Sweet Potato and Honey Pecan Mash, 195
Swiss chard
  Chard and Cannellini Beans, 254

T

Tea
  as dehydrating, 92
  iced, for flavoring water, <u>116</u>
Testosterone, for muscle growth, 301
Thermogenesis, <u>48</u>, 64–65, 70, 74, 86, 102, 172, 276
Thiamine, in Greek yogurt, 82–83
Thirst, hunger confused with, <u>49</u>, 91, 128
3-Day Fast-Track
  cooking for, <u>336</u>
  for couples, <u>26</u>
  food combinations for, 103
  foods to stock for, 112–13, 126
  food tracker use after, 337
  men's food trackers for, <u>145</u>, <u>149</u>, <u>153</u>
  men's Ghrelin Hunger Scale for, **144, 148, 152**
  men's meal plans for, 142–43, 146–47, 150–51
  preparing for, 100, 124–27
  purpose of, 6, <u>31</u>, 47, 110, 111, 122–23, 158, 159, 307
  quiz determining readiness for, <u>111</u>
  for recovering from setbacks, 170, 175
  reflections on, after completing, 154–55
  results from, 94, 123–24, 268
  rules for, 127–29
  skipping, 110, 114, 123
  success stories about, <u>68</u>, 122–23, <u>174</u>, <u>266–67</u>, <u>336</u>
  women's food trackers for, <u>133</u>, <u>137</u>, <u>141</u>
  women's Ghrelin Hunger Scale for, **132, 136, 140**
  women's meal plans for, 130–31, 134–35, 138–39
Tilapia
  Lemon Tilapia with Curried Cauliflower, 232
Time-out, for preventing stress eating, 24
Tofu
  Meatless Monday "Meat Loaf," 246
Top Five Ingredients to Avoid list, <u>81</u>, <u>99</u>, 100
Trans fat free labels, <u>96</u>
Trans fats, 76, 77, 96, <u>99</u>
Treats. *See also* Desserts
  guidelines for eating, 108–9
  special-occasion, 6
  sweet, 83, 86, <u>103</u>